Six in the Easy Chair

Six in the Easy Chair

Edited by John Fischer

University of Illinois Press

Urbana / Chicago / London

ACKNOWLEDGMENTS

I acknowledge with deep gratitude the help of Mrs. Ellen Davis, a former member of the *Harper's Magazine* editorial staff, who did much of the preliminary research for the book and whose editorial suggestions were invaluable.

I also am grateful to Professor W. W. Howells of Harvard University; to Lois M. Blagden, Mary M. Degener, and George W. Martin, Jr., the heirs of Edward S. Martin; and to Mrs. Avis DeVoto for their permission to reprint the Howells, Martin, and DeVoto essays.

Contents

Introduction

The Easy Chair is the oldest column in American journalism. It began in the October 1851 issue of *Harper's Magazine* and except for a lapse of eight years it has appeared regularly ever since. In all that time it has been conducted by only six men. Because the character of the magazine has been remarkably consistent, all found themselves speaking to much the same kind of audience; and the latter five tackled the job with similar purposes in mind. Consequently the column has served as a lens with a reasonably fixed focus on American life. A selection of Easy Chairs over the decades, then, should reflect something of the changing nature of our society, as seen by a particular kind of journalist. That, presumably, is the reason why the University of Illinois Press asked me to edit this book.

The Easy Chair is grotesquely misnamed. It has never been easy for me, nor, I suppose, for any of those who occupied it before me. As my family and editorial colleagues can testify, I am as peaceable as any man who ever cursed a typewriter; yet the column has kept me embroiled in almost continuous combat for more than fifteen years. In the beginning that astonished me, but I soon learned that it is an inescapable part of the job. Four of my predecessors also got their share of angry mail, threatened law suits, abuse from politicians, and occasional poison-pen letters. None of us, so far as I know, actually suffered a horsewhipping, though some were promised.

To be sure, the column did not start out that way. Originally it was intended to be "an agreeable and entertaining collection of literary miscellany," something like "The Talk of the Town" would be in the early days of *The New Yorker*. Its tone was set by the opening sentence of the initial Editor's Easy Chair: "After our more severe editorial work is done . . . we have a way of throwing ourselves back into an old red-backed EASY CHAIR, that has long been an ornament of our dingy office, and indulging in an easy and careless overlook of the gossiping papers of the day, and in such chit-chat with chance visitors as keeps us informed of the drift of town talk, while it relieves greatly the monotony of our office hours."

That column was written, though not signed, by Donald Grant Mitchell; and the opening passage at least was pure fiction. He was never editor; that was Fletcher Harper, the youngest of the four brothers in the publishing firm of Harper & Brothers, which had launched its New Monthly Magazine in the previous year. (Most histories list Henry J. Raymond, who later founded the *New York Times,* as first editor of the magazine. In fact, he seemed to work as managing editor, under Fletcher Harper's close direction.) Despite its title, The Editor's Easy Chair was never written by the actual editor until my own time. Moreover, so far as the firm's records show, Mitchell never had an office on the premises—and I doubt whether any employee of the diligent Brothers Harper was ever permitted an easy chair, or the leisure to muse in it.

The truth is that Mitchell was a free-lance writer, who had earned considerable popularity with his books of essays and travel, published under the pen name of Ik. Marvel. He was an engaging, dilettantish young man-about-New York, well suited to producing a gossip column; but for reasons which are unrecorded he did not last long. Within two years the Easy Chair passed into the custody of George William Curtis, and its character changed immediately. Apparently Mitchell continued to make contributions to the column from time to time until 1859, but even during this transition period the dominant personality clearly was Curtis's.

For Curtis was an irredeemable crusader. In his youth he had been a practicing communist, as the word was then understood, at the Brook Farm commune, and much of the idealism of that short-lived social experiment stuck with him for the rest of his life. He was a founder of a radical and disruptive organization, the Republican party; he was an early campaigner against slavery and for women's suffrage; and in later life he was largely responsible for the first civil service reforms—which he believed, and hoped, would wreck the machinery of both political parties. It did not. But he and his fellow-agitator at the House of Harper, the cartoonist Thomas Nast, did succeed in wrecking the Tweed Ring, the most corrupt political gang that ever afflicted New York City. Both his temperament and the evolving nature of the column (as I shall explain in a moment) set him steadfastly against The Establishment. Curtis wrote the Easy Chair for thirty-nine years, far longer than anyone else, and all that while it was a running affront to the genteel and the comfortable.

Like Mitchell, he began his career as a travel writer. He first met the Harper brothers when he brought them a book manuscript entitled "Nile Notes of a Howadji." (*Howadji* being his rough transliteration of the Arabic word for *traveler*.) It and his subsequent volumes of travel notes and essays were successful, and he soon found himself in demand as a lecturer, as do popular authors to this day. He also became an editor of *Putnam's* magazine; when it failed in the financial panic of 1857, Curtis assumed its indebtedness—although he had no legal obligation to do so—and this debt of honor ate up a large share of his income for many years.

Perhaps that is why he worked with such ferocious energy. In addition to his lyceum tours, his books, and his monthly contributions to the Easy Chair, he took on the job of political editor of *Harper's Weekly,* a companion publication to the monthly. It became a second weapon in his crusades against slavery and Boss Tweed; and he was in good part responsible for its remarkable coverage of the Civil War. (Winslow Homer was only one of its artists reporting pictorially from the Union battle fronts.)

Somehow Curtis also found time for a parallel career in public affairs. He campaigned hard for Lincoln, in the process acquiring a national reputation as a political orator. As a reward he was offered several diplomatic appointments, including the ambassadorship to the Court of St. James's. Because he was morally opposed to the spoils system, he turned them all down; but under the Grant administration he did accept the chairmanship of the first Civil Service Commission. When Congress refused to accept his recommendations for reform, he resigned—but continued the fight as president of the National Civil Service Reform League. Then, only two years before his death, he was named chancellor of New York University, after long service on its board of regents.

When Curtis died in 1892, the Easy Chair was dropped until 1900, probably because the magazine had a hard time locating a worthy successor. Then it was revived under the ministrations of another radical:

William Dean Howells. Although he was an avowed socialist, a de-
fender of anarchists, and a dissenter from the prevailing values of
his America, he was never as active in politics as Curtis. Instead he
was an archetypical literary man—pioneer of the realistic novel, poet,
critic, playwright, essayist, and (again) a travel writer. Henry Steele
Commager observed that "No other American ever commanded such
wide and prolonged literary influence in his own lifetime . . . . Except
Mark Twain, he was the most representative of American writers in
the long period between the Civil War and the First World War."

The son of a printer, Howells himself went to work at the age
of fourteen as a compositor for the *Ohio State Journal;* by the time
he was twenty-one, he was its news editor. He was an autodidact.
His formal education probably added up to less than two years in
classrooms, but he had a gluttonous appetite for reading, and he taught
himself a working command of the main European languages. His
chief contribution to practical politics was a campaign biography of
Lincoln, which turned out to be pivotal to his career. It led to an
offer of the American consul's office in Venice, which he accepted
cheerfully since (unlike Curtis) he was not squeamish about patronage.
In those days the job was far from burdensome, so Howells spent most
of his five years there reading, writing, and getting acquainted with
European culture. He returned at least as well educated as most graduates of Harvard. Inevitably he produced a couple of travel books.

After stints as an assistant editor of *The Nation* and of the *Atlantic
Monthly,* he served for ten years as editor-in-chief of the *Atlantic.*
In 1881 he resigned to return to full-time writing, and soon after
moved from Boston to New York, where he took up an association
with Harper & Brothers which was to last for the rest of his life—as
author, columnist, and literary advisor. Both in style and content his
Easy Chairs were markedly different from Curtis's; but many of them
sounded a similar note of discontent with the quality of contemporary
society.

So did those of Edward S. Martin, who took over the column after
Howells's death in 1920. He too was a professional writer for most
of his working life, although he never attained the eminence of his
two immediate predecessors. A graduate of Phillips Andover and Harvard, he was one of the early editors of the *Lampoon,* the Harvard

humor magazine. After a brief try at practicing law, which bored him, he turned to newspaper work and free-lance magazine writing until 1883, when he started a publication of his own—the original *Life,* a humor magazine modeled on the British *Punch.* (Aside from the name, it had no connection with Henry Luce's later venture in pictorial journalism.) It was relatively short-lived.

During the years when he was running *Life* and the Easy Chair, Martin continued to produce a formidable output of light verse, essays, and current history, collected in more than a dozen volumes. He retired from the Easy Chair in 1935, at the age of 79, presumably from sheer exhaustion.

Enter, then, Bernard DeVoto, a banty rooster from Utah who enjoyed a fight more than any man I ever knew. I can't pretend to speak of him with objectivity—not only because he was a close and revered friend, but because he influenced so profoundly my own work. He liked to describe himself as "a hack" and "a literary department store"; in fact, he came close to being a Renaissance man of the writer's trade. I can think of no one else who had such a wide range of interests, and handled all of them with such competence. He was a historian who believed—almost uniquely in his generation—that history should be a branch of literature, rather than a hermetic academic exercise. Consequently he won both the Pulitzer and the Bancroft prizes, token rewards for five volumes on the American West which (I suspect) will never be superseded. He was a prolific novelist, although none of his fiction has the survival value of the best of his other work. He was a literary critic who still provokes controversy.

Above all, DeVoto was a combat journalist who charged headlong into any public controversy that got his dander up. He was a passionate conservationist, decades before concern for the environment became fashionable. Long before anybody heard of Ralph Nader, DeVoto was defending the consumer against shoddy products. He fought against censorship, McCarthyism, cattlemen who tried to steal the public lands, literary dogmatists, benighted drinking habits, bad restaurants, and slippery politicians. More about him later.

Well-organized people, I understand, conduct their lives according to a rational plan. Mine has been a series of accidents. On the evening of November 13, 1955, DeVoto—who had been seething with vigor and vinegar that afternoon—died of a heart attack. Since I was then editor-in-chief of *Harper's,* and another column was due at the printer within three weeks, I made a hurried effort to enlist someone to take his place. One after another the likely candidates turned me down, each first taking a few days to think it over. Time was running short, so finally in desperation I wrote a column myself. I then thought of myself as a pinch hitter, serving only until I could find a permanent writer for the Easy Chair. Instead I have been writing it, with occasional help from guest columnists, ever since. I should have been able to locate someone who would do it better, even if not as brilliantly as DeVoto. The truth is that I enjoyed it, and therefore lacked diligence in my search for a replacement.

At this point it may be useful to say a few words about the purpose of a column—the Easy Chair in particular, although I think most of the specifications apply to other columns as well.

DeVoto once described his job as "criticism of society," a definition that seems fair enough to me, as I believe it would have to Curtis, Howells, and Martin. Ideally, however, I think it should be something more: call it analytic reporting.

For no sensible reader, it seems to me, will be interested in a writer's opinion on any subject unless he knows the facts on which it is based and the line of reasoning by which the judgment is reached. Consequently the reporter-analyst is under an obligation to be informed on any subject he takes up—not only from reading the source material, but from first-hand observation and discussion with experts in whom he has confidence. This may sound like a truism; but you would be surprised how many writers are willing—indeed, eager—to brandish smoking-hot opinions on practically any subject, whether they know anything about it or not. Sincerity and commitment, they believe, are enough. They are mistaken; worse yet, they are ineffectual, because an argument without an underpinning of fact is not likely to be persuasive.

It helps, too, if the columnist has some active personal involvement in public affairs. However skilled he may be as observer and reporter, he cannot really understand the workings of society unless he has served some time in the boiler room. Thus Curtis profited from his immersion in politics, Howells from his term in the consular service and in newspaper editing, Martin from his venture in publishing, DeVoto from his work as advisor to the government on conservation, and I from various forays into public service and political campaigns. An outside example is Walter Lippmann. He could never have written so solidly about foreign affairs if he had not served in the War Department and on the staff preparing for the Versailles peace conference, just as a man who never sailed could not report competently on the America's Cup races.

Such involvements, however, impose on the columnist another obligation. Inevitably they affect the way he thinks and feels. It is his duty, therefore, to let his readers know about his biases and emotional commitments, so they can make due allowance for possible distortions in his vision.

We all know that complete objectivity is impossible—or so at least the psychologists and economic determinists keep telling us. An honest reporter will nevertheless believe that an approximation of objectivity is worth pursuing like the Holy Grail; and when he realizes that he, like Galahad, may never get his hands on it, he is obliged to point out where his grasp falls short. A member of Parliament is honorbound to "declare his interest"—that is, to tell his colleagues when he has a personal stake, financial, emotional, or any other kind, in the subject under debate. The same holds true for a writer. Thus when I was writing some months ago about poor people and their migration from farms to cities, it was only fair to point out that my views had been largely shaped by my work on a government Commission on Rural Poverty, and that I then owned a small interest in an Oklahoma farm. Similarly, if I were commenting on the automobile industry, my readers would have a right to know whether I hold stock in a motor company. (I don't.)

Another requisite for a columnist is independence. Many New Leftists hold as an article of faith that no writer for any periodical (except perhaps for the so-called underground press) can be really independent: that he must be a puppet of The Establishment, which manipulates him through the publication's ownership, or its advertisers, or maybe the wicked banker who holds a mortgage on the plant. I have no hope of disabusing such true believers. For the more open-minded, however, I would like to note that so far as I can discover such hands have never been laid on this column. Certainly during my own tenancy and DeVoto's, its independence has never been questioned by any editor, advertising manager, or officer or stockholder of the company; and I believe the same to be true of our predecessors. This is not a matter of piety, but of simple common sense. The only value of a columnist—or, for that matter, any reviewer or critic—lies in his absolute freedom to speak his own mind, subject only to the laws of libel.

There was a period before my time when the House of Harper was deeply in debt to the Morgan banking firm. Throughout those years the magazine's columnists and other writers were just as critical of Wall Street and the shortcomings of American business as at any time before or since. I suspect that they sometimes brought on an epidemic of near-apoplexy in the Morgan board room, but no hint of bankerly displeasure ever reached the editorial floor. So at least I was assured by the late Frederick Lewis Allen, who was both editor of the magazine and biographer of the elder J. P. Morgan.

This does not mean, of course, that a columnist lives in a vacuum, insulated from all pressures and contamination. Pressure is his working habitat, like a deep-sea diver's. Readers berate him and sometimes cancel their subscriptions. Offended advertisers do occasionally drop their contracts. Whole regiments of press agents seem to lie awake nights thinking up new ways to seduce him. Do-gooders incessantly remind him of his duty to save mankind by giving their causes a plug. Life at times may seem to him like on long session with an encounter group, armed with real knives. But these varieties of pressure are no threat, so long as he is shielded by a thick skin and a bristly conscience.

The most aggrieved complaints come from people who honestly believe that the columnist is a malicious rocker of boats and upsetter of apple carts. This was as true in Curtis's time as it is today, and not by coincidence. The complainants, in fact, have a point. For the very nature of his work pushes the reporter-analyst, much of the time, into the role of enemy of the status quo—a role which beneficiaries of the status quo naturally resent.

Any reporter who examines carefully an existing institution—the seniority system in Congress, for instance, or the tenure system in our universities—is bound to be struck by its imperfections. If it is human, an institution is by definition less than perfect; and the longer it has been around, the more imperfect it is likely to get, because of universal human reluctance to change with the times. The conscientious reporter-analyst, then, inevitably devotes much of his energies to sticking knives into patches of dry-rot, wherever they show up in the fabric of society. If he accepts without question a glorious tradition, a foreign policy which worked a decade ago, a political arrangement which seems entirely satisfactory to the people in power, he is not doing his job. His duty is not to commemorate, but to set off alarms; to demonstrate that changing our ways, though uncomfortable, may be the price of survival.

This does not mean, of course, that his critical stabs are always well aimed, or that his conclusions are necessarily correct. Like a baseball player, any columnist whose batting average reaches .300 is doing better than he, or his readers, can reasonably expect. But even when he is wrong, I think, he can serve a useful purpose: he can help his readers arrive at conclusions of their own.

Here is where the columnist has an advantage over the free-lance writer, whose articles show up sporadically in a dozen different publications. The column offers continuity, a fixed point of reference.

For many years I read Walter Lippmann's column three times a week. At least half the time I disagreed with him. Nevertheless I found him enormously useful; by watching his mind sift and evaluate events, I learned to appraise them in my own way. This was possible only because Lippmann's column appeared regularly in the same place. His readers had a chance to learn his unspoken assumptions, his moral stance, even his unconscious biases. We learned to make allowances for them, just as one figures the magnetic deviation of a compass. This, it seems to me, is the chief justification for any column, in newspaper or magazine. It enables the reader to become familiar enough with a given point of view so that he can use it to work out his own intellectual bearings.

That has been the main purpose of the Easy Chair, as I understand it, for well over a century. Its critique of society is by nature ephemeral, and has little to do with literature. But I hope that DeVoto was right when he once remarked that this particular kind of journalism "is not important, it is only indispensable."

In winnowing the selections for this book from the more than 1,300 essays that have appeared in the Easy Chair, I have followed two principles. First, I have tried to give a fair sampling of the work of each of the six men who have conducted the column—enough to indicate his style, the way his mind worked, and his approach to the subjects that concerned him. Second, I have tried to choose those essays of most interest to the readers of today. As a result, I have drawn relatively lightly from the earlier years, since many of the issues that seemed urgent then are now forgotten or obscure. Moreover, the prose style characteristic of a more leisurely era now sounds quainted, mannered, and occasionally tedious. To my surprise, I found this true even of so recent a writer as Howells. Consequently I have included here what some readers may think is an undue proportion of the columns written by Martin, DeVoto, and myself.

Within each section the selections are not arranged chronologically, but in the order which seems to me to make for the best reading; the date is of course given for each item. I have supplied titles for items by Mitchell, Curtis, and Howells, originally untitled, as well as for three essays of DeVoto's.

The months I have spent in sifting through the millions of words (perhaps six million, at a rough estimate) written by my predecessors have been rewarding for me. The essays have given me a more intimate sense of the temper and thought of earlier times than I have ever gained from formal histories; and they have brought me into close acquaintanceship with men I would have enjoyed as friends. I hope I have been able to pass some of these rewards along to the readers of this book.

I/Donald Grant Mitchell
1851-ca. 1853

In the nineteenth century most literate Americans had a lively interest
in the outside world but little opportunity to satisfy it. For a family
of ordinary income, sightseeing abroad was out of the question. Many
people, including some of my ancestors, never in their lives journeyed
more than fifty miles from the places of their birth. Moreover, before
the day of the press associations no American newspaper could afford
anything like systematic coverage of events overseas. A few of the
better ones had correspondents in London and Paris, but the rest of
the world they covered with meager excerpts from the foreign press,
supplemented occasionally by letters from free-lance writers.

As a consequence, the writing of travel books, and travel articles
for the few magazines then being published, became a major literary
enterprise. In the early issues of *Harper's,* for example, a large share
of the editorial space was devoted to reports on the arts, industries,
fashions, and scenery of other countries. And anyone who visited a
really exotic place—Turkey, say, or the interior of China—almost inevitably produced a book about his experiences.

It was natural, then, for a young man with literary ambitions to
try his hand at travel writing. Donald Grant Mitchell is a case in
point. He was the son of a Connecticut farmer, who prospered enough
to be able to send young Mitchell through Yale. After his graduation
in 1841 he took over the running of the farm, apparently with considerable competence, since by 1844 he had saved enough money to embark for Europe and the precarious career of a free-lance writer. Most
of his early stories were published in the *Morning Courier and En-
quirer,* one of the better New York newspapers of the time.

His first book, a collection of travel pieces, appeared in 1847 under
the title *Fresh Gleanings.* It was followed three years later by *Battle
Summer,* an account of the French revolution of 1848. Both sold reasonably well, but his first really major success was a volume of light
essays, *Reveries of a Bachelor,* which he brought out in 1850. A sequel,

Donald Grant Mitchell

Dream Life, attained equal popularity the following year. It was
Mitchell's demonstrated skill as an essayist, presumably, that led the
Brothers Harper to invite him to write a column for the monthly
magazine they had launched in 1850.

His handling of the assignment was, it seems to me, somewhat perfunctory. As the following selections indicate, Mitchell was given to
moralizing—about the need of American women for more exercise,
the sad state of Broadway traffic, and the scandalous reception in Washington of Lola Montez, the most notorious courtesan of that era. But
he didn't bother to look up the correct spelling of her name, or rather
pseudonym; in fact she was not Spanish, as she claimed, but Irish,
originally christened Marie Gilbert. And when he couldn't find anything local to moralize about, Mitchell filled up his column with cau-
tionary tales from the foreign press.

Evidently Fletcher Harper felt that this sort of thing was not good
enough, for George William Curtis—another young journalist who
had learned his trade as a travel writer—soon began to contribute
items to the Easy Chair and then took over full responsibility for the
column, probably in 1853. The exact date cannot be determined,
because the column was then unsigned and early records of the magazine were lost in a fire. Internal evidence suggests, however, that
Mitchell made only occasional contributions after that date; his style
is quite different from Curtis's.

Subsequently Mitchell served for a year as American consul in
Venice, before settling down for good as a farmer and book writer
in Connecticut. He produced more than a dozen volumes of history,
essays, and fiction, respected in their day but now of interest only
to literary historians. The following excerpts from his first column
and from four later ones are enough, I think, to convey the flavor
of his writing.

Women and the Outdoor Life

October, 1851

WE have forewarned our reader, or should have done it, that we shall shift our topic in these our after-dinner musings, as easy as the turning of a leaf. Our eyes have just now fallen upon a passage in Mr. Greeley's last letter from Europe, in which he speaks of the appearance of the English women, and commends, with a little more than his usual ardor of expression, their perfection of figure. He attributes this, and very justly, to the English lady's habit of out-of-door exercise. We had thought that this fact was known: that it was known years ago, and that our fair country-women would catch a hint from it, that would throw color into their cheeks and fullness into their forms. And yet, sadly enough, our ladies still coop themselves in their heated rooms, until their faces are like lilies, and their figures—like lily stems!

We have alluded to the matter now, not for the sake of pointing a satire surely, but for the sake of asking those one or two hundred thousand ladies, who every month light our pages with their looks, if they do indeed prize a little unnatural pearliness of hue, and delicacy of complexion, beyond that ruddy flush of health (the very tempter of a kiss!) and that full development of figure, which all the poets, from Homer down, have made one of the chiefest beauties of a woman?

If not, let them make of themselves horsewomen: or, bating that, let them make acquaintance with the sunrise: let them pick flowers with the dew upon them: let them study music of nature's own orchestra. Vulgarity is not essential to health: and a lithe, elastic figure does not grow in hot-houses.

For ourselves, we incline heartily to the belief, that if American women have a wish to add to the respect, the admiration, the love, and (if need be) the fear of the men, they will find a easier road toward that gain, in a little vigorous out-of-door exercise, and a uniform

13

attention to the great essentials of health, than in any new-fangled costumes, or loudly applauded "Rights."

We have grown unconciously heated with the topic, and this added to the 90° by Fahrenheit, which is steaming at our elbow, must cut short the first installment of gossip from our red-backed easy-chair.

New York in Winter

March, 1852

NEW-YORKERS have a story to tell of the winter just now dying, that will seem, perhaps, to the children of another generation like a pretty bit of Munchausenism. Whoever has seen our Metropolitan City only under the balmy atmosphere of a soft May-day, or under the smoky sultriness of a tropic August—who has known our encompassing rivers only as green arms of sparkling water, laughing under the shadow of the banks, and of shipping—would never have known the Petersburg of a place into which our passing winter has transformed the whole.

Only fancy our green East River, that all the summer comes rocking up from the placid Sound, with a hoarse murmur through the rocks of Hell-Gate, and loitering, like a tranquil poem, under the shade of the willows of Astoria, all bridged with white and glistening ice! And the stanch little coasting-craft, that in summer-time spread their wings in companies, like flocks of swans, within the bays that make the vestibule to the waters of the city, have been caught in their courses, and moored to their places, by a broad anchor of sheeted silver.

The oyster-men, at the beacon of the Saddle-rock, have cut openings in the ice; and the eel-spearers have plied their pronged trade, with no boat save the frozen water.

In town, too, a carnival of sleighs and bells has wakened Broadway into such hilarity as was like to the festivals we read of upon the Neva. And if American character verged ever toward such coquetry of flowers and bon-bons as belongs to the Carnival of Rome, it would have made a pretty occasion for the show, when cheeks looked so tempting, and the streets and house-tops sparked with smiles.

As for the country, meantime, our visitors tell us that it has been sleeping for a month and more under a glorious cloak of snow; and that the old days of winter-cheer and fun have stolen back to mock at the anthracite fires, and to woo the world again to the frolic of

15

moonlight rides and to the flushing play of a generous hickory-flame. . . .

As for political chat at home, it runs now in the channel of President-making; and the dinner-tables of Washington are lighted up with comparison of chances. Under this, the gayeties proper are at a comparative stand-still. The Assembly balls, as we learn, are less brilliant, and more promiscuous than ever; and even the select parties of the National Hotel are singularly devoid of attractions. Lent too is approaching, to whip off, with its scourge of custom, the cue of papal diplomats; and then, the earnestness of the campaign for the Presidency will embrue the talk of the whole Metropolis.

While we are thus turning our pen-point Washington-ward, we shall take the liberty of felicitating ourselves, upon the contrast which has belonged to the reception of LOLA MONTES, in New York, and in the metropolis of the nation. Here, she was scarce the mention of a respectable journal; there, she has been honored by distinguished "callers."

We see in this a better tone of taste in our own city, than in the city of the nation; and it will justify the opinion, which is not without our support, that the range of honorable delicacy is far lower in the city of our representatives, than in any city of their clients. Representatives leave their proprieties at home; and many a member would blush at a license within the purlieus of his own constituency, which he courts as an honor in the city of our Caesars! We wish them joy of their devotion to the Danseuse, whom—though we count as humble as themselves in point of morals—we believe to be superior, mentally, to the bulk of her admirers.

The Welcoming of Lola Montes

May, 1852

SO M E little time ago we indulged in a pleasant strain of self-gratulation, that the extraordinary woman, Lola Montes—danseuse, diplomate, widow, wife, femme entretenue—should have met with the humblest welcome upon American shores, and by such welcome given a lift to our sense of propriety. It would seem, however, that the welcome was only stayed, and not abandoned. The cordial reception which our national representatives have given the Bavarian Countess, was indeed a matter to be looked for. Proprieties of life do not rule high under the Congressional atmosphere; nor is Washington the moving centre of much Christian enterprise—either missionary or other. But that Boston, our staid rival, should have shown the danseuse the honor of Educational Committees, and given her speech in French and Latin of the blooming Boston girls, is a thing as strange as it was unexpected. We observe, however, that the officer in attendance upon Lola, pleads simple courtesy as a warrant for his introduction, and regrets that newspaper inquiry and comment should make known to his pupil-protegees the real character of the lady introduced. It certainly is unfortunate—but still more unfortunate, that the character of any visitor should not be proof against inquiry.

Lola, it seems, resents highly any imputation upon her good name, and demands proof of her losses.

Her indignation is adroit, and reminds us of a certain old "nut for the lawyers," which once went the round of the almanacs:

"Will Brown, a noted toper, being out of funds, and put to his wits, entered the beer-shop, and called for four two-penny loaves of bread. After ruminating awhile, with the loaves under his arms, he proposes to exchange a couple of the loaves for a mug of ale. Bruin of the bar assented to the bargain. Will quietly disposed of his ale, and again proposed a further exchange of the remaining loaves, for a second mug of the malt liquor.

Will quietly discharged his duty toward the second tankard, and as quietly moved toward the door. Bruin claimed pay. Will alleged that he had paid in two-penny loaves. Bruin demanded pay for the bread; but Will, very imperturbably swore that he did not keep the bread, and challenged poor Bruin to prove his indebtedness."

On Generals as Political Candidates

August, 1852

THE two great hinges of public chat are—just now—the rival candidates, Generals Pierce and Scott; serving not only for the hot hours of lunch under the arches of the Merchants' Exchange, but toning the talk upon every up-bound steamer of the Hudson, and giving their creak to the breezes of Cape May.

Poor Generals!—that a long and a worthy life should come to such poor end as this. To be vilified in the journals, to be calumniated with dinner-table abuse, or with worse flattery—to have their religion, their morals, their courage, their temper, all brought to the question;— to have their faces fly-specked in every hot shop of a barber—to have their grand-parents, and parents all served up in their old clothes; to have their school-boy pranks ferreted out, and every forgotten penny pitched into their eyes; to have their wine measured by the glass, and their tears by the tumbler; to have their names a bye-word, and their politics a reproach—this is the honor we show to these most worthy candidates!

Solving a Growing Traffic Problem

November, 1852

HOW does it happen that no other city of the world, of whatever magnitude, is so hampered with the plethora of street-goers, as ours? If we are not misinformed, a foot-passenger has a reasonable chance of picking his way across the London Strand, or Oxford-street, or Thread-and-Needle-street, without any serious risk of life or limb; but surely, the same can not be said of the lower half of Broadway. In Paris, where the omnibuses will transport a man from one corner to another, in any and all directions, there is nowhere such crush and jam as belongs to our terrible Broadway.

One reason of this difference will at once suggest itself; viz., the fact that Broadway is more peculiarly the great thoroughfare of our Island City, than is any one street of any other city of the world—not even excepting the Corso of Rome. It is the spinal marrow, to which all other streets are but the vertebrae. But besides this, another reason may be found, in the foul haste which pervades everything like business, or travel; that undue haste which shatters our boilers, and makes our rivers race-courses, drives the very carmen to infuriate speed upon our highways, and infests every Irish cab-driver. We are even now plotting a railway to take us from our breakfast into Wall-street, and we shall soon have a railway to Greenwood! We live and die by steam!

European travelers all remark that our streets are full of men "in a hurry." There is no place for quiet walkers; they are hustled off the trottoir; they are knocked down by sharp hand-cart-men; they are jostled by the women; we are in a state of nervous tremor; we all need the cure of quietude.

But quietude works best by system; and system is the best medium of real force and progress. On this text we should like to preach.

As a beginning of system, why may not all those heavy materials, which cumber so much the street in their passage from the North River docks to the old wards upon the southeast of the town, be denied the passage by Broadway, and be transported by the parallel avenues?

What is to forbid a healthful municipal enactment, forbidding cars of merchandise to appear on Broadway, except they are for the delivery of freight at some store-house immediately upon the street? What is to prevent the entire exclusion of enormous timber, and boilers, which day after day choke up the thoroughfare, and which only take the transit by Broadway to humor the caprice of some indolent driver, who solaces his loitering habit with a sight of the shop-windows and the equipages? What lies in the way of street-cleaning, whether by shovel or brook, at an hour of the morning when the street current will meet no check, and when no passers-by will be choked with dust, save the lack of that energetic system which we beg leave to propose?

Must it always be, that our town should remain a by-word and a reproach, for its slack municipal management, and its want of all the healthier regimen of an advanced civilization? We make no apology for talking in this strain even to our country readers; those who have been beleaguered upon the street for a half-hour together, will join in our petition for reform; and we have no doubt that easy transit through our thoroughfares, is as new to the wish of our country visitors as to our own.

II/George William Curtis
1853-1892

There was nothing dilettantish or perfunctory about George William Curtis. He came from a New England family that believed profoundly in the Protestant ethic and the religion of hard work. Moreover, while still in his teens he met Ralph Waldo Emerson, who lectured frequently at the school Curtis was attending in Providence. He soon became both a friend and disciple; and from Emerson he learned that the world needed changing, urgently and drastically, and that it was his personal responsibility to bring about that change. Curtis took up the challenge with all the idealism and energy of youth—and, untypically, he maintained both the energy and the idealism for the rest of his life.

At Emerson's suggestion he and his brother enrolled as boarders at Brook Farm, the Utopian community near Boston. Today it would be called a commune. Its residents—probably not much more than a hundred at its peak—were dedicated to high thinking and plain living. Their purpose was to demonstrate in a cooperative, semisocialist enterprise that Emerson's transcendental philosophy could be a practical way of life.

For all his enthusiasm, Curtis was too hard-headed an observer to overlook the weaknesses of this undertaking. Years later in one of his early Easy Chairs he wrote: "There was plenty of steady, essential, hard work, for the founding of an earthly paradise upon a New England farm is no pastime. But with the best intention, and much practical knowledge and industry and devotion, there was in the nature of the case an inevitable lack of method, and economical failure was almost a foregone conclusion. But there were never such witty potato patches, and such sparkling corn fields before or since. The weeds were scratched out of the ground to the music of Tennyson or Browning and the nooning was an hour as gay and bright as any brilliant midnight at Ambroses's."

His association with the Brook Farm intellectuals was the beginning of Curtis's higher education. Apparently he never thought of enrolling in a college, but throughout his late teens and early twenties, he and his brother Burrill systematically taught themselves European languages, literature, philosophy, and practical agriculture. For a couple of years they rented a small farm near Concord, where they could raise most of their own food and continue their studies in the company of such men as Emerson, Hawthorne, Channing, and Thoreau. Neither Harvard nor Yale could have offered a better faculty.

Their father, by this time a prosperous New York banker, was glad to help finance this venture in self-education; and in 1846, when George was twenty-four, he put up the money for his sons to spend two years in traveling through Europe and the Middle East. George sent back a steady flow of dispatches to New York newspapers, and soon after his return he published his first book, *Nile Notes of a Howadji,* at the age of twenty-seven. It was a moderate success, but it offended his father. As a conscientious reporter, George Curtis had included a few passages about the harems and dancing girls of the Muslim communities. These father thought too sensuous, if not downright immoral; but he soon forgave them.

With the publication of another Howadji book the following year, Curtis was well launched on a career as writer and lecturer. He contributed articles to *Harper's Magazine* and to *Putnam's,* of which he was briefly an associate editor; and about 1853 he began the association with Harper & Brothers, the publishers of his books, which was to last the rest of his life.

Curtis's contributions to the Easy Chair, our main concern here, took only a small part of his phenomenal energies. He also wrote verse, novels, and volumes of essays; served as political editor of *Harper's Weekly* from its founding in 1857; made a national reputation as a literary lecturer and political orator; and became an early and influential member of the Republican party. His editorials in the

Weekly were his chief weapons in his crusades against slavery, municipal corruption and the Tweed Ring, and the traditional system of political patronage. (His ally in these campaigns, incidentally, was Thomas Nast, the *Weekly's* leading cartoonist, who gave the country three lasting symbols: the Republican elephant, the Democratic donkey, and the Tammany tiger.) Curtis's Easy Chair essays were usually more gentle, casual, and "literary"—but in them, too, he often campaigned for his favorite causes.

In the first two of the following selections, for example, he argued the case for women's rights—not merely to political equality, but the right to use their talents in all fields on an equal footing with men. They would not sound out of place today in a women's liberation publication. Incidentally, the Ida Lewis he mentions is commemorated still by the Ida Lewis Yacht Club, with headquarters not far from her light house.

The next three essays are typical of Curtis's political Easy Chairs—a satire on the workings of the spoils system, a comment on the violence of party feelings, and his observations about the presidential campaign of 1876.

Determining the Sphere of Women

June, 1869

AT the close of a stormy March day of this year two soldiers were crossing from Newport to Fort Adams in a sail-boat managed by an inexperienced lad. When they were partly across a blast suddenly struck the craft; the boy was confounded, the boat capsized, and for half an hour, clinging to the keel, the hapless men and boy struggled with the waves. Then the hold of the boy relaxed, and he sank; but a boat had put off from the Lime Rock Lighthouse, about half a mile away, and before the men were exhausted it had reached them, and they were saved. The persons who saved them were Ida Lewis and her brother Hosea, children of the keeper of the light.

Ten years ago in the same harbor four young fellows were upset in a boat, and the same girl hastened in her skiff to rescue them. A little later three drunken soldiers stove a hole in their boat not far from the light. Two swam ashore, the third was saved by Ida Lewis when nearly exhausted. Two years ago some men were driving a sheep upon the wharf in Newport. The animal plunged into the water, and three men running along the shore in pursuit at length found a skiff and put out into the harbor. A heavy sou'wester was blowing, and the skiff was swamped. Once more Ida Lewis pushed off for them, and bringing them safe to shore, returned and landed the sheep. In the next winter a scape-grace stole a sail-boat from the wharf and made off. But the gale drove it upon the little Lime Rock, a mile from the light; and the thief clung to the mast from midnight until morning, when Ida Lewis saw him, and rowing to his relief, found him, as she said, "shaking and God-blessing me, and praying to be set on shore."

This is a girl in her twenty-eighth year, slender, blue-eyed, with light brown hair, frank and hearty, and likely to be more famous next summer than any Newport belle. Let us pray that she may save herself from the storm of notoriety and flattery as she has saved so many lives from the sea. Or, still better, as she is betrothed, let us hope that she may be safely married, and with a changed name have left the Lime Rock Light-house before Mrs. Grundy reaches Newport.

But the heroic story of which these are the incidents suggests some very improving reflections upon the sphere of woman. No one can read the report in the newspapers, no one certainly read the brief telegraphic notice upon the following morning, without a thrill of admiration and sympathy. But are we to understand that such emotion was natural and proper? Are we to believe that it is "feminine" for young women to row boats in storms? Is it "womanly" to tug and strain through a tempest, and then pull half-drowned men into a skiff? Is not the Heavenly appointed "sphere of woman" the nursery? and is there not very grave apprehension of the "female sex" disappearing altogether if such conduct is approved? The brother Hosea, in the first instance related, was in his place, undoubtedly. He was a stout youth, and it was an occasion that demanded brawn and vigor and skill. But, my dear Sir Piercie, would you wish to have seen your sister, et cætera, et cætera?

There was the inevitable Grace Darling also, who in the early dawn, thirty years ago, rowed with her father from Longstone Light, and at the risk of her own life saved the lives of nine persons from the wreck of the *Forfarshire* steamer. Then there was Mrs. Patten, who steered the wrecked ship to port. There were Molly Stark, Joan of Arc—where will these things stop? What is to become of the sex, and womanliness and feminineness, and all other pleasing qualities, if general applause shall be unguardedly lavished upon conduct which, if our sisters, et cætera, et cætera?

Dear Sir Piercie, what an intolerable deal of nonsense is talked and written and sung and, above all, preached about women, and their sphere, and what is feminine, and what isn't—as if we men necessarily knew all about it! The other evening the Easy Chair heard something which sounded so familiar that it might have said it itself; and it was in this vein. Here comes a man and says, "Isn't it curious that it is the nature of melted lead always to run into bullets?" And while I am wondering I observe that he has a bullet-mould in his pocket, into which he pours the fluid metal. Or another bland gentleman remarks: "How beautifully Providence ordains that pear-trees shall grow like vines!" And he takes me into his garden and shows me a tortured tree trained upon an espalier. These worthy philosophers might as wisely inform us that Providence beautifully ordains saints to be chops and steaks, and then point us to St. Lawrence upon his gridiron. What determines the sphere of any morally responsible being? Perfect freedom of choice and liberty of development. Take those away and you have taken away the possibility of determining the sphere.

Now, speaking soberly, no man will be such an—let us say donkey, as to insist that it was unfeminine in Ida Lewis to pull off in her boat to save men from drowning. It was no more unfeminine than to sing a babe to sleep. And if this be so, then it was perfectly womanly to learn the use of oars—to acquire the means of doing so great a service to her fellow-creatures, a service which touches the heart and the imagination, and, as in the instance of Grace Darling, will become a poetic tradition.

When we have come as far as this there is certainly no need of asking whether such actions fall within the sphere of women, or whether they are competent to row boats. Ida Lewis has shown that she can row to some purpose, can row indeed to such purpose that every generous heart applauds. This seems to settle the whole vexatious question about women. Indeed there is really no more question about women than about men. And unless the whole debate upon the subject of the rights of men, which has shaken society now for so many years, and often to such tremendous results, is folly, that upon the rights of women can hardly be smiled away.

The original impediment is the apparent difficulty of persons who are otherwise intelligent to understand what they are talking about when they begin to discuss the proper sphere of womanly activity and interest. Some few weeks ago, for instance, there was a meeting at the end of the winter term of the Female Medical College under the immediate charge of Dr. Elizabeth and Dr. Emily Blackwell, with Dr. Willard Parker and other eminent surgeons and medical men in the faculty. The object of this college is to give to women just as profound and thorough a medical education as any man can receive, and it was hoped that the meeting might tend to direct public attention and sympathy to the subject. There was an admirable address by Dr. Emily Blackwell upon the history of the intention and progress and condition of the college, and a speech to the students by one of the faculty, and two or three speeches by Dr. Parker and others upon the general subject of the professional study of medicine and surgery by women.

One of the speakers took the ground that what was really wanted was an opportunity to prove by experiment whether such an institution were desirable; and necessarily he stated that the question was not whether women were competent to become efficient and skillful physicians and surgeons, but whether they should be allowed the same liberty of choice and freedom of development which men claimed for themselves. That many women might fail was very possible, as certainly a great many men failed; but it was the perfection of owlish folly to begin by a theory of the sphere of women, or a guess or a prejudice as to their capacity.

To thinking persons this was undoubtedly a sufficiently trite and obvious statement, but it really goes to the root of the matter. Dr. Johnson advised his friend to try to divest his mind of cant, and what people usually need in approaching the consideration of such a question is to divest their minds of theory. Even some very accomplished and trained scientific men find it very difficult to observe scientifically—that is, with a sole regard to the fact, and not to the possible suggestion or use of the fact. If we wish, therefore, to know whether women are competent to do this or that, we must do as we do with men, allow them perfect freedom of choice and opportunity.

Now imagine a person listening to such a strain of remark, for the obviousness of which perhaps the orator should have blushed, and then gravely writing to a newspaper that the orator's remarks were nothing but stale rhetoric about liberty and rights and some supposed hostility to women—without the slightest allusion to the only important point, namely, whether women are competent to be good physicians and surgeons. Here you see is a worthy person who has not even a tolerably remote idea of the ludicrous position in which he places himself. "It is not," says the orator, "the business of men to theorize about the competency of women to do this or that, because competency can not be abstractly determined, especially by traditionally prejudiced minds—the business of men is to allow the utmost freedom of choice, not to hamper it with doubts and wonders and surmises and suspicions. Give women every opportunity of education that men have, and if the maternal instinct of a woman is not strong enough to overbear her fondness for a quadratic equation—to paraphrase Sydney Smith's witticism—let the maternal instinct in that woman go. It certainly is not the duty of men to keep women ignorant in order that they may continue to be women." And no sooner does the luckless speaker take his seat than the worthy person who has been gravely listening shakes his head and exclaims, "Tut, tut! mere froth of words! Why doesn't this gentleman leave his various faces and tell us whether women are competent to be doctors?"

To answer this question in the briefest terms—"Because nobody but women themselves can tell us, and they will never have the chance to tell us if we undertake to decide for them in advance."

This view seems to include all the aspects of the question. There really is no occasion for the horror which some good people express, as if a woman who thinks she is quite as capable of voting for a school trustee for her children as her gardener, who lately came from Tipperary, is therefore a kind of moral monster—a woman trying to unsex or de-womanize herself. She may or she may not wish to do it, as is the case with men. But that the idea should seem repulsive or strange can only excite a pleasant smile upon the part of any body whose mind has ever seriously moved upon the subject. Mr. Hoar, a Representative in Congress from Massachusetts, recently said before a committee of the Legislature of that State that he had known in Concord a woman fitted by her accomplishments to fill any chair in Harvard College, and every one who knew her knew that she was equally competent to every duty in her household. Now this lady, so far as the Easy Chair knows, never asked nor wished to vote for school trustees or for any other office.

Such women are known to every body—not, indeed, of the accomplishments of the lady to whom Mr. Hoar referred, because her attainments were unusual, whether among men or women. But there are plenty of women every where who in general judgment are superior to men. All that is or can be asked is that they enjoy the same opportunities as men, without any theory of their competence or incompetency. Possibly the worthy but uncomfortable listener who was waiting to hear whether certain men supposed that women can be learned and skillful doctors will, upon further reflection, perceive that he was waiting for a very ridiculous thing. Suppose that Dr. Parker had said, "I don't believe that woman ought to study medicine, or will ever attain any skill in the practice," would the worthy listener have retired from the pretty little theatre with the conviction that Dr. Parker's opinion settled the matter? Would he not, being a just and reasonable person, have instantly answered, "I don't want Dr. Parker's theory upon the subject. I want the women themselves to prove it."

The very point upon which the most intelligent women insist is that men shall not interpose their opinions and prejudices as the laws of nature. They insist that the form of the vine shall not be considered the type of the pear-tree merely because men think it pretty and convenient to train it upon an espalier. The worthy listener complains that somebody did not say whether he thought the tree naturally grew in that form. No, he did not. Somebody said that if you wish to know the natural form of a pear-tree you must leave it to show for itself.

Women as Journalists

October, 1883

IN speaking a month or two ago of the various employments now open to women the Easy Chair did not especially mention what is called journalism, as it omitted to specify many others. But there is one general remark to be made upon the subject which is suggested by a recent inquiry. The nature of the work to be done is not changed by the fact that it is a woman who undertakes it. It may be done better, more delicately, more shrewdly, more honestly, but it is the same work, and requires the same qualities, whether the worker be a man or a woman. There are, indeed, some special branches of labor upon a newspaper, such as that which relates to the dress of women, to needle and other work of the kind, with which women are naturally more familiar than men, and women will therefore treat them more satisfactorily and intelligently. But "a woman's duty upon a newspaper" is substantially the same with that of a man.

Perhaps the most conspicuous and noted of women who have been employed in journalism was Harriet Martineau. For some years she wrote editorially for a London paper. Her articles were upon the current public questions of the hour—the policy of the government at home and abroad, the characters of eminent public men, and the various problems of political economy. There was no editorial contemporary of Miss Martineau's who was more fully equipped for the office of public censor, and the volume of obituary biographies which was collected from her contributions to the paper are as admirable and vivid as any which appeared in any journal of the time.

There was, however, nothing which Miss Martineau selected to do, or which was suggested to her to write, which could be defined distinctively as a woman's work on a paper. She wrote articles not as a woman, but as an editor, as Mrs. Somerville studied astronomy not as a woman, but as a scholar. If the Easy Chair may take an illustration close at hand, it would say that any woman who is anxious to know what is a woman's work upon a paper or in journalism has only to turn to the *Critic,* a weekly literary journal in New York. The *Critic* is edited by a woman, but it depends for the just and we hope assured success which it has achieved upon the ability with which it is edited, upon the tact with which public sentiment and interest are perceived, and upon the skill with which the books for review and the writers of the reviews are selected.

In such an office there is nothing which belongs peculiarly to sex, or which requires different training in a woman from that of a man. Miss Martineau was one of the most accomplished and shrewdest observers and students of politics and public affairs then living in England. She was much more capable of wisely directing the government than many men who were likely to be called into the administration. Her political views, especially upon economical subjects, were singularly enlightened and sagacious, and her series of tales illustrative of the principles of political economy were among the chief educators of public opinion in England. Her *History of the Peace* is a work so instructive and admirable that it is quite indispensable to the English legislator who would know both the course of politics in England during the first half of the century and the influences which really controlled those politics. But in all this there was nothing which was peculiar to a woman.

For that part of journalism, therefore, which concerns the treatment of great political and industrial questions, and comment upon public affairs, a woman must look for her outfit and qualification not in any distinction of sex but in taste and education and literary faculty. For that other part which involves the treatment of special topics, or the work of selection and adaptation for the paper, her main reliance must be upon her quickness, intelligence, industry, experience, and temperament. Her womanly qualities, her patience, devotion, tranquillity, and conscientiousness, will be always most serviceable, but the work of journalism as such is of no sex, any more than that of setting type.

Office-Seekers and Office-Holders

September, 1857

OU R correspondent belongs to no corps, and is attached to no organ of public opinion. He is a private, and not a public writer of letters, and his communication is of the most confidential character:

"DEAR EASY CHAIR AND FATHER-CONFESSOR,—I acknowledge it, with my pen in my hand, and with tears in my eyes! It is true, and I will not add denial to disgrace. I have been an OFFICE-SEEKER. I came here for an office, and here have I waited from the fourth day of March until this day, an office-seeker still, and nothing else, until—and here, believe me, that I find in this avowal a lower deep of degradation—I have become an OFFICE-HOLDER. Let me confess. You know my tendencies as a politician. I was always one, from that first leader in the *Bogville Trumpet,* in the campaign of 1840—in which I established beyond controversy that Colonel Johnson did actually kill Tecumsch, and that General Harrison was not present at the Battle of Tippecanoe—down through every succeeding contest, local or national, to the last. I never asked for nor wanted a place for myself, and when I went into the canvass, and stumped my native State for Buchanan, I did it, I will not say out of pure patriotism, but as a matter of course, and without a thought beyond the success of my party. You are probably aware that we did succeed—and what then? My evil genius tempted me in the form of a Collectorship. It was vacant, for the incumbent died just about the time of the election. It was moderately lucrative, and was just the place for me. My friends said I ought to have it. Stripe, the editor of the *Trumpet,* and our leading man in the party, never says much, but he has a wink which we all look up to and respect; and when I broached the subject to him, he winked in the most encouraging and satisfactory manner. Now, Easy Chair, I am not going to tire you out by going through a description of the process by which this coveted office gradually grew to be the desire of my heart, inseparably linked with those visions in which, in common, I suppose, with all young men, I too indulged, and which in my particular case may be specified as the Future, Fame, and Fanny. Suffice it to say that when I went up to the Inauguration in company with Stripe, I was fairly in training as a competitor for this prize, and, as soon as the Cabinet was organized, I went to the Secretary of the Exterior, on whom I had some claims on the score of family connexion, stated my case and my claims, and asked his influence. The Secretary charmed me by his manners. He took a deep interest in the state of crops in our part of the country, and made several inquiries as to the number of inhabitants in Bogville, and other matters of local interest there, which inspired me with a profound sense of the comprehensive grasp of his mind. He promised to aid me, and took a prodigious pinch of snuff. This emboldened me to seek an interview with the President, who, by a remarkable coincidence, made very much the same inquiries as the Secretary respecting the state of our crops and population, a circumstance which led me to infer that the affairs of Bogville were occupying no small share of the attention of the Executive, and that I could not be overlooked in the scrutiny. I went to the hotel and reported progress to Stripe. He winked for several seconds with his left eye, indicative of assured confidence and a calm conviction of success. So I went to bed happy, and dreamed that I was planting corn around the Bogville Custom-house, and taking the census of its inhabitants arm in arm with Fanny.

"The next day I expected my commission, but it did not arrive. I waited a week, a fortnight, and then consulted Stripe. He was on the eve of departure, having been mysteriously occupied with the delegation from our Congressional District, and had but a moment to spare; but there was encouragement, and I may say certainty, in his wink, and he left by the next train.

"About noon of the following day I began to feel that I was an office-seeker. It had never occurred to me before. The sensation came over me like the first chilling premonition of an ague fit. It was requested to settle my bill to date—the tone of the request revealed its motive—and as I pulled out my purse and paid the clerk, I felt that with the fifty dollars which he called for I parted with all my self-respect. Every man in the house knew my errand; every eye was upon me, morning, noon, and night; every other office-seeker recognized me as his fellow, and hated me for my pretensions; and even in the tipping of the whips of the hackney-coachmen, as I stepped from the hotel-door to the sidewalk, there was something that looked as if they were pointing me out as an object of derision.

"I fled from the place? No. I could not fly; I was chained to it by a fascination which I can not fathom or describe. The expected office held me as its victim, and would not let me go. Day after day wore away, and I began to hold up my head again. I made acquaintances with my companions in the hope of patronage; and, miserable tide-waiters that we were, we sat together and watched for the moving of the waters, and counted our chances and made wagers as to our prospects. I felt my manhood wasting away under this wretched proba-tion; but my vision had become so intently fixed on the single point of my desire, that every other object was obscured, and my whole existence turned on this single point.

"I was summoned at last to the Department of the Exterior. The Secretary was as affable as ever, and held out his hand and his snuff-box in the most fraternizing manner.

" 'There was a batch of appointments put through at the Cabinet meeting this morning,' said the Secretary, 'and yours among them.'

"The news did not thrill me. I took it as quietly as if he had asked about the crops again. I had lost even the capacity of satisfaction at my own success. Three months before, and this announcement would have brought my heart to my mouth, and to my imagination the whole Future, every thing of Fame, the *tout ensemble* of Fanny. I was alarmed at my own apathy.

" 'To be sure,' he went on to say, after a liberal pinch, "it isn't exactly what you asked for—in fact, quite a different sort of affair. But I suppose it is all one to you; we have to do the best thing we can, and, bless me! to a young man like you, a Consulship is a hundred per cent. better than a Collectorship at Bogville.'

" 'A Consulship! Do you mean to say, Judge—?'

" 'I mean to say, my dear North, that the place you asked for was promised by the President, six weeks ago, to sombody else, and filled yesterday, and there is a prejudice, you know, against putting two men in the same office at once. They do such things in New York, but we manage it differently here. Besides, nobody ever gets the place he asks for; and this is the first lesson in these matters, which the veteran beggars (no offense to you, North) understand so perfectly, that they make a point of applying for some office they do not want, in the hope of getting some office that they do want. Because a man does not get a seat in the Cabinet, it does not follow that he may not be sent to Kansas as Governor and Dictator. In your case, by way of compensation and special favor, you are appointed Consul at the port of Girgenti.'

"The Furies! This was a blow which at once annihilated me, or rather the counterfeit office-seeking substitute for myself which had usurped the place of my better nature, and the shock brought back my stray senses.

"My punishment was just, and I accepted it. I swallowed the disappointment without a wry face, and took my destiny as if it had been a joke. The indignation with which at first I intended to reject the proffered office was lulled into silence by the thought which flashed across my mind, Why not carry out the joke, and avail myself of this grand excuse to see the world? If I can not be a Collector to please myself, why not be a Consul to please—nobody?

" 'Only, my dear Judge, can you give me the faintest idea where Girgenti is?'

"Here followed a pinch which might have suited the nose of Slawkenbergius.

" 'Upon my word—why really, it is in Portugal, or Spain, or Italy, is it not? Certainly it is somewhere. You ought to know, if any body, as you are Consul there. Go into the next office and consult the encyclopedias, there are two of them—and North, by the way, have you got any tobacco about you—fine cut?'

" 'I am sorry to say that I have not,' I replied, 'but, I have got a small box of blue pills, capital correctives. Will they do just as well?'

"The secretary did not take; he rarely takes any jokes except his own; so we shook hands and parted. I got to the bottom of the stairs before it occurred to me that I had not asked him the name of my successful rival. I went back, but it was too late. The statesman was deep in dispatches relating to the great case of reprisals for the capture of two lobster cars on the coast of Cape Cod by the crew of the British smack *Luncheon,* and 'No admittance' stood out as if in letters of white chalk on the countenance of the grave gentleman of color who kept guard at the door. I must ascertain at once who is Collector of Bogville. What grieves me most of all in the matter is the disappointment which I know my old friend Stripe will feel, and my utter loss of confidence in his winks. This is a severe blow. I have followed Stripe's wink as my guiding star. It has been a beacon in my darkest hours. And now it is no more than the wink of any body else. It would only twitch to bewilder, and twitter to blind. I can not even submit to him the question which perplexes me—Shall I go and see the world under cover of this proffered parchment? What do you advise, most sagacious Easy Chair? To hear is to obey.

"And do you know where Girgenti is?

"Yours, penitently and inquisitively,

"WESTERN NORTH.

"P.S.—I have discovered all; treason has done its worst. It is *Stripe himself who has been appointed Collector of Bogville.* Who could have believed it! My eyes are opened, my trunk is packed, and my mind is made up. I will demand satisfaction for every wink—no, for that final and most perfidious one with which he left me to my fate and went off with the Presidential promise in his own favor. I will practice with hair-triggers at eyelids, and if I can get a side-shot at the Collector, and take his off close under the eyebrows, I shall feel that I have done the State some service. Again I ask, do you know where Girgenti is?

W. N."

Party Spirit and Fear of Ruin

April, 1877

THE political history of the English-speaking race is the history of party spirit. Macaulay said of the House of Peers: "It is certain that no man has the least confidence in their impartiality when a great public functionary, charged with a great state crime, is brought to their bar. They are all politicians. There is hardly one among them whose vote on an impeachment may not be confidently predicted before a witness has been examined." American experience does not entirely confirm this opinion. The most famous impeachment in our history, although decided by a political assembly, was not decided by party spirit, and it is to the American branch of the English-speaking race that we must look for the most signal self-restraints of that spirit. Contrary to the general impression, and notwithstanding the melancholy head-shakings of many prophets of evil, it is plain that the fury of party was greater at the beginning of the century than it is now, both in England and in this country. Our Congressional debates are often hot and angry, but we seldom hear such remarks as those which were made in the British House of Commons in 1782. The orator was speaking of the Prime Minister, and he said that "if Lord Shelburne was not a Catiline or a Borgia in morals, it must not be ascribed to any thing but his understanding." It was no tyro or shallow-pate who said it. The orator was Edmund Burke. And Fox said that he had no doubt that the ministry "would now strengthen themselves by any means which corruption could procure."

In this country, party feeling was never more intense and bitter than during the Genet troubles under Washington's administration, and in the discussion about the Jay treaty, nor has any President been so personally insulted as Washington upon his retirement, except in one recent instance, in which the offender acknowledged the enormity of his conduct and apologized. That fact alone is full of significance. The election of Jefferson was another Saturnalia of party spirit. There were multitudes of intelligent men who thought it presaged the destruction of all that was most precious in our system of government, and who apprehended a kind of cataclysm of immorality and wickedness, in which the nation would disappear. They were mistaken. It did not follow that because their side of the shield was golden, the other side might not be silver, or even *vice versa.* When the bill abolishing the slave-trade passed the House of Lords, Lord St. Vincent declared that the British Constitution and the great bulwarks of society had been swept away. That is always the opinion of every body who feels strongly when his plans have been baffled and his party beaten. It is but natural, for an honest and well-meaning man belongs to this or that party because he believes that it more truly promotes the public welfare. Just in the degree of his sincerity, therefore, is his apprehension under defeat. When we add to this the interests of patronage, the pride of power, the greed of ambition, we have all the elements of tremendous strife.

The best sedative in times of great political excitement is history. When a party is beaten, it thinks the country is going to the dogs. In the life of Lord Shelburne, an interesting chapter of English history at the end of the last century, it appears that his lordship said a hundred years ago—although he was a disciple of Lord Chatham and a friend of America—"The moment that the independence of America is agreed to by our government, the sun of Great Britain is set, and we shall no longer be a powerful or respectable people." Lord Shelburne was very positive. But it happened that he was the minister who afterward virtually concluded the negotiation for peace and the acknowledgment of independence. He was as positive as Benedick when he flouted women. He was as sure as Fisher Ames when Jefferson was elected. But he lived to see America independent, and to say that he meant to prepare for the rising of the star of Great Britain with greater lustre than ever. In this country the opponents of the Constitution of 1787—our happy Constitution—were quite as sure that that terrible instrument would destroy popular liberty as Lord Shelburne was that the British star would set if America became independent. " 'Tis really astonishing," said Richard Henry Lee, "that the same people who have just emerged from a long and cruel war in defense of liberty should now agree to fix an elective despotism upon themselves and their posterity." "Some of the powers must be abridged," said Samuel Chase, "or public liberty will be endangered, and in time destroyed." Joshua Atherton congratulated anti-Constitution members of the New York Convention that they had the opportunity "to save our devoted country from impending ruin." George Clinton said of the same Convention: "The friends to the rights of mankind outnumber the advocates of despotism nearly two to one."

Nor was the opposition confined to words. The spirit of party was fierce. Mr. John C. Hamilton asserts that there was a party combination to take the life of his father, the great champion of the Constitution, by the duel; and Colonel Oswald did certainly challenge him, but upon explanation withdrew the challenge. On the 3d of July, 1788, twenty days before the New York Convention adopted the Constitution, came the news of the ratification by Virginia. The friends of the new charter marched to the fort in Albany, read it aloud with exultation, and fired a salute. The next day, the Fourth of July, the opponents of the Constitution, who believed that its adoption would be the setting of the star of American liberty, marched to the fort and burned the charter. Its friends, rejoicing in prospective victory, attempted to pass triumphantly the house where the other party were holding their celebration. But the latter fell upon them and drove them back. The Constitutionalists rallied, and approached by another street. But again the other party were ready, and had planted a small cannon loaded with stones to repel the assaulting column. The Constitutionalists pressed on, and as the dragoons at their head began the charge, the anti-Constitutionalists tried to fire the cannon. But it had been spiked, like the gun in Governor Dorr's assault upon the Providence arsenal in 1842, or the priming was wet, and it would not explode. A conflict followed, and the stony battle of Green Street is historical.

In the city of New York, after the Constitution was adopted, its friends resolved to punish its opponents by destroying the press of the publisher Greenleaf, whose paper had been the organ of opposition. They assaulted his house. He fired a pistol among them, and gallantly defended his castle. But the mob triumphed. Greenleaf and his friends fled, and the publication of the paper was suspended for many days. The rioters also proposed to visit General John Lamb, a tough old soldier of the Revolution, who was Collector of the Port under the State government, and who was subsequently appointed to the same position under the new Constitution by President Washington. Lamb was as brave as a lion. He made due preparation. Four veterans of the war, two young men, and a colored servant who had attended Lamb at the battle of Monmouth, composed the garrison of the house. The general directed in person. His house was on the south side of Wall Street, midway between Pearl and William streets, about the present site of the banking house of Brown Brothers. He had laid in fifteen or twenty stand of arms, with proper ammunition and side-arms. The lower doors and windows were barred, the hall was barricaded with the furniture of the dining-room, the stairway was obstructed in the same manner, and the garrison was massed in the second story. The boys were stationed at the magazine to hand fresh muskets and to load. The general placed each man, with strict orders not to fire until he should begin the action, and all the lights in the house were extinguished except at the arsenal. Loop-holes were cut in the window-shutters for observation, and the general calmly awaited the assault. The rioters arrived. They filled the street in a dense throng. They roared, threatened, and challenged. But there was no reply. The house was dark and silent. The leaders of the mob held a council of war. They decided that the house was either deserted or garrisoned. They knew General Lamb, and concluded that it was probably not deserted. Then embracing the better part of valor, and shouting defiance, they withdrew.

The Constitution so bitterly opposed was adopted. But it has not ruined our devoted country, as Joshua Atherton feared, nor have the rights of mankind been imperiled, as George Clinton believed. The desponding American to-day, as he hears gloomy forebodings that we have surely reached the end, that liberty has now been finally overthrown, and that only accumulating disaster remains, should carefully inquire whether Jeremiah belongs to a party that has won or lost, and remember Lord Shelburne, Burke, Benedick, Clinton, and the Constitution that was to destroy America.

Political Passions in America

December, 1876

ONE thing, at least, is shown by the political contest from which the country has just emerged. It proves that the theorists are mistaken who assume that society can not stand the strain of a really popular canvass, or an appeal to universal male suffrage involving such enormous interests as those of a change of administration. Three or four months since, the Easy Chair quoted from the diary of John Quincy Adams, less than forty years ago, his apprehension of the consequences of the system of monster meetings which came in with the Harrison campaign of 1840. The general characteristics of that exciting time have been reproduced in every subsequent national canvass, except that during and since the war the aspect of the canvass has been naturally somewhat more sober. But, upon the whole, the essential good humor and toleration in the larger part of the country have been much the same. Even in the election which immediately preceded the war, the general character of the canvass was unchanged. It was full of significant signs to the acute observer, but the gayety, the music, the banners, the transparencies, the general festivity of the mass-meeting, were the same.

The celebrated tourist from New Zealand would probably be chiefly impressed by the real self-restraint and good nature of our great political meetings. Hogarth's pictures and the English memoirs show a kind of brutality at the British hustings which is unknown among us. The rioting, the brickbats, the disorder and terror, which attended an old English election have had little parallel in this country. There have, indeed, been election riots, but very few and exceptional. We naturally find the explanation in our system. The universality of the suffrage gives every man a sense of responsibility and importance which is essentially conservative. In England, the mob that chaired the member was not a mob of the voters. In a population of eight millions a hundred years ago there were but a hundred and sixty thousand voters in England. It is a favorite fancy of clubs, and one which comes in

43

with the old Madeira after dinner, that general suffrage is the source of all our woes. But the practical question is not so much what we might have been without it, as what we shall do with it now that we have it. Garland says in his *Life of John Randolph* that that wayward character cherished fond dreams of a patriarchal society as the best of all—a society in which a baron lived in a fine castle, surrounded by swarms of happy dependents, whom he guided and befriended, and who looked up to him as their protector. Many other Americans besides John Randolph have dreamed the same dream. The fancy lurks in that fine old Madeira. But, in that Arcadia, Randolph always means to be the baron, and not one of the happy dependents. It is like Disraeli's picture of the political ideal of "Young England" in *Coningsby* and *Sybil*. In other years the Easy Chair has heard from the lips of an accomplished college president the same glowing praises of a political and social system of superiors and inferiors. But the implication was the same. The painters and the poets of that visionary realm always reserve the best places for themselves.

When we consider the intense and profound excitement of such a summer and autumn as those just ended, the passionate appeals to prejudice and political hostility, the natural personal rivalries and jealousies, with the general irresponsibility of declamation among a fluent people, arising from a half admission that all is fair in politics, and above all these the sincere conviction of so many honest thousands that the prosperity and progress, if not the actual existence, of the nation are at hazard, the tranquillity of the election itself and the prompt acquiescence in the result are very agreeable facts. They are certainly significant signs of the peculiar "capacity of this people for self-government," whatever may be true of other people.

The old Madeira philosophers, however, are apt to smile in pleasant contempt of the general aspect and character of the mass-meeting. They see immense enthusiasm for frenzied rhetoric and the most shallow sophistry. They hear false issues raised and lustily cheered. Or they observe that second-rate and even immoral men are gladly hailed as leaders. But such philosophers require that every voter and attendant at a mass-meeting shall be as well-informed, as clear-headed, as high-minded, as they are themselves. The striking fact at a great popular

meeting is the general good sense, the interest in discussion of principles, the sympathy with a high and patriotic view. Passion, brilliancy,
whimsical and epigrammatic extravagance, are, indeed, greatly relished,
but, after all, with the same invincible good humor. The crowd cheers
the sayer of a good thing, but not necessarily all that it may be made
to mean. The applause for men and leaders, also, is given to what
the crowd believes of them, not to what a better-informed man may
know to be the truth. If Dick Turpin leaps the turnpike bar handsomely
and throws a gold sovereign to a poor cripple by the way, it is the
manly dash and act of generosity which the crowd applauds. The cheers
are not approval of theft. If the shouters knew that this gay horseman
had waylaid honest laborers to steal their purses, and that the money
he flings so jauntily was filched from a poor widow, they would pull
him from the saddle. And when this is made plain, they see him
ride by to the gallows with satisfaction, while they do not refuse admiration to the pluck with which he wears his nosegay and stands
under the tree.

The better the man, the more the crowd likes him. It may, indeed,
be very much mistaken. But it applauds what it believes him to be;
and the duty of the philosopher who deplores the kind of man that
the crowd cheers is to show what kind of man he is. The Easy Chair
has heard the name of Mr. Jonathan Wild loudly and warmly cheered
at a public meeting, and other Easy Chairs have been exceedingly dis-
gusted with the applause. But the crowd knew that Wild had thrashed
a sneak thief whom he saw stealing a blindman's dog. Nobody denied
that he had done that. And when Mr. Wild's political opponents declared that he had himself picked the blindman's pocket, the crowd
attributed the story to malice, and would not believe it. It has no
time to investigate closely, and it will not trust the tale of his opponents. But if one of themselves, whom they know to be their friend,
points out to them the proof, they will not reject it. When Tweed
gave fifty thousand dollars' worth of coal to the poor, the poor saw
and felt only his generosity; and if his opponents had charged that
it was stolen, the poor would have mobbed them, and carried Tweed
on their shoulders. But if one whom they trusted had traced that coal
money from the earnings of the laborer, through his rent and the

taxes of his landlord, into the public treasury, the laborer would have seen that the coal was bought with his own money, which Tweed had stolen, and his cheers would have changed into curses.

If the applause be wrongly timed, it is the fault of the platform rather than of the floor of the meeting. It was a shrewd young preacher who went to fulfill an exchange, and when the sexton said to him that if he saw any body sleeping in the pews, he would stir them up, said, "No, no; if you see any body sleeping, come up into the pulpit and stir me up." Let no Madeira philosopher reproach the crowd with cheering an unworthy person until he has done his duty by telling the crowd what he knows of the person and his character and conduct. It is not his Jonathan Wild, but their own, that the crowd cheers. And if honest people wish to keep Mr. Wild out of politics, they must not leave it to his opponents to show what he is.

But all of us, friends and foes of Mr. Wild, have a right to be glad and proud of the way in which we endure the strain of a contest like that which has just ended.

III/William Dean Howells
1900-1920

Around the turn of the last century a man could be sure that he was really famous when he saw his name and portrait on a cigar box label. That was one of the honors conferred on William Dean Howells; like other literary immortals, such as Robert Burns and John Ruskin, he had a cigar named after him. He also was elected the first president of the American Academy of Arts and Letters in 1908 and was continuously reelected until his death. Best-selling novelists traditionally are sneered at by the critics, but Howells was—at the apex of his career—given the reverential treatment. For decades he was the best known American writer in Europe, including Russia. His judgments as a critic and editor could make or break other authors. He was praised by characters as diverse as Karl Marx's daughter, President Rutherford B. Hayes, and Henry George. He was proclaimed as "the dean of American letters" so often that the phrase made him wince.

The glory, alas, did not last out his lifetime. He lived to see his reputation overshadowed by those of two close friends, Mark Twain and Henry James, both of whom were published, like Howells, by Harper & Brothers. The realistic novel, which he practically invented, was taken over by more forceful writers, such as Frank Norris and Theodore Dreiser—and then went out of fashion. A final humiliation was that one of his manuscripts (not an Easy Chair) was rejected, shortly before his death, by *Harper's Magazine,* which had been eager to get every word he would give it for more than three decades.

Even Van Wyck Brooks, his generally admiring biographer, admitted that Howells wrote too much: "Two out of three of his novels had been inferior to the best." And in his later years, he plainly was out of touch with the times, a man of the nineteenth century who had little to say to the twentieth.

The same thing might have been said of *Harper's Magazine* during the twenty years Howells wrote the Easy Chair. That was the final period of the editorship of Henry Mills Alden, who hung on to the job for fifty years, far too long for any editor. He and the magazine declined together into a kind of tired gentility—and the best that can be said for many of Howells' columns is that they fitted perfectly the publication in which they appeared. It is probably fortunate that Howells died shortly after Thomas B. Wells took over the editorship in 1919, because in the process of reinvigorating the magazine Wells certainly would have replaced him with a more contemporary mind.

As the foregoing suggests, I find Howells the least interesting of the writers who contributed to the Easy Chair. In selecting six of his columns for inclusion here I hope that I have at least been fair to him. They indicate, I believe, some of his characteristic views: his lack of enthusiasm for the American political process, his appraisal of the publishing scene, his opposition to capital punishment, and his championship (radical for that time) of women's rights.

Authors and Publishers

February, 1906

I T would be interesting to know, if one might, how general the appeal of Mr. Henry Holt's recent *Atlantic Monthly* essay on "The Commercialization of Literature" has been. After the passion of love, and, formerly more than now, the principle of religion, there is scarcely any human affair so intimate in its hold upon the majority not immediately concerned in it as the relation of authors and publishers. It seems of such universal indigeneity that one cannot help wondering what interest supplants it among those extremely low forms of savagery in which no analogous relation exists. But this inquiry must be postponed to the more immediate duty and pleasure of recognizing the charm of Mr. Holt's treatment of his subject, and the skill with which he has brought it home to the popular business and bosom. Literature might or might not seize the widest attention; but the commercialization of literature is something that must make a mercantile community sit up as one man. This is what Mr. Holt has perceived, and the effect of his admirable paper is as final as anything in that mystical region can very well be.

It might be said that literature was always commercialized, else there would never have been any such thing as the publishing business. But the commercialization of literature which Mr. Holt means is that very immediately modern condition of the publishing business in which books are run like lines of dry-goods, and advertised like baking-powders and patent medicines. It sounds very undignified and even disgraceful, but the condition which seems so immediately modern is quantitatively rather than qualitatively novel. Within the memory of men who we hope will live long to recall the fact, the contributions of a distinguished statesman to a trashy, but otherwise irreproachable, periodical were announced with an iteration of *Edward Everett writes for it, Edward Everett writes for it,* line after line, and column after column, till the whole wide page of a New York daily paper echoed the cry. This was full fifty years ago; and probably there were other instances of depravity among publishers, not so glaring, we dare say, which we cannot now remember; but we are sure that no immediately modern explosion of publicity has been more scandalous. In fact, the student of the actual publishers' announcements will agree with us, we think, that there is almost nothing of the brute vociferance in them which marked that earlier proclamation. There is rather the vice of a too jaunty knowingness in some of them, where, for instance, the advertising man, putting on the airs of criticism,

> Assumes the god,
> Affects to nod,

and attempts the analytic and synthetic in singing his wares, as if he were an "indolent reviewer." He forgets, apparently, that a chaste sobriety of statement is the best thing, if he would catch the eyes of any but the groundlings. Possibly, however, it is the eyes of the groundlings which he mainly wishes to catch, and here is the danger, if not the disgrace, the hasty observer of conditions might say. A little reflection might convince such an observer that there is at least not so much danger, so much disgrace as appears. The advertiser is dealing with a condition which evidently he knows, and he is dealing with it according to his lights. He understands what will catch, if not what will keep, that vast, half-taught, half-bred multitude, which has lately so increased, and seems to be growing ever greater, involving the question whether culture will assimilate it, or it will assimilate culture. Whether written for it or not, most books are published for it, and whether authors live by it or not, publishers do live by it.

Publication, therefore, is commercialized, and it always has been so; but literature can be commercialized only when it aims to sell, by aiming in unworthy ways to please. It must aim to please if it would exist; but it must please by being true, by being beautiful. It must make its public; that is a long process, but the effect is lasting. It must not let the public make it, for then it is made an end of as an art; it is indeed then commercialized, like any other ware.

Some people say that this is what literature, in the imaginative forms, now does. They say that the authors of the novels which are destined to sell have got such an accurate measure of the popular tastes that they know exactly how to meet them: with what proportion of passion, adventure, suspense, relief, mystery, self-devotion, villainy, comedy, tragedy, lubricity, morality, and the rest. They know, fatally well, what the public wants, and they supply it, just as any other shop would. If this saying is true, we have the commercialization of literature as an accomplished fact; and if it is not true, there is no other commercialization possible, and we need not be afraid. No methods of advertising books can harm literature; the tricks of the trade may be indefinitely multiplied; the publishing business may be vulgarized till no self-respecting man will own himself a publisher; literature may be peddled or huckstered about in any fashion; cried from carts like bananas or oranges; pushed by agents, and foisted upon the unwary by bunco-men. Still it cannot be tainted, cannot be degraded, cannot be commercialized. Its corruption can be wrought only through the authors of it; the publishers of it cannot hurt it.

Of course they do not wish to hurt it; they wish by all means to help it; they would not probably go into a business which scarcely offers the rewards of the leanest of the learned professions, and in which few fortunes are made, if they did not somehow love books. They like the look of them, the feel of them, if nothing else; their own imprint is a pleasure to them. They like even the authors of books, even the authors of books they have lost money on; and they would rather enrich all their authors than not; next to themselves there is no one they would like so much to enrich. When they see a popular novelist rolling in his automobile, they like to think that but for them he would be trudging beside them on foot. Their relations with authors are very intimate, very tender; and they are more so than other business relations, because they somehow feel his helplessness, his generic haplessness. It may be that there is something peculiarly winning in the literary temperament; we would like to think so; or it may be that publishers are of exceptionally affectionate natures, or that their business is one which singularly softens and subdues the asperities of the mercantile relation. The process may go so far as to lead publishers into the belief that they are fonder of authors than they really are; it may even deceive the authors in some such effect.

It is, in fact, the superstition of the young author that the publisher takes his book because he loves him; and he repays the publisher's supposititious passion with an undying ardor, until some other publisher approaches him, and alienates his affections by the offer of a higher royalty. Mr. Holt touches upon this point in deploring the instability of the relation between the author and the publisher. It appears that the alienators of authors' affections are much more active than formerly, and that they stay at no means of corrupting novelists and poets. But this is the blame of the publishers and not of the authors, and again there is no commercialization of literature. That, if its artistic ideal is maintained, is as pure as ever, just as the heart of a lady released from its allegiance by the divorce court is as essentially true as ever, and may be so transferred to a new object of devotion. Besides, the inconstancy of authors is no new thing. There is a potential fickleness in the tribe, which no one knows better than themselves, and some of them go so far as to make a principle of their inconstancy. It was the serious belief, humorously avowed, of one of our best and finest that a change of publishers was very wholesome and desirable. He contended that it kept each of the author's successive publishers on the alert to hold his favor, and inspired the latest with an energy to outdo all the rest in pushing his venture. He was an author whose ideal never faltered, who always meant and always did the best that was in him, with the beautiful results we were all glad to know. Yet he preached and practised a system which Mr. Holt regards as one of the regrettable features of the present demoralization.

To his contention Mr. Holt, who sees in the impermanence of the old (perhaps prehistoric) relation of faithful authors and publishers the work of that most baleful of middlemen, the literary agent, would oppose the familiar doctrine that an author's books, if kept together in a single publisher's hands, will help sell one another. This we have ourselves always believed, and we hope it is true; but the author of whom we have spoken believed that the books so compactly grouped were allowed to sell one another without the publisher's help. In fact (and this is an awful secret told only in whisper), authors never think that their publishers have pushed their books quite enough. They may affect a polite goose-flesh at the shameless advertisement of their productions, and they may wish the odium of it to fall altogether upon their publishers, but they wish the disgrace to keep on, and to increase in space and frequency. To their mighty gorge whole pages of all the newspapers would not be too much. They are insatiable, and perhaps they are unreasonable; but perhaps they are not unreasonable if, recalling with difficulty the titles of their earlier books, they never find the public reminded of them from year to year by the publisher who is keeping them together. He is keeping them together, they say in their hearts, with such a vengeance that apparently he has no wish to share his treasure with others. So they come to doubt that good old doctrine, and fall away into denial, or at the best lapse into a condition of cold agnosticism.

Yet with all this, literature is not commercialized, even in the greedy souls of its authors. It cannot be commercialized, we say again, unless it is made to sell, with an eye single to its sale. As for the publisher's or the bookseller's methods, they are not yet enough commercialized, they are not yet truly business methods. In most other manufactures a well-known brand brings a better price than a brand ill known or unknown. But in the book trade it is not so. A book by an author of established repute and unquestioned merit sells for no more than a book by an author of no literary excellence, or of no attested worth. The new author, the trashy author, sells for the same price as the author whose name is a measurable warrant of worth. Apparently the size, shape, and quality of the material put into a book fix its value. There is no other standard known to the trade; and therefore it seems that its methods are not businesslike. The publishing, the selling, of books needs to be commercialized at a vital point. At present it is ridiculously naïve. It still proceeds upon the theory that "A book's a book, although there's nothing in't." If a dealer in dry-goods were to put upon his counter a "beautiful line of alpacas," say, of which he knew nothing as to material or texture, or of which he knew that both were bad, and offered them at the same rate as alpacas of recognized superiority, what would be thought of his wisdom, his morality? If a dealer in wet-goods (as they are sometimes called) were to invite his customer to buy a raw or acrid vintage at the same cost as "a fine old crusty port" or a delicately tempered champagne of exquisite bouquet, because it was put up in the same kind of bottle, how long could he hope to keep the custom even of the newest millionaire who was trying to educate his palate? Yet upon precisely this principle the bookseller would indiscriminately offer his wares to the millionaire who was trying to form the library of a gentleman.

We think that Mr. Holt has miscalled his pleasant essay, and that he has really written of the demoralization of the book trade. He has written of this very knowledgefully, of course, and very justly, but, upon the whole, we feel not hopefully enough. It has great odds against it and it is in a bad way, as it always has been, but not in the worst way. It has only measurably against it the mortal enmity of the law by which the author innocently suffers, and if he lives long enough, perishes, as regards his property in his books. After a term of forty-two years, under a constitution guaranteeing equal rights to all citizens, he is singled out by the malice of the statute, and deprived of his ownership in every book of his which has come of that sad age; he is treated like a malefactor in jail rather than a benefactor at large; and the very publisher who complains of his inconstancy can safely be the first to seize his work and profit by it without offering him any portion of the gains from it.

This ought to be a great consolation, and all the greater if the aggrieved publisher refuses, as he nobly does, for the most part, to seize the advantage of the author which the statute gives him. In all forms of business man is superior to his conditions, and their amelioration through the human equation might very well persuade both author and publisher that the tie between them is more than usually sacred. Their alliance is not really more sacred than the relation of ordinary business partners, but it eventuates often in lifelong friendships, and in every case it is more honorable than that of patron and client which it replaced. The lexicographer now no longer "waits in the outward rooms" of my lord, or is "repulsed from his door," but takes his unabridged dictionary to an enterprising firm who straightway urge the public to "get the best," and provide for his declining years, or at least till those of his copyright shall have reached forty-two.

The relation of the author to his publisher is altogether of a gracefuler and sincerer friendship than the relation of patron and client, in which literature lived before it was at all "commercialized." Even when the rising young author, whom his publisher has helped up, in a genuine liking for him and his literature, takes flight to another publisher paying more, the first bears his desertion more in sorrow than in anger. He reflects that there is a great deal of human nature in man as well as genius, and he does not think too hardly of the inconstant, though he may think him something of an ingrate. At least Mr. Holt does not, and there is no part of his essay which is more amiable than that dealing with this nice, this difficult phase of the subject. In these days it must be an unfortunate young author indeed who has not received much personal kindness from his published, over and above the bargain. The glad young author feels the kindness to the bottom of his heart, and none may say how deeply that heart is wrung when duty to himself obliges him to accept a larger bid from another publisher for his second book.

Mr. Holt tells us that publishers now tempt authors away from one another much more shamefully than they used, offering them in advances and superior percentages temptations too strong for their weak natures; but he does not so much blame the authors. He knows their fragile make, and he will not visit a severe censure upon them. In fact, he discovers some excuse for them; they have a right to profit by their success in better bargains for the future; and he perceives that they may do so without derogation artistically. He would perhaps have them behave more sagaciously than they are capable of doing, and to look well before they leap from one height to a loftier acclivity. They may meet the fate of vaulting ambition; they may come croppers, and he would not like that for them.

The young author scarcely forebodes any such fate; for the young author, when the praiseful book-notices come flocking in, imagines his future secure. He cannot understand the cynical calm of his publisher; he begins to have his suspicions, he does not know of what. Yet unless some other publisher, or worse yet, some literary agent, comes to tamper with his constancy, he remains true to that first love which Mr. Holt would perhaps imply as the lifelong dream of his first publisher. Their fidelity to each other is typical of the final nature of their tie, for the author cannot go back from the publisher to the patron, and we do not see what he could forward to. Of course, some sort of cooperation is always possible, and authors joined in a species of trade-union might publish one another with a union label, and penalties for non-union authors, in the nature of boycotting, or, in extreme cases, of personal assault. But there is much in the jealous nature of authors to forbid the expectation of anything in this kind. Probably, as long as the actual economic conditions endure, we shall have authors and publishers on the present terms, with, we trust and believe, an ever-increasing amity.

On Political Campaigns

December, 1912

NOW that one of the several recent candidates for the Presidency has been chosen by an overwhelming plurality of the Electoral College and a sweeping majority of the popular vote, or that the election has gone to the House of Representatives, and by a tie there has been transferred to the Senate, with the effect of making the actual Vice-President our Chief Magistrate, it seems a fortunate moment to inquire into an interesting psychological phase of the contest so happily ended.

If there is one thing on which we practical Americans are more agreed than another, it is that we are severally and collectively governed by our convictions. We believe that we put our convictions far before our affections as rules of conduct, and further still before our emotions. Nothing, we believe, has any effect with us but reason, the severe logic of sound principles. It is our national habit to inquire into the history of the men seeking to serve or rule us—it seems much the same thing—and to accept or reject them as we find them to have been or not to have been invariably truthful, just, honest, humane, virtuous, and actuated or not in public life by the finest ideals of private life. This is what we believe, and yet the history of almost any political campaign, and especially the campaign which still shakes the Indian Summer air with its reverberations, scarcely seems to justify our belief.

We had reached this point in our cogitations when we suddenly felt the need of a disinterested spectator whose unprejudiced criticism we might invoke, and we fortunately thought of a certain Chinese philosopher who used to visit the civilized countries of the Old World in the eighteenth century, and offer his countrymen the fruits of his impartial observations in a series of letters home. No sooner had we thought of this savant than he appeared with a promptness that might have hushed us in a superstitious age, but which so exactly jumped with our occasion that we did not lose a moment in laying our misgiving, or call it quandary, before him. He seemed to have arrived in the office of the Easy Chair after a sojourn in our national midst so long as to have covered all the political events of the past six months, and he had not the least hesitation in confirming our latent doubts. He approached the matter in hand with a knowledge of our political history such as few who have lived it enjoy, and almost his first remark expressed his surprise that we should always devote so much of our time and strength to the investigation of the moral and personal history of the different men whom we proposed to vote for or against.

When we answered him that we made this sort of inquiry for the satisfaction which could come only from an instructed judgment of them, he said, with the polite perplexity which is so charming in Chinese philosophers, "But I cannot understand how, since this is so, you seem never to have acted from that judgment. It appears that almost from the beginning of your national history the characters of your popular favorites have been shown such as to shock great minorities of your people without affecting the opinion of the majorities. How is this, if you act from judgment based upon faith in the integrity and honor of the men chosen to office among you?"

In reply we felt obliged to begin by disabling the capacity of any foreigner, however amiable and enlightened, to understand a people so complex as ourselves and then we begged him to explain a little further. Naturally he complied with our request by further question. He asked whether we really thought that a single voter's mind had ever been changed by anything proven for or against any one of the admirable men chosen or rejected in the recent election.

We could only try to smile compassionately in saying that the sort of inquiry made had been for the purpose of influencing the minds of voters who were not yet of fixed opinions. "What we call the floating vote," we said; and then he wished to know whether such a vote was large, and we explained that it was the unknown quantity in our problem, but probably it was not important. We thought ourselves very frank in this, and when the philosopher demanded what caused the great changes which had from time to time taken place in our political opinions, we answered that it was something which appealed to the conscience, as in the memorable revulsion, sixty years ago, from pro-slavery rule. Often, we owned, the motive was slighter, and there

were cases in which many voters could give no better reason for trans-
ferring their allegiance than that they thought we needed a change.
"Measures, not men," we quoted a faded formula.

"But I noticed," the philosopher returned, "or I thought I noticed,
that in the recent canvass comparatively little was said about measures
and a very great deal about men. The several candidates were accused
of every inveracity, hypocrisy, imbecility, every species of incivism,
of a willingness to ruin their country for the gratification of their
selfish ambition."

"Certainly, there was something of that sort," we admitted, and
then our overweening truthfulness obliged us to add, "There was
everything of that sort. It was a canvass embittered in unparalleled
measure by personal disappointments and resentments."

"But those accusations, so freely made, did they have any sensible
effect on the result?" the philosopher pursued, and we were forced
to own:

"No, we can't honestly say they had."

"But they were addressed to the reason, the conscience?"

"Yes, apparently they were."

"Apparently? I don't understand."

"You must realize that in this country every man has his reason
and his conscience in his own keeping. Many things may be addressed
to them, but it is quite for each voter to say whether his reason or his
conscience shall be affected by those things."

"In the way of argument, yes. But if the things are in the way
of fact?"

"Then," we explained, "each voter is competent to decide for himself
that the alleged facts are lies."

The philosopher drew a long breath. "I see! Then it was all to
no purpose?"

"We cannot say that, exactly. With the unimportant exception of
the unknown quantity, the floating vote, every American citizen enters
into such a contest with his mind made up through cold reason in
a process something like this: 'I, A B, being of sound mind and perfect
in wind and limb, have decided that C D is the fittest man to be
President because I like him and trust him, and because, as I am neither
fool nor knave, I could not like or trust a bad man, or any but the

best man. I do not care what others may think or say of him; I believe in him, and I shall vote for him in spite of anything, even, that he thinks or says himself.' "

Our statement silenced the philosopher for the moment; he winked his Oriental eyes, at once almond and oblique, and then we saw him gathering head for another question, which came in the words, "But isn't this decision rather temperamental, the effect of sentiment, of emotion?"

"It might be," we said, "in a person who was sentimental or emotional, but we invite you to realize that the Americans are never so. Each of us, as has been exemplified, being neither fool nor knave, may safely trust the decision which he reaches intuitively as well as logically. The sum of such decisions gives the triumph of reason in our elections."

"Yes, that is so if the decisions in a certain case form a majority. But what of the minorities which, if united, would sometimes form a losing majority over the winning plurality?"

"That is a matter," we explained, "which may be safely left to take care of itself. The wisdom of our system is proved by the fact that it works. Everybody acquiesces in the result."

"Yes, yes!" the philosopher said, with perplexity. "But we are leaving the question which we began with. Why, if you all enter into a political canvass with your minds made up, whether logically or emotionally, do you spend so much time and money in the endeavor to change one another's minds?"

"It is impossible to answer that question, unless by the supposition that the discussion releases the electricity latent in the body politic and ultimately tends to establish the civic health. It may be said that, while our opinions are logical, our actions are mystical; all may understand the first, few (especially foreigners) the last. In monarchical countries no such release takes place; and such countries suffer indefinite discomfort and malaise, or else relieve themselves by violent explosions called revolutions. When they are also constitutional countries, some relief is afforded by the parliamentary elections, the parliamentary debates; but the process is seldom so drastic as that which you have witnessed in our recent Presidential canvass, and not so completely effective. The change of executive takes place through the succession of the hereditary heir to the throne; and though possibly the vast majority of his subjects know him to be dissolute, mendacious, feeble-minded, nobody dreams of urging the facts as reasons why he should not be king."

"I know all that," the philosopher submitted. "But, if you will excuse me, all that does not convince me you are right in your premise."

"What is our premise, pray?" we demanded, rather sardonically.

"That your citizens reason to their preferences in their choice of a candidate. If they reasoned to it they would be open to reasons against it, often in the form of undeniable facts, now absolutely wasted. It appears to me, if you will excuse my saying so, that your people are politically actuated in their preference by affection, by emotion; that they *feel* their way, and are therefore not to be moved from the end which is also the beginning."

"Prove it!" we cried.

"How does one prove such a thing? You admit that the fact has this appearance?"

"And if it has?"

"Well, then, I think your premise is wrong. You could only be right in it when there is some great moral, fundamental question before you, like the slavery question; otherwise you do not act politically from conviction; you act from fancy, from prejudice. What has become of the motives which actuated their followers in the support of Clay, of Blaine, of Bryan, to name only popular favorites who failed? Their followers loved these men; they could not tell why because they had not reasoned why; they might have reasoned why convincingly, but they did not reason at all. You are forgiving my frankness?"

"Oh, by all means. It is very interesting. But you don't call the initiative, the referendum, and the recall great moral, fundamental questions, then?"

"In answer I will ask whether you consider them of the proportion and the quality of the slavery question?"

"No, certainly not."

"Well, I should say your people did not vote on them; they voted on the men who favored or opposed them; and in this they obeyed their affections, they acted from their emotions. The characters of the different candidates had nothing to do with their decision for or against them; it was their natures which attracted or repelled the voters' liking. They felt that they would be safe with this man or that because, irrespective of his actions, even of his expressions, they knew he was this or that kind of man; and they knew he was so because they felt it in their bones."

The philosopher smiled, not more, we fancied, from satisfaction in his argument than from pleasure in his apt use of the concluding phrase.

His amiability, if not his argument, was irresistible, and we admitted: "There may be something in what you say. But we are glad you have agreed with us that when there is a question of vital importance, like the slavery question, before our people, they act from their reason. By the way, how is it with you in China when it is not a question of foot-binding or cutting off queues, but only a choice between men, all equally patriotic?"

"Ah," the philosopher said, in the act of vanishing back into the eighteenth century, "we are only just commencing republic."

The Suffragettes

June, 1913

THE history of the most momentous civic reform known to the race has embodied during the last three months a variety of facts which the votaries of the Easy Chair cannot ignore if they would maintain their well-earned repute for philosophic observance of human events.

As if it were not enough to have broken windows, filled postal boxes with tar and corrosive acids, assaulted the persons and blown up the houses of Cabinet ministers, overpowered protective as well as preventive policemen, and outraged the sensibilities even of black-guards, the English suffragettes went, in early March, to the opposite extreme of throwing a petition for the female vote into the carriage of the King and Queen as their sacred majesties were driving to open Parliament. At the time this exercise of the meekest of the subject's constitutional rights was regarded with ungovernable fury by many who questioned aghast what the suffragettes would do next in the furtherance of their cause: possibly kneel in the mud as their dread sovereigns passed and join in a service of song invoking the help of those peculiarly powerless potentates. It did not actually come to that, but no one can ever say what the suffragettes will do or will have done next. What is certain is that the crowning impropriety of petitioning sacred majesty in such a manner (instead of writing to its secretary as they should) is the least offensive of the many advertisements which the suffragettes have employed to keep the cause of female suffrage before the people, as they declare it the object of their atrocious indecorums to be. The King seems to have understood something of the kind, and so far as his helplessness under the constitution availed, he interfered to save the fair petitioners from the virtuous ferocity of the bystanders.

That was a good advertisement for the principle of monarchy which, in these days, is by no means wanting in just and kind kings to endear it to the people. George the Fifth is apparently a king whom any of the earlier Georges might well have patterned by in this, if not in other things, and the contemporaneous mob of half-drunken and wholly savage republican sovereigns who, under the patronage of the local police, insulted and hustled a peaceable suffrage parade in Washington might profit by the King's example, and another time recognize the right of petition. The assertion of this was what the women's Washington parade amounted to; but the right of petition, to be sure, has never been tenderly regarded at Washington in times past; there were times when Congress itself denied it if exercised against slavery; and men still living can remember how rudely it fared with Coxey's Army when it came to petition Congress for Good Roads. But that was long ago, and now it is not a question of owning men and women, or of improving the highways, but of letting women, equally with men, own the means of making the laws which all must obey, or ought to obey.

This is as far as we think any one can safely go in defense of the suffragettes or the suffragists, and we make haste here to begin picking our steps. There is no doubt but the methods of the English militants have been very exasperating, and the witnesses rather more than the sufferers have been exasperated beyond endurance. There are men in this country, at our safe distance of three thousand miles, who would have the militants condemned to almost any penalty short of hanging. Such men would have them punished by both fine and imprisonment, and if they attempted a hunger strike would let them perish miserably, or at least suffer as much as many innocent people are said now to suffer in our tenements. But the authorities on the ground do not find the affair so simple. They probably find the militants' offense as rank as their impatient friends and counselors here do; but possibly at the bottom of their hearts they may have a guilty sense of having paltered with the cause so dear to the militants. We do not say they have this sense; saying such a thing would be something like justifying the militants, and we who are averse to all war could never do that. But we say if the authorities have it, then that sense of guilt may embarrass them in being as high-handed or mailed-fisted as they would like to be, or we at our distance would like them to be. It is not a question of their government's losing dignity by bringing in a suffrage bill under apparent compulsion from the militants. To refuse that for such a reason would be as ignoble as the behavior of our own citizens who are now threatening not to take off their hats in elevators where there are women if the women persist in demanding the vote; or as those who pretend they would give up their seats to women in the streetcars if the women renounced their pretensions to the franchise. The sly rogues know very well that they now keep their seats for the comfort of it, and that if women renounced all hope of their civil rights they would not offer them a single one of their places. As for the chivalrous deference now shown the sex by uncovering in elevators, it has its comic side, which must be evident to the most ardent anti-suffragist. A man keeps his hat on as he stands outside of the elevator with ladies; as soon as they go inside together he takes it off, unless he suspects them of being suffragists.

It is not to be supposed that these conditional and modified favors are the only ones which anti-suffrage men stand ready to do women if women will not ask to vote. Of course, as compared with equal rights such unequal privileges are not to be overestimated. That they are not valued enough, however, is almost sufficient evidence that women are unfit for the franchise. If anything more were needed to convince men of this it might well be the ungraciousness of some women in despising that supremacy in the home which their lieges in the club and the saloon offer them. The ingrates ask, "What home?" if they have none, and they have the indelicacy to imply that the men had better provide them each a home if they wish her to be supreme in it. In large degree such women prefer the vote, and the very women whom men have established in homes, and who have no excuse for their ingratitude, would rather be citizens at the polls than sovereigns at the firesides. The poison, or say the iron, of civic ambition has entered into the souls of such a vast number of women that the time-honored *métier* of wifehood and motherhood does not satisfy those even who are wives and mothers; when they are not, the mere notion seems to make them furious.

As for the chivalrous deference which all knightly spirits now offer them in lieu of the right to help make the laws which govern them, which tax them and punish them, they have a contempt too deep for words. They boldly question the fact whether they would lose so little as this deference if they got the vote. In a good many states they already have the vote, and they deny that the men in these states are ruder to women now than they were before. Whether this is really the case or not we cannot say, but we suggest that it might be useful in states where women are still unfranchised to have each man, when he comes to register before election, make sworn answers to some such questions as: Do you now always give up your seat in the car to a strap-hanging lady? Do you always take off your hat on entering an elevator where there are ladies? What are your views on Votes for Women? If the elector answers that he is opposed to the vote, but does neither of the other things, which may be supposed for argument's sake to render women supreme in the home, he might be disfranchised at any election deciding the question of votes for women. If he can truthfully answer that he does these chivalrous things as due compensation for the vote withheld, he might be allowed to vote, but he ought to bring at least two reliable witnesses who would certify that they have seen him do the things habitually.

As the reader must by this time perceive, the problem, though in some respects soluble, is not of the simplicity of the Gordian knot; it is not much easier to cut than to untie. In our country the impatience of women for the vote is expressed not in brickbats or petards or petitions, but in parades, such as we have seen in New York holding their way unmolested, and in Washington hustled and insulted by the friends of woman's supremacy in the home. Besides the parade as a means of publicity for the suffrage cause, the American suffragists have invented pilgrimages to the state and national capitols, joyously known to the press as hikes. The hike certainly does attract notice, but of how great practical effect it is remains to be seen. What is already apparent is that the women who hike are in earnest about it; they are not in the hike for their pleasure, or even for their health. Already the hike has ceased to be an object of derision with our press, which is so fond of a joke. Possibly some dull, thick-witted witness, seeing these brave women as they drag footsore through snow and mud and dust, bearing banners of a strange device, may try to take a little thought, and may come at last to wonder why his mother and sister and wife should be without the right he knows to be mostly muddled away on himself, and should have no more voice in making the laws which govern them than the cattle in the fields. Perhaps he may come to imagine the heart-burning of the women who have long realized this, and are willing to make those cruel pilgrimages in order to remind him and his like of the wrong done them.

But the reader must not suppose that in recording these facts, grave and gay, of a pathetic and serious struggle we are subtly working round to a defense of the English militants. We indeed see no harm in their having petitioned sacred majesty for help where sacred majesty could render none. But that is not saying we would have the cause of woman pour corrosives or adhesives into postal boxes, or assault Cabinet ministers or blow up their houses, or break windows, or burn railroad stations. We hold these things, however difficult of punishment by the English government, as altogether wrong. Somehow they ought not only to be punished but prevented, and it is at this point that we venture a suggestion (very modestly and timorously indeed, and under favor of superior wisdom) which may contain the possibility of a solution. It appears from all the English suffragists have said, and from much they have done, that they want the vote. Well, then, we say, let the English government give them the vote, and trust to the chance that they will do what it hitherto has been unable to do: that is, prevent, and, when they cannot prevent, punish the outrages which they have been practising for several years past to the scandal of Christendom and to the peculiar abhorrence of the knightly gentlemen who would like us to believe they now give up their seats to women in cars and take off their hats to them in elevators.

It would be very interesting to see how the suffragettes, when once they had the power, would deal with such lawbreakers as they have been. They would deal efficaciously, we have no doubt, for women are born managers and rulers, and would stand no sort of nonsense from themselves when it came to a defiance of their power. Even as we write these prophetic words there comes the tale of how successfully the militants dealt with the disturbers of a suffrage meeting in Glasgow, which a strong force of students from the university proposed to break up. By some means their fell design became known to the women, who grappled efficiently with it. They did not invoke the help of the police whom they had themselves so often foiled. They hired in a force of mighty sons of toil from the docks, and when the students began to make trouble the sturdy mercenaries acted as "bouncers":

they thumped the studious youth, they obliged them to the hygienic but humble office of vacuum-cleaners of the floor, and then such as they did not throw into the street they thoroughly reformed and made over into quiet, law-abiding citizens, if they did not convert them to the suffrage cause. It is not positively known that the sons of toil were themselves suffragists, but they could not have better befriended the cause if they had been. The appeal to their strength whether by argument or money, was a stroke of political genius which the world is destined to recognize more and more in women. Here was no trifling with the emergency such as they were used to at the hands of men whose meetings they themselves broke up in times past. These men, if they had been as wise as the women have shown themselves, would not have confronted the militants with squads of mild-mannered police-men or a mob of chivalrous male spectators; they would have invoked the help of a corps of "daughters of the plow," or their equivalent in brawny cooks and vigorous housemaids, who would have dealt with the militants as the docklaborers dealt with the students. It is rather against our contention that in a meeting in Hyde Park, held since the meeting in Glasgow, the suffragettes failed to provide themselves with a guard of dock-laborers, and were pelted with mud and howled down by an audience differing from them in opinion. But in a conten-tion like this one cannot have everything one's way. Meanwhile, mili-tancy goes on rejoicing in every species of violence short of homicide.

Concurrently the English government has been behaving as obstruc-tively as it knows how. It is trying to keep the militants from doing these wicked things; but it is confronted by difficulties from within and without. There seems to be a disposition lingering from the old chivalric impulse in men, even statesmen, to give up their seats to women in the cars and to take off their hats to them in elevators which prevents the government's using the insurgents with the frank severity employed with men in rebellion. The hunger strike has fairly carried the day. Suffragettes, when sent to jail, have refused to eat, and forced feeding has been condemned by public sentiment. In Par-liament itself a leader of His Majesty's opposition has denounced it as cruel; but His Majesty's government cannot let the prisoners die; it has to let them go, and do more and more violence. The suggestion (we think from His Majesty's opposition) that the militants should be deported has not yet been tried, but it is not certain that this would work; it would not be fair to innocent nations, and the militants might be sent back as a sort of anarchists from the foreign parts to which they were exiled.

It is true that the government can still hold out against such women in one way; it can always refuse to bring in a bill for their enfranchisement, and it is refusing to do this with a good deal of passive persistence. Or it was doing it two months before this writing will reach the reader. By the time the news of to-day becomes the annals of tomorrow, militancy and passive persistence may have become reconciled, and votes for women may have become the law of the land in Great Britain.

It is becoming, rather slowly but rather surely, the law of this land; and here we will breathe a word of consolation in the ears of the chivalrous men who would prefer to keep on giving up their seats in cars and taking off their hats in elevators to voteless ladies. It seems to be the peculiar dread of these polite persons that if women are enfranchised the vote of the ignorant masses will simply be duplicated and the vote of the enlightened classes reduced to a yet more desperate minority than it is at present. On the surface of the fact this is undeniably true, but beneath the surface it will be found that the vote of the enlightened classes has been increased through the minds and merits of the women of the masses. It is only among the rich and idle that women are the inferiors of men; it is only in what calls itself the best society. Below that the women are the superiors, and the farther down you go you find this truer and truer. The women of the lower classes do not drink, they do not even smoke, as some women of the upper classes do. They keep the house, and they make the earnings of their husbands and themselves go far in the practical application of political economy, which is only domestic economy "writ large." Over the washtub and the cook-stove and the cradle they have worked out problems which the enlightened classes have not yet thought out. Almost always they are the betters of their menkind in mind as well as heart; and when they get the vote they will naturally come to the help of their brethren of the enlightened classes, as far as these are truly enlightened, and by their accession they will reduce the ignorant and vicious majority.

The Accomplishments We Value

August, 1913

NOT very long ago one of our contemporaries, by no means the least esteemed, indulged the fancy of inviting its readers to vote upon a very interesting, if not a very important, question. The question was, Which ten Americans living were the most useful to their fellow-men, or which could their fellow-citizens afford to insure for the largest sum because they were of the greatest value to the community; or, in other terms (but still the terms of the same conundrum), If Congress should decide to award ten prizes to the most deserving men and women in the country, and leave the choice to a popular referendum, who should get the largest number of votes?

Something more than a thousand of our contemporary's readers voted in response, and in large part gave their reasons for electing Mr. Edison, Miss Jane Addams, Mr. Carnegie, Mr. Roosevelt, Mrs. Helen Gould Shepard, Dr. Alexis Carrel, Colonel Goethals, Mr. Bryan, President Wilson, and Mr. Luther Burbank, here named in the order of their priority. Many other distinguished and beneficent citizens were chosen by respectable minorities, from Dr. Booker T. Washington, for spreading light among his people, to Mr. J. D. Rockefeller, for putting by means of his philanthropic monopoly another kind of light "into millions of homes, even the humblest"; Mr. Orville Wright, "for his improvements of the aeroplane"; Dr. Wiley, "because of his services in behalf of pure food"; ex-President Taft, for his endeavors to establish international arbitration; Mr. John Mitchell, for his devotion to the cause of labor; Miss Helen Keller, "as an inspiration to handicapped lives"; Miss Ida Tarbell, "as an exposer of social and financial rottenness." Captain Peary was gratefully remembered for the discovery of the North Pole, although that pole has not yet been found of great practical benefit to the nation. In the absence of actual hostilities, Admiral Dewey and General Wood may have been sufficiently chosen in the third or fourth ten of our benefactors, but in spite of the prodigious prevalence of the letters and arts among us in these piping times of peace, not one "poet, novelist, dramatist, actor, musician, artist, architect," as our contemporary notes with apparent surprise, "received votes enough to bring him anywhere near the topmost ten." Ministers of the gospel fared no better; with our authors and artists, they were evidently "not regarded as useful or indispensable members of society."

We cannot share the feeling of our contemporary at this unavoidable conclusion, and we do not refuse to accept the average thousand voting on this referendum as fairly representative of our whole hundred millions. Each of the ten men and women chosen as our best unquestionably stands pre-eminent among living Americans for some definite, absolute, tangible benefaction in his or her way. As our latest and shrewdest observer has noted, we Americans have a dominant passion for "getting results," as those ten have got; results that we can lay our hands on and feel advantageous in our daily lives. Yet it is in no poverty of imagination that a great and good woman is popularly ranked next to the tireless inventor who works his wonders continually for the advantage and convenience of the community. The voters recognize that she has "got results," as unquestionably as he, and it is not incredible that if the matter were left to Mr. Edison himself he might vote Miss Addams into the first place.

Such an effect of magnanimity in him would not be alien to the nature of the representative Americans voting him most indispensable among living Americans. These are none the less generous in their admiration because they seem so aridly practical in their preferences. As a people, however, we prize and honor those who utilize principles more than those who discover them. Not the genius which divined the steam-power, but the ingenuity which put it to work on land and sea is the greater in our eyes. Not Franklin who rent the lightning from the sky, but Mr. Edison who lights, heats, moves, and amuses modern civilization with it, and makes it talk, sing, and do everything but think, is supreme in our regard. Not to Langley, who surprised the secret of the aeroplane, but to the brothers Wright, who applied it, do we render our highest praise and warmest thanks. Yet when it comes to asking which among us is greatest and best, our dry utilitarians cannot forget a woman who is greater and better than anything she has done. In their way they feel the beauty and nobility of her nature; they revere these next to the molecular activity of the unrivaled inventor's life.

The Americans who have so frankly put themselves on record by their votes, and their reasons, have apparently no misgivings as to their judgments or their qualifications for judging. Not only Miss Addams in her dealing with the saddest sin of every age is in a practical way "getting results," but also Mr. Roosevelt, "by an ability to achieve results," is held "pre-eminent in the realm of national affairs"; and for kindred virtues the eight others of the ten are confidently ranked above their fellow-citizens. We are not, or not yet, finding fault with the test employed; it is a very direct and a very specific test. What has a man done that he should be called great? What has he tangibly accomplished for the general use? "By their fruits ye shall know them" was said long ago by One who spoke as having authority; and surely this is the same as trying men by the results they have got? Perhaps it is, and perhaps it is not; perhaps those fruits were the fruits of character rather than the fruits of action; for there seems to be a difference, though it is not palpable to the hand of the greater employment.

It is not from our passion for "getting results" that we can best and most value the woman who has so surpassingly applied Christianity at Hull House. There are other passions of the heart which must have their share in our veneration of her. There is such a thing as *being* good, which is as real and as conceivable as *doing* good, and which was before that and beyond it. The benefactions of Mr. Carnegie are many, but there are those who will feel that he was worthy to be elected third of our first ten because he has owned that the means of this came from the work of others, rather than because he had founded libraries and served the cause of peace and scientific research. We should not deny that the great surgeon who among his other wonderful achievements has learned how to "keep the heart alive one hundred and twenty days apart from the body to which it belonged" is worthy of the highest honor and fame; but why ignore the painter who can put soul into a picture?

Is it perhaps the Great American Mistake to do so? Does not it show a certain crudity of nature in us that we ignore even the existence of the arts and letters as national glories and blessings? Has it always been as it is now, and if it has not, have not we been advancing in the wrong direction? Is not our present practicality a recrudescence which we have sunk to through our passion for getting results, for material advantages such as we can see, feel, hear, touch, and taste, rather than such as appeal for appreciation to the heart and soul? Would not it be possible to prove that artists had as high claim to popular gratitude as our inventors, our charitable millionaires, even our reformers? At the door of the Luxembourg Gallery are certain figures and groups in bronze, rendering so vividly the fact of the poverty which exists in Paris that they wring the heart with pity and remorse. If there were a plebiscite in France, would the artists who created these be quite ignored in a vote which should choose the greatest inventors in aviation and automobiling chief of the French nation? Is not something like such a gross insensibility to what is essentially the highest result to be got in any civilization, manifest in the American vote which does not register a single ballot for any sculptor of ours? Or has no sculptor of ours got such a result?

In these conjectures we are asking the reader to follow us in a region where we do not blame the voters of our contemporary for not being able to penetrate. As far as they could go, we do not think they have gone astray; we even think they have chosen very well on their chosen ground. No living author has been considerably mentioned in their referendum as having contributed to the greatest good of the greatest number, as having "got results" of the sort that materially benefit the masses of men and women eager for light, heat, housing, and health. But perhaps even on that higher ground where the esthetic fames pine forgotten the finest results have not been achieved in the divine or heroic measure demanded by the tests employed. If we were bidden to think which of our best sellers deserved a place beside Mr. Edison, or Mr. Burbank, or Dr. Carrel, we should have some hesitation. No living author whom we recall among our hosts of novelists has "got results" in any such sort as our inventors and investigators have got them; and Mrs. Stowe alone among the immortals who are dead has surpassed those successful favorites in "getting results," if her great novel superlatively promoted the emancipation of the slaves.

The time was, easily within the recollection of any man who has survived his generation, when the American ideal was higher living instead of the higher-cost living which comes of greed for the cheapening of the creature comforts, the grossly appreciable advantages, material, mental, and moral. Yet our present recrudescence is not wholly ungenerous, if our lower ideal is that not a few but all shall share these advantages; that none shall be left behind or aside in the race for them. But undeniably we had once a fineness of ideal from which the present ideal has coarsened. In that former time our literature expressed a longing for the beauty which is truth; neither Longfellow, nor Lowell, nor Whittier could be content with the lovely line alone; its curve must lead to the strait and narrow path which few find but none need miss; it was sometimes even forced to this office. The clear, cold voice of Emerson called from the crystal air of Concord in the duteous accents which we seem to fail of in the voices of Indianapolis and our other literary centers. The greatest novel of that day, the best seller of almost any day, flamed from a passionate ardor for humanity. The incomparable romances of Hawthorne bore a message to the conscience of every reader. If a vote upon the question put by our contemporary had been taken in that day, would none of these authors have been elected among the ten whom their countrymen could least spare? Or would not Channing, Beecher, Parker, Hale, have been remembered as our benefactors along with the first electricians, reformers, philanthropists, and scientists of their different epochs?

There is really no saying. If we had a writer like Tolstoy living among us and of us, would he be counted as one of those Americans whom we should award the prizes of the highest desert as an unrivaled benefactor of his countrymen? If he would, it must be by a criterion altogether different from the criterions which the public school and the Sunday edition and the specialized magazine have taught us to use. Our good men and true, our good women and true, are known to such as have chosen among them by this referendum through the paragrapher and the interviewer, and we are not saying that they are known amiss, any more than we are saying that the choice among them is an error. Very likely the chosen are what they have been voted; their excellence is a visible and palpable thing, and the excellence of other kinds of Americans who in their different sort may have meant as well by their fellow-citizens is simply not evident to the general apprehension. For that reason the arts and letters have been passed over, and the applied sciences, economics, politics, which get results for knowledge, comfort, health, and even humanity, have their reward.

If once it seemed different, will it ever be different again, and shall the great actor, author, painter, sculptor, preacher be counted a supreme friend and helper of a grateful generation? That depends a great deal upon how the coming generation is taught; a great deal more, possibly, upon whether those who entertain and even edify the passing generation can come somehow to its ground and dwell there neighbors and friends with it, as those heroes and heroines of the average choice seem somehow to have done.

Capital Punishment

March, 1915

W I T H the American habit of taking the ironical attitude toward moral problems which urge themselves over-vexatiously for solution, one of our public functionaries came forward in the latter part of last year with a proposal which would let people feel how it was themselves in a certain exigency of his office. At that time the governor of Arizona found himself with eleven men (or it may have been thir-teen—thirteen would have been a more dramatic number) to be put to death, just after the people of his state had voted against the aboli-tion of capital punishment. It is not very clear whether the governor had or had not the power to pardon these miserable men, or to commute their sentence to the milder penalty of imprisonment for life (if it is milder; opinions vary even among the criminals themselves), but it appears certain that the governor was averse to killing them even by law, and was wroth with that majority of his fellow-citizens who favored it, and whose vote seemed to have left him no choice in the matter but mercy or massacre. He appears not to have liked solely taking the responsibility which logically divides itself among the agents of the law in such cases, making the prosecutor, judge, jury, and ex-ecutioner alike sharers in it. He appears to have felt it a hardship that the majority of his fellow-citizens should not also share the blame, if it was blame, of putting those eleven or thirteen men to death, and he proposed trying what he could do to make them realize what they were making him do. The men should be put to death, yes, but not privately. They should be put to death publicly, in the most con-spicuous manner possible, and he invited his fellow-citizens to be present (we suppose with their wives and children) and see the triumph of the law over crime.

We did not follow the course of comment and we cannot say just whether journalistic criticism accused the governor of being more a coarse humorist or a pestilent sentimentalist. His proposition was probably regarded as either a bluff or a play to the gallery, which applauds freely when its feelings are touched. But it appears that after his bold challenge to his fellow-citizens the governor began to hedge. Somehow (as well as we remember) the number of the doomed men was reduced to six, and the executive heart inclined to mercy in the case of these fewer examples of justice. We are not sure but the date of their sentence passed without its execution; as happens with so much in our contemporary history, the ultimate fact was lost in the mists of actuality, and the student of civilization was left to employ himself with the academic question of the moral effect of a return to public executions after they had been disused for generations. In the course of this study he may have had to inquire whether the governor ought not to have been regarded as an enemy of progress in proposing such a thing seriously, or as an erring humorist of coarse fiber in suggesting it ironically.

We do not know what conclusion the student has finally arrived at, and it is in the absence of returns from him that we venture to ask the reader to consider the question with us. If he is a reader as well stricken in years as ourselves he can barely remember hearing some yet older survivors speak of a *hanging* which he had witnessed with five or six thousand of his fellow-citizens, largely drunk and disorderly under the instruction offered them by the great civic lesson. The custom began to decay when capital crimes were finally reduced from the theft of a shilling to murder alone; but Thackeray, in one of his early papers, wrote of a public execution which he seems not to have enjoyed seeing, and Tourguénief has described a decapitation in Paris which he witnessed with the conviction that the law had committed a horrible crime. It was in fact considered an immense advance in practical Christianity when men were strangled and beheaded in the sacred privacy of their prison walls, with only a few incorruptible witnesses to attest the fact and two physicians to verify the death. Men still in the first frosts of autumn will remember with what satisfaction the electric chair was hailed as a happy substitute for the gallows-tree. It was to function in a yet greater secrecy, if possible, and something was to be added to the effect with the imagination of the general by the refusal of the state to admit reporters, or even to allow the friends of the criminal to bury his body, which was to be consumed with quicklime in a hidden grave as soon as the doctors had done with it. Of course, as in all questions where the liberty of the press is concerned, these rigors soon gave way; the details of the electrocution were painted by the daily papers in the most animated colors, till the reader wearied of them. And it was also quickly realized that his punishment could not be continued after the death of the criminal without cruelly afflicting his hapless kindred. Until the novelty of the electric chair had worn off the public execution of death sentences was practically restored; but when the popular curiosity concerning it was once sated, the inviolable secrecy largely maintained itself again.

We are not advised whether the governor of Arizona had a choice between the two usages when he mooted the participation of his fellow-citizens in his responsibility, as witnesses of a spectacle once considered vital to their well-being. So far as the event was concerned, we are still in the dark. If there is a Recall in Arizona, the vote on capital punishment may have been subjected to it, and the affair settled in that way, by a repentant majority. But what appears certain from a contemporaneous expression of abhorrence for the death penalty by an official in our own section is that the West can no longer claim a monopoly of advanced penology. At almost the very moment when the governor of Arizona was inviting his fellow-citizens to countenance its infliction, the newly appointed warden of the cherished bulwark of our civilization at Sing-Sing was avowing his abomination of it. Unless we misremember his reported words, he declared that he would never see it inflicted, while he also declared that it ought never to be secretly inflicted, as it ostensibly is at present. He may have felt, with the governor of Arizona, that those who liked it ought to see the thing done. The order of events is uncertain in our recollection, and perhaps the latest feat of our metropolitan gunmen was not yet performed; but this recalcitrant warden might now point to the fact that the state-killing of four gunmen for a ruthless assassination had eventuated, before the year was out, in a quite parallel crime. He could invite the friends of the established penology to observe that deterrent punishment apparently does not deter except in the case of criminals who have ceased to live, or who are shut up for the time in some of the stone pens all over the country for their respective misdemeanors, and that the only way to make punishment truly deterrent is to make it anticipative. But he seems rather to have wreaked himself in expressions of pity for all sorts and conditions of criminals, and in propositions for the amelioration of their lot. Naturally this has given their chance to the paragraphical publicists, and they have not spared him some gibes and thrusts for his emotionality. Intrenched in the fact that deterrent punishments do not deter, if inflicted after the fact, and that prisons are the breeding-grounds of crime, they have brought him to such confusion as they could by teaching that the lot of the criminal should be made heavier and not lighter, in order that crime may more and more abound.

To be sure this is not their logic, but the logic of the facts, and perhaps the warden feels that the logic of the facts is on his side, and does not greatly mind the paragraphic publicists, though they are many and often, and he is only one and now and then. What appears beyond question is the failure of the old system of penology. The captives of the state are apparently made worse by the hardships accumulated upon them, not for their reformation but for their suffering. In the first place, their sentences are atrociously out of proportion to their offenses. The death-sentence alone bears a sort of rough relevancy to the deed punished. The man done to death has really taken the life of a man, and there is a diabolical proportion in taking his life; but the man who goes for years to States-Prison for grand larceny or for months to the Island for petty larceny is the victim of injustice which seldom fails to make him a life-long criminal.

If we could trust the gay cynicism which mocks at the appeal for kindness to the prisoner, we must suppose that more and more severity was what was needed to make a better man of him. But with the logic of the facts the friends of the thing that is or that has been have nothing to do. If they had they might appositely ask themselves where the deterrent force of punishment lay, if within the year after those four men were put to death for a ruthless assassination quite the same sort of murder was done by the same sort of men. The lives which the state took might almost as well have been spared, and it may be that in view of such a possibility the new warden at Sing-Sing proposes to himself more mercy and not less in dealing with the captives in his power. In a certain light it is grotesque, of course, his proposing such a thing; the wise old world has not aged so much without knowing better than that. It knows, or it thinks it knows, that prisons were meant for the punishment of prisoners, and not, as the warden supposes, for their reformation. It knows that when a man is sent to Sing-Sing it is to make him sadder, but not better. It is to subject him to a slavery under conditions which seem often fixed not by the law but by the will of his immediate masters. It is to take him from his family, his wife and children, or his father and mother, who trusted him, however mistakenly, for their support. It is to put him to hard labor for five, or ten, or twenty years, not for the behoof of these dependents of his, but for the profit of such contractors as buy his services from the state, and at the end to cast him back upon the world empty-handed, dishonored, hopeless, helpless.

One of the foibles of the new warden is to propose paying the prisoner the wages he earns, and this might not be so ridiculous, if he ended there. But he proposes treating the prisoner compassionately in conditions which his own voluntary experiment of prison life has taught him were cruelly hard. That he made this experiment is much against him with his critics; it attaints him of sentimentality, of the love of a histrionic pose. If he had been a real criminal he would have known that the hardships he saw and shared were the right thing for them, whatever arbitrary will invented and inflicted them. His brief experiment counts for nothing against the long experience of the world that the only way to better bad men is to do the things to them that would make good men worse. The application of this system is what prisons are for, and always have been; and it will outlast such empirical penology as that of the Western prison-camps where unguarded criminals work out their sentences in the open and are paid the wages they earn. It is not to be expected that the Sing-Sing warden's dreams of bettering his wards by bettering their conditions and changing the object of their imprisonment will last nearly so long even as the attempts of these empirical penologists in the West to humanize the terms of their prisoners' captivity.

All such emotional endeavors must avail nothing against the im-memorial inhumanities of man to man as practised in the prisons which so densely dot the surface of the earth. What these are like the reader may learn from a book by a man who has lately come prominently before the world, and who was trained for the work of writing it by efficient knowledge of "the criminal classes." We mean our minister to Belgium, Mr. Brand Whitlock, and his graphic study of prison life called *The Turn of the Balance.* One would consent to be a little illogical, a little ridiculous even, in the hope of helping better the atrocious conditions which this book reveals. Perhaps "reveals" is not quite the word, for the facts were always open and scarcely needed revelation, except as all the facts of life need revelation by the spoken or written word for that immense majority of purblind people who have them constantly under their eyes, but must have them somehow dramatized before they can realize them.

To these the heroic bluff of the Arizonian governor and the philan-thropic ideals of the Sing-Sing warden may have their appeal. At any rate, it is interesting to note that the ironical attitude of the governor has been his defense against the criticism which has accused the serious warden of sentimentality. If he had proposed in capital cases to have the prosecutor, the judge, and jury share among them the necessary incidents of executing the sentence of the convict whom they had jointly brought to his death, it would have been humor which the paragraphic mind could have tasted. Or if he had proposed having the suffering of the prisoner intensified, say, by giving him frequent intelligence of his innocent family, how they were sharing his guilty condemnation through want of the earnings which the state was stealing from him, this would have been something appreciable to the humorists of the satirical press. The warden would then have given the delight which we Americans all feel in a joke, and which was imparted by the sugges-tion of the Arizona governor. Yet the Sing-Sing warden should not altogether lose the courage of his convictions. He might remember that some of the divine precepts of our religion were not inculcated by means of a self-defensive irony. He might read the Sermon on the Mount and some other homilies and parables of the New Testa-ment, and consider how few of the things there seem to have been humorously said, with a view of better imparting the ideals embodied. He might read the confessions and essays of Tolstoy, and from their plain and single discourse fortify himself in his direct condemnation of the prison usages which he would abate. We could not promise him that in the end he would not seem ridiculous to the keen wit of his fellow-citizens or the dense culture which has plunged the world in manifold murder. If he minds such things much, he must continue to suffer from them, and find what solace he can in the good which he may or may not accomplish.

But we would not be thought to condemn irony altogether. Even the gospel is not destitute of it. " 'What is truth?' said jesting Pilate," and when he "would not stay for an answer," he had clearly been having his joke, or been thinking he had. That fine spirit, that subtle wit, that nimble essence, will not be exorcised by any sense of the pathos, the tragedy of life. It helps the governor of Arizona out with his lesson to his fellow-citizens, but it lends its smiles to those who mock at the Sing-Sing warden's aspirations for those unfriended wards of his. It can say it is not enough that he feels for those in bonds as bound with them. It is all right that he should feel so, but he ought to put on the air of jesting at their scars even though he has felt their wounds in his own experience. It is our American nature not to take ourselves too seriously; we like our Lincolns to laugh out their heartbreak; we are rather helpless in that matter. While we discuss such points as whether people who wish to have hanging go on ought not to look on at the hanging, and, perhaps, prosecutor, judge, and jury occasionally lend a hand in a thing they morally share in; or as whether such a philanthropist as the warden of Sing-Sing should seem so much in earnest about his aims and ends of mercy, we would like of course to keep a sober countenance, but we may be temperamentally unable to hide a covert wink to the other great nations which have presently got so far beyond any such polite polemic. They might not see the wink, but there should be those among us at home not so lost in the contemplation of the activities beyond seas who must find a relish of involuntary irony in the discussion of such fine points just at this moment of multitudinous massacre over there.

On Women Living Their Own Lives

March, 1920

WITHIN a year or so past we took occasion to blame a certain type of English fiction for its complaisance with the life of men and women wrongly living together without apparent shame or sense of sin. We ventured to doubt whether this was a veracious picture of our elder-sister civilization, and we questioned its usefulness even as a study of the ideal. One of the characters who apparently grieved no more than her partner for their transgression, was the daughter of a mother who had erred in her time but who had suffered lasting remorse for her error, and we ventured to doubt whether the daughter's impenitence was not less true to the actual conditions in England. As for the conditions in our own country, they did not come in question at the time, and it is only since reading Judge Robert Grant's studies of *The Law and the Family* that the recognition of our own social faults has contributed to a larger trust of the English realism which we reprobated.

It is true that Judge Grant's view of our society may have been shaped by his knowledge as a probate judge, of the effect of divorce upon the national character. Apparently divorce has become little less frequent than marriage with us, and it seems not much more deleterious. In both the main motive seems to be love, though the course of this popular passion is more circuitous in divorce than in marriage, but Judge Grant's study of it is by no means so cynical as the view which we are falling into in our report of it. He may be somewhat swayed by his larger official experience of the legal human putting asunder of those divinely joined together, but his view of the whole matter is scientific, and, like the other chapters of his very interesting book which relate to feminism—for divorce seems primarily feministic—is past all fiction in the elements of appeal to the intelligent reader. Besides the chapters less directly bearing upon womanhood, such as "Women and Property," "The Third Generation and Invested Property," and "The Perils of Will-making," there are those more entirely devoted to them in "Domestic Relations," "Feminism in Fiction and Real Life," and the "Limits of Feminism Independence and Marriage and Divorce." What it all comes to is the recognition of their influence in our conditions, which seems to have arrived through the prevalence of divorce. If this view of the case is the result of a probate judge's involuntary familiarity with divorce, it seems chiefly through divorce that woman "realizes that she has renounced the static condition of slave, drudge, parasite, plaything," and is "experimenting with herself and with man—experimenting with a vengeance, in our democratic hope of providing a living wage for everybody, abolishing the double standard of morals, and putting an end to war. When women talk of inequality to-day it will generally be found that what they have in mind is the sex relation." Nearly all the fiction in novels and plays he thinks has dealt with it "because of a lurking growth in the feminine mind that the sexual relations may be casual without detriment to the eternal scheme of things." Motherhood outside of marriage may be intentional from the love of it, as in an instance he cites, and there may be a woman who gives herself to it without shame or the sense of sin or the intention of continuing in her relation with the chosen father of her child.

It is a rather revolting instance, but if our civilization is passing to the rule of a renewed matriarchy, it may not be the most revolting instance of that condition. Such a fact must go far to reconcile criticism to the fiction which we reprobated as an improbable report of English conditions, and it is interesting as a proof of the entire abeyance in New England to the tendency of the strongest feeling and sentiment.

Mr. Brooks Adams, in his *Emancipation of Massachusetts,* has invoked anew our sense of the awfulness of the Puritan ministers in dealing with Antinomianism, Quakerism, Witchcraft, and other unpuritanic question of their right to worship God after their exclusive opinions. They did not go so far as Torquemada or Simon de Montfort, but they went as far as they could, and this was such a long way as banishing Ann Hutchinson and sending her into the wilderness to be killed by the Indians, and whipping Quaker women on their naked backs from town to town, in the freezing winter weather, not to name frequent exile when exile meant scarcely less than death. The ministers were men of strong convictions and relentless consciences, and they would have made short work of the convictions of the equal suffragists whom Mr. Adams himself, indeed, would not willingly suffer to prevail, as Judge Grant forebodes in the body politic.

It is apparently through his official acquaintance with the increase of divorce that this jurist so tolerantly studies the different phases of feminism, which we understand him to regard not as a political advance or an effect of suffragistic opinion, but as the triumph of women's endeavors for personal freedom in the thing nearest her heart. The desire to "live her own life" has its effect in raising her to a selfish supremacy as yet unequalified by those endeavors for moral reform which the friends of her political equality had promised themselves from her. These had hoped that woman's suffrage would, for instance, immediately involve the endeavor to rid civilization of the social evil which neither science nor religion had hitherto availed against. But apparently there has been no generally concerted movement against this horror; women's rule has left this where it found it, or where men's rule had kept it from the beginning of time. What we see is a constant extension of divorce; but whether divorce is a sin in itself, or only a sin against marriage, or against the family, there is no more proof than woman's enjoyment of her greater freedom through its extension as a gift from men or a spoil of her increasing power. One sees more and more divorced people who are often remarried, but in their behavior they do not seem different from people married "of the first intention," as used to be said of the healing of surgical wounds. They are sometimes husbands and wives of repeated remarriages, but one would not surmise the fact from meeting them in society; one might like to find them more obvious than they are, but one does not; and how far the feminine parties to divorce will characterize the feministic rule there is no saying; one had better not try saying; and one learns nothing very different by inquiring into the history of feminine rule in former ages.

Just what the primitive form of feministic predominance through the civic and domestic state known as matriarchy was, the student will not rashly decide. It seems to have established women in a certain supremacy through her uncertain hold upon the father of the children left to her through her impermanent relation with him. Whether something like it may return through the general theory and practice of the young woman whom Judge Grant instances as desiring motherhood so much more than marriage that she preferred to dispense with that means altogether, is very doubtful. Her example is revolting rather than inviting to the imagination, and one rather prefers that the reign of feminism should not involve it. There is no reason why it should, in fact; and the supposition of it offers a gratuitous insult to that ideal. This has been realized through what may be a lingering effect of that allegiance which the sons of men feel that they owe to the mothers of men. Every step toward the independence of woman has been taken with the help of men and she has been established in her supremacy, if she is now supreme, by the loyalty of her sons and brothers, and even husbands. She has been established by these in property rights equal with theirs, as the reader shall learn to his advantage from Judge Grant's interesting book, and if her desire to "live her life" has liberated her from the bonds of matrimony by well-nigh unlimited divorce, she can always say that the men began it. Whether this is entirely true or not, who can tell? Who can tell whether free divorce is an evil or not? Has it been tried long enough to authorize a general opinion on the point such as exists concerning marriage? It has not been generally held that marriage is an evil; if it is, the remedy is almost freely at hand, and if divorce will not satisfy there is always the safeguard of remarriage with some untried partner, or even the husband who has once failed to help the wife "live her life," and who may not yet have experimented in living his own.

Feminism, whether it is a return to something like matriarchy or not, has at least freed itself from the color of "funniness" which it began with. Possibly its political apotheosis has arrived partly through the American man's sense of humor; it has "made him mad" at some moments in the past, but at more moments it has made him laugh. It has struck him as something incomparably droll; even the men who advocated it have seemed as "funny" as the women who demanded it. The swift changes of opinion which women were subject to were as delightfully funny to him as if he had never himself been of more than one mind. The women who in the day of our pacifism used to sing, "I did not raise my boy to be a soldier," seemed to him deliciously inadequate to the situation, but it must be owned that in their swift conformity to all the demands of the hour when the boys they had "raised" became soldiers, the mothers' heroic self-devotion lost all tint of absurdity. Now that feminism is to be put to the dry, commonplace tests of civil life it will be seen whether its supremacy will be as "funny" as women's endeavor for equality was. When their failures, selfish or unselfish, begin to work the mischief which men's mistakes have wrought we shall hardly laugh; they will not seem so "funny" as their struggle for power used to seem. If they show that they know how to rule us for our good, as they sometimes have shown in their immemorial quality as wives and mothers, we shall not necessarily smile at our submission to a phase of perfected matriarchy. Some of our feminist rulers, especially those "not over thirty," may call to our faces the derision of other times by their preposterous hats and impossible heels; but the ruling majority among our women rulers will sober us by the good sense and dignity which they will bring to the work of managing a world which many men now freely confess that men have "made a mess of."

IV/Edward S. Martin

1920-1935

When Thomas Bucklin Wells took over the editorship of *Harper's*
in 1919, the magazine was in deep trouble. During the latter decades
of Henry Mills Alden's editorship, it had failed to keep up with the
fast-changing spirit of the times, and as a consequence had lost readers,
advertising, and money. Wells, who had served as an associate editor
under Alden, saw clearly that if the magazine were to survive some
drastic changes would have to be made immediately. He moved quickly,
therefore, to create a new format with modern typography and cover
design, bring in a new galaxy of authors, and shift the editorial mix.
What he wanted was much less emphasis on fiction and literary essays,
and far more on discussion of contemporary problems, which were,
in the years following World War I, both plentiful and novel.

One of his key decisions was the selection of a successor to Howells
in the Easy Chair. His choice of Edward S. Martin was characteristic
of his whole new editorial policy. As Martin said in a newspaper
interview soon after his appointment, he was "not a literary man."
He was a professional journalist who had established a national reputation with the incisive editorials he had written for *Life, Scribner's,*
and *Harper's Weekly.* He had a broad background in public affairs,
including a law degree, a tour of duty in the State Department, and
experience in both newspaper and magazine editing. From the beginning his Easy Chair columns were concerned almost entirely with current issues—political and moral—and his position was usually anti-
establishment. Martin was an early opponent, for example, of the prohibition laws; he favored American entry into the League of Nations
and forgiveness of war debts; and his views on education were far
from orthodox. Curiously, he was the only Easy Chair author who
seemed to feel strongly about religion. (Curtis had been a fairly nomi-
nal member of the Unitarian church, which was said to believe in
"One God, at most;" Howells seldom touched on a religious subject.)

Although it is hard to measure the influence of any journalist, Martin

Edward S. Martin

evidently did have a considerable impact on public opinion: his columns were widely quoted and reprinted in newspapers throughout the country, and many of his unorthodox views ultimately became public policy. Two of the following essays indicate a prescience that was extremely rare (and unheeded) at the time; as early as 1927, when the Great Boom was nearing its peak, he seemed to forsee the Great Depression which was to follow two years later.

Prohibition and Democracy

April, 1922

T H E enforcement of prohibition meets with some obstacles and furnishes food for thought to two large groups in the community—the people who want it enforced and the people who occasionally want something to drink. Just at the moment it seems as if the people who want a drink are somewhat ahead of the other group in the competition; at any rate, the group that wants enforcement seems to think it necessary to make extra effort. To *Harper's Magazine,* as doubtless to hundreds of other periodicals, has come a communication from the Committee for Prohibition Enforcement of a much-respected and powerful organization of women, which announces that the committee has adopted a program, the items of which it communicates. The fifth item is to the effect that all the ministers be urged to preach and teach the necessity for respect for and observance of the law. The sixth item runs, "That every theatrical manager, movie manager, and editor, whether of a daily, weekly, or monthly publication, be requested to see that all jokes ridiculing prohibition and its enforcement are eliminated from any production, film, or article coming under his jurisdiction, and that the matter be treated with the seriousness that the subject merits; and that this resolution be thrown on the screen and printed in the different papers and magazines throughout the country."

The demand for protection from jokes is often made and always implies that there is something that needs to be joked about. There is a sin called "sacrilege." If we joke about things that are sacred to enough people, it gives a kind of offense which, even if the law does not punish it, it is not safe to excite. There is a sin of blasphemy, which we suppose the law will still punish if it is gross enough. It will be agreed that the considerate people do not jest about sacred things, nor even about things which, though not sacred to themselves, are sacred to the people they are talking to. Well, then, is prohibition one of these sacred things we must not talk about? Are amendments of the Constitution and the Volstead law to rank with the Ten Commandments and the Sermon on the Mount as not being safely subject to derisive comment?

Something like that seems to be in the minds of the women whose communication we have received, who include item six in their program, but if so, their attitude is wrong. A constitutional amendment is not sacred, much less a Volstead Act. It is the Volstead law that the jokes on prohibition are aimed at more than the amendment. If we cannot joke about an act of Congress, then indeed things have come to a restricted pass. If a law is bad, one of the ways to beat it is to laugh it out of court. If that is being done about the Volstead law, the ladies who want that law enforced would do well to examine it and see why it is not enforced, rather than try to stop jokers from laughing at it.

A letter writer to a newspaper says, "If it is true that a community gets the kind of government it deserves, it is equally true that a law gets the kind of obedience it deserves." His assertion may be disputed, but still, if the Volstead law is not being respected, is it certain that it deserves respect? It is a law in the process of being tried out. If it is good we want it enforced. If it is bad we want it amended, but we do not want to be choked off from discussing it or testing it. There is no power in Congress to say what is right or wrong. The most that Congress can do is to say what is lawful or unlawful. The distinction is important. The practical judge of whether a law is right or wrong is the general community to which the law applies. If that community will not back up the enforcement of the law, it will not be enforced. It is yet to be demonstrated how far the Volstead law, as it stands, is enforceable. If its fruits do not please a majority of the people who live under it, it may have to be modified so that it will stand for something that is near enough to the popular judgment of what is right to win popular support. There is a great deal of good in the present prohibition movement. It put the saloons out of business. It checked the brewers and distillers in their overstrenuous efforts to sell their products. It accomplished benefits which probably could not have been accomplished except by the kind of clean sweep that the amendment was. But it was necessarily a rough job—an experiment to be tried out in practice. If its rules need modification, they may get it or they may not, but if not, they may be practically modified in enforcement.

Who is boss in this country? Is it the President, the Senate, the House, the Supreme Court, the state authorities, the newspapers, the lawyers, the ministers, the doctors, or possibly the women?

None of them! Public opinion is the boss. In the long run, what public opinion demands it gets. Laws to be of any worth have to have sanction. That is, there must be something to make people who violate them feel that they are doing wrong. The laws of nature have abundant sanction. If you fool with the law of gravitation, you get bumped. There is no trouble about the enforcement of the law of gravitation. Nobody goes around begging you not to ridicule it. It takes care of itself, and if you flout it you pay the consequences. The Ten Commandments have a sanction of long experience. Some of them are obsolete, but the others are respected, and, though they are not directly enforced by the courts, laws based on them are so enforced. Public opinion hereabouts rests very considerably on the Ten Commandments. They have shaped the habits of thought and deportment of many millions of people, including most of those now living in this country.

The trouble with the present enforcement of prohibition is that it has not yet got moral sanction enough to make it effective. Public opinion will back up the law in closing the saloons and restricting and regulating the sale of intoxicants, but it does not follow it, for one thing, in defining a beverage with an alcoholic content of one half of one per cent as intoxicating. When it comes to that, public opinion laughs, because that is contrary to its experience. Furthermore, public opinion shows as yet no particular fervor about achieving a total stoppage of alcoholic supplies from those who want them. No serious stigma attaches to violations of the Volstead law by private buyers. Fines and like embarrassments may result, but not disrepute. A good many fairly decent people seem to buy what they want, and do not conceal it. The people who thought before the law was adopted that it was wicked or inexpedient to drink intoxicants, still think so. The people who thought otherwise continue to think otherwise. Many people drink less than before the law began to operate, but a good many other people drink more, and buy much worse beverages at much higher prices. To some extent prohibition seems to have made drinking popular by diminishing the individual discouragement of it and putting the responsibility for the maintenance of temperance on a law and the officers who enforce it. That may be only a temporary effect, but if it turns out that the Volstead law, as it is, cannot be enforced at the present time, there may possibly be an effort to tinker it—to put it into such shape that public opinion will stand back of it and give it a sanction. The alternative would be to wait and see what effect time will have on men and habits. There is nobody to tell us that we shall be damned if we disobey the Volstead law, and so long as juries refuse to convict persons who violate it, it stands modified in practice. Nevertheless, drinks are very dear, and apt to be poisonous. It has accomplished that.

Since public opinion is so potent in this country, it is worth while to inquire what it is and who makes it. It is the voice of whatever civilization produces it. It is made by schools, by churches, by newspapers, by organizations of all sorts, good and bad, by politicians, by banks and business interests, but the best of it is a product of life and comes out of the minds and reflects the experience and influence of individual people.

The organizations, political, commercial, religious, that seek to shape public opinion all use propaganda. We all know what that means because we have all had such a surfeit of it. During the war we were flooded with it and everyone learned what it was and how to use it. It is put out by speakers, on the movie screens, and in print wherever possible. Organization secured prohibition, but organization is not public opinion and may for a time override it. Organization works on the run with noise and big headlines and meetings and even with threats. Public opinion slowly takes form in the minds of individuals. There comes in Lincoln's saying about the impossibility of fooling all the people all the time. Propaganda may overwhelm private judgment for a time, but private judgment keeps on working after propaganda ceases. It digests what has been offered to it. The common facts of life continue to appeal to it and impress it. It views what propaganda has accomplished and slowly and deliberately considers whether it is good, and if it concludes that it is not good it ceases to back it and then there has to be something different, something that looks like improvement.

Who are the people who finally make public opinion in the United States? They are the great mass of people who furnish the population and do the work of the country—the farmers, the other working people, from the bankers and lawyers and ministers and doctors to the miners and ironworkers and railroad men and factory hands and plumbers. Out of that great mass of people, spread across the continent and furnishing it with human life, slowly emerges public opinion. It will be sound and liberal and wise, or foolish and intolerant, according as that great company is more intelligent or less. Its intelligence will be tested partly by the ability to think things out and trace effects to right causes, and partly by instinctive acceptance of good leadership instead of bad. Men are very unequal in their abilities to think things out, but in their instinctive actions they are more alike. The recognition of truth is a good deal instinctive, and it is to that that leaders who know the truth and speak it have to appeal. In that great mass of the population there must be people whose heads are far enough above the heads of the group to see farther than the group sees, and whose experience of life is broad enough to make them liberal. People are prone to think that what is strange to them is necessarily sinful, or, if not sinful, at least hostile, but if there are people in sight whose characters they respect, though their habits of life are different from their own, it helps to get them out of that notion. Democracy must have leaders, but it must produce them. It need not go out of itself to find them. They must and will be the fruit of its own body. If the body is good the fruit will be good.

The great service to democracy is to keep its body sound. If that can be done it will never lack leaders. And how about the body of our democracy? Is its quality, its soundness, improving or decreasing? There are races in the earth that have slowly developed a capacity for democratic government and can make it go. There are other races that have shown only a limited capacity for it. Our democracy was founded by men who came from a country whose people had worked steadily for centuries toward democratic government. They and their descendants have kept a school here in which the principles of democracy have been taught to all comers. It has been a successful school, but how is it keeping up?

It is immensely important that these States should continue to be a sound school of democracy—that they should not undertake the training of more pupils than they can handle, or be swamped by too great a deluge of newcomers. An appreciation of that importance prompts Congress to check immigration, and, though that is an unwelcome expedient, it may be time that it was pressed. Two results should be helped by cutting down immigration—for a while fewer new pupils would come into the country, and the native-born citizenship would get more encouragement to provide, themselves, the population of the country. If there had been no immigration to speak of since 1850, but only the natural increase of the population of the country at that time, there would still have been plenty of people in this country. There are those who regret that such a result did not happen, but that is probably a mistaken regret. The destiny of the United States seems to be to perform a service to all races, a service in the direction of which most races are represented. We now have all Europe represented here in considerable force, and Asia and Africa sufficiently. If the United States had been populated by the families that were here in 1850 that would not have been true. The family that we have seems to accord better with the service that is required of us. To train and educate that great family in the way it should go, so that the public opinion that comes out of it shall be sound and wise and helpful—that is the task to be done, not only for ourselves, but for all the world.

The biologists are strong for purity of race and, of course, there is something in that. They point out how horses and other animals are bred, how the thoroughbred stock justifies itself, and how the greatest improvement in animals is won by judicious inbreeding. They would produce supermen by the same methods that produce successful race horses, but they know they cannot do that, and are content to emphasize the necessity of keeping the strong and valuable breeds of men as clear as possible from intermixture with weaker stocks, and races not weak but too different to blend with to advantage.

That is good sense, and doubtless accords with the purposes and practice of nature, but it is something very difficult of accomplishment by law or regulation, and it is not enough. Given luxury enough and circumstances favorable to demoralization, and even the best races will eventually drive after material things and go to pot. Animals do not do that. They cannot accumulate property or power and use it to buy ease and luxury. Once they are domesticated they are under direction. But man is much more complex than the animals and is his own master and responsible for his own course. The important influences to keep him moving upward are spiritual. The main factor in improving him is religion. First by instinct and presently by observation and reflection he recognizes the existence of an invisible life to which he is related and out of which seem to come the ideals which he struggles to realize. Biology is important. It is the science of a process, but religion is much more than that, it is the greatest factor in progress.

The New Inquisition

June, 1929

TWO very large and serious matters await handling by the people of the United States. One is the War Debts. The other is the New Inquisition.

As to the War Debts—the moneys due us from our Allies in the late disturbance in Europe—it is questioned by many observers whether we do well to continue to try to collect even so much of them as now, after some abatements, is found to be due us. The justice of the collections is not so much debated as the expediency. Many persons, by no means moved by sentimental considerations, think we should have done better, might still do better, to wipe the whole mass of War Debts off the slate. Secretary Mellon, thought by so many people to be rather canny about money, suggested several years ago that good trade relations with Europe were worth more than all these debts. If the four gentlemen from the United States who at this writing are trying to settle the reparations problems of Europe had power to do as they thought fit about these moneys due to the United States from their late Allies, we might have a real solution of incalculable value. For these four Americans are large-minded men, not scared by rows of figures and used to voluminous transactions. What they would agree upon would probably be wise and just; but their powers are limited, and they can use only what they have. Some great rumpus in the world such as now and then gives power to governments to spend the taxpayers' money in war may presently confer on our government or its repesentatives the power to cancel or reduce these debts; but until then they seem likely to drag along, impeding the reorganization of Europe and embarrassing the relations of nations.

It does not take any great degree either of foresight or far sight to remark that the relations of the United States with the two greatest nations of Western Europe are especially important by reason of the disturbed state of the world. In Europe Italy is experimenting with a remarkable Absolutist, or perhaps it would be nearer truth to say that a remarkable Absolutist is experimenting with Italy. Spain leans in the same direction—towards the substitution of authority for representative government. Turkey and Russia are speculating with the same formidable principle. In Germany apparently the party that cleaves to representative government is strong and hopeful, but there is another party, also pretty strong, that seems still to adhere to the persuasion which carried Germany into the Great War. Beyond the Ural Mountains, and all the way to the Pacific Ocean, there is a great unrest and unusual military activity. Who then stands for civilization on the basis of Democracy, the basis on which still rests the Government of the United States? Who but Great Britain and her Dominions and Colonies, France, Switzerland, the Low Countries, and the Scandinavian peoples? Divers newly made kingdoms or republics in Central Europe should doubtless be included in that group, but the powerful factors in it are France, Great Britain, and the United States, who have common interests in the world and would have to get together again if anything happened which was serious enough to warrant it.

All this is a consideration when we think about War Debts, though to act upon it is difficult until something happens to make action imperative.

Our other big job is to deal with the New Inquisition. We were threatened, when Mr. Hoover came in, with a drive to crush out the opposition to the Dry edict. The Jones Law gives power to judges to punish trifling offenses against the Volstead Act by fines of ten thousand dollars and five years' imprisonment. What that amounts to we are about to ascertain since it has just begun to be effective. A group of lawyers in New York, shocked by the possibilities of the injustice and oppression in this new law, offered to undertake without charge the defense of persons in danger of injustice under its terms, whereat arose cries of rage from the leading inquisitors. Cherrington and Poland were shocked at the temerity of these lawyers; Mrs. Willebrandt yapped at them. Clinton Howard, Chairman of the National Law Enforcement Committee, would have them not only disbarred but tried for treason. Nevertheless, they are quite respectable characters as well as lawyers in excellent standing. In the first case hereabouts under the Jones Law the culprit pleaded guilty and got three months in the Federal House of Detention; but the Judge said he would not be so lenient again and that future defendants would be given at least six months in the penitentiary. That prospect may deter arrested persons from pleading guilty and, if they have a jury trial and are represented by competent lawyers, it will be interesting to see how many cases come to trial, what verdicts the juries bring in, and whether the existing Federal courts can handle the liquor cases that come to them without prejudice to other duties.

Senator Wesley Jones, the author of the Jones Law, has had his picture in the paper and his biography published. Jones, it seems, is a Senator from the State of Washington. He is said to know a good deal about agriculture, shipping, commerce, irrigation, and other matters that come before Congress, but to have very little personal knowledge of rum. He is a hard-working, clean-living person and, noticing that there has been an Amendment to the Constitution and a law passed to stop drinking, he thought that drinking ought to be stopped and put his mind on devising means to stop it.

Torquemada seems to have been a nice man, very correct in his personal habits, not embarrassed by a seraglio, no accumulator of personal money from estates forfeited through his activities, and altogether a respectable character. He thought that people ought to believe what he believed and the Roman Catholic Church required, and his mind was hospitable to charges against Jews. He was able to pull the leg of Queen Isabella, a pious woman without much sense, and got enormous power, which he used for the detection, examination, and extermination of heretics. Possibly in Spain in his day he had a considerable popular support. He made interesting spectacles, and the King and Queen regarded him as a holy man. He could reward as well as punish. The people on his side of the theological fence probably approved of him, but he was never a really good asset of the Roman Catholic Church. Even the Popes of his time were chary of supporting him. He was useful in that he personified the horrible consequences which may ensue in giving power to clergymen over the lives and property of their fellow-creatures.

That is what Congress did when it passed the Eighteenth Amendment and the Volstead Act and now lately the Jones Law. It gave power to clergymen over the lives and property of their fellow-creatures. They can use the secular arm to carry out their judgments, just as the Inquisition could and did. The Federal prisons are crammed to-day with persons convicted for the violation of these laws imposed on us chiefly at the instigation of the Methodist and Baptist clergy. Prohibition, as we see it, is the product of the Baptist and Methodist churches. Even Doctor Fosdick supports it for the Baptists; and for the Methodists there are thousands of clergymen including bishops, shouting hymns, preaching sermons, and carrying fagots for the executioners.

This is really an appalling situation. Nobody is going to start an armed rebellion about it, but we may see all the means employed by which minorities resist oppression. Hunger strikes have done something in some cases. We may see hunger strikes. It is curious that when a great evil has to be overcome it often happens—one may say it usually happens—that someone has to die to do it. Jones, of Washington, seems to be a reputable man, but think of him as making laws about drinking for the State of New York! The cure of the predicament in which Prohibition has put the country seems to be the substitution of mild and comparatively wholesome drinks for spirits poisoned or otherwise. The United States can produce very good wine in any quantity for which there is a market, also beer. It can probably regulate the sales of both so far as is expedient. Presumably that is what we shall come to in the end, but what these zealous fanatics will succeed in doing to us meanwhile is something no one can foretell.

Meanwhile very serious complications constantly arise. At this writing a ship of Canadian registry has been sunk by a Coast Guard vessel in the Gulf of Mexico, one of the crew drowned and the rest of the crew carried in irons to New Orleans. The vessel sunk was undoubtedly in the business of bootlegging, but whether she was near enough shore to make her a lawful subject of the attentions of the Coast Guard is at this writing still undetermined, and further proceedings are awaited with lively interest. In Aurora, Ill., on March 25, Mrs. Lillian D. King was shot and killed by Dry agents in her home and in the presence of her son and her unconscious husband. The Dry agents, it appears, had broken into the house on false information and clubbed the husband into insensibility. New outrages of like character transpire daily.

The battle against the saloons was a righteous fight. The saloons were a nuisance. The liquor dealers and the brewers thought, with few exceptions, about nothing except to extend their traffic and make money. By advertisement and by the opening of innumerable saloons they constantly enlarged their sales. Their operations were under the control of government by taxation and a license system, but they were not controlled enough. The Eighteenth Amendment and the Volstead act put these lawful rum sellers and beer sellers out of business. That was what the Anti-Saloon League professed to wish to do, but that was really only part of its purpose, which was really to suppress the use of all alcoholic stimulants whatever in the United States. That has so far seemed to be beyond the power of the League and of the laws they have secured. The effort to dry up the whole country has produced crime and disorder to a calamitous degree. The effort has been, not to make laws suited to the people affected by them, but to remake the people to suit the laws. That effort runs into formidable difficulties. In Michigan a law which made felonies of breaches of the Volstead Act and provided drastic punishments for successive offenses brought down a life-sentence on a mother of children and excited such disgust that it had to be repealed. Wisconsin, in a referendum, has gone Wet by a huge majority.

The great defect of the inquisitors, the leaguers, and the supporters of the Methodist Board of Morals is their lack of understanding of human life. The Christ whom they claim as their religious leader had this understanding, and that is the great strength of the religion that He founded. These Methodists and Baptists who have invented new felonies and let loose the police on us are apostate Christians. Their backs are turned on the spirit and the teachings of the Master. They profess to be good; all fanatics profess to be good; but the verdict of history on fanaticism is not very flattering. It does not favor Torquemada, and it will not be overloaded with eulogies of Wayne B. Wheeler (a layman) and his clerical backers. People have been fooled into supposing that in giving support to Prohibition and Volstead they are upholding righteousness. Twenty centuries ago in Judea the greatest claimants to righteousness were the sect of Pharisees, denounced by Christ in stinging words that have come down through the ages without abatement of their force. Prohibition as we know it, as we see it, is profoundly un-Christian in purpose and method. To say that, is to indicate the reason why it is bound to fail. Its psychology is wrong.

What is there then to do? Shall opponents of Volstead, and possibly of the Amendment, organize as the Drys did, concentrate on one purpose and bring to bear upon legislators an influence that will offset the coercion of the Anti-Saloon League and the Methodist Board of Morals? That would be one way. Possibly resort will be had to it, but it may not be necessary. It may be that public opinion and the impossibility of enforcing the present laws in communities that do not approve them may compel revision. It has become evident that to enforce laws to determine what people shall drink in communities opposed to such interference is a greater evil than the drinks concerned. Many people think that the fight against the Drys is a fight for rum. In some cases it is, but in many other cases drinks are not the main consideration. For the better and more formidable characters who are out to beat the Drys the fight is one against clerical despotism, against men who in the name of Christ attempt to regulate life by means abhorrent to the Christian spirit. That is not a new thing in the world. The Puritans tried it in England and New England. The Roman Catholic Church has often tried it. The Jesuits have shown remarkable examples of it as in Paraguay, the Mormons have done pretty well at it. If you can get an obedient people under the domination of religious leaders who have some business sense, you can produce remarkable results in industry and external deportment, but do such gains last? They may last long enough for the consummation of a special purpose. The discipline of an army may be maintained while a war lasts; the discipline of a nation, even though it is harsh, can be maintained throughout an emergency; but in the long run, and especially with peoples used to self-government, compulsion cannot win.

What is going to happen when the worm turns? What is going to happen as the popular opinion spreads that despises the informers, the wire-tappers, the dry agents with guns, the Coast Guard ships with more guns, the Methodist and Baptist clergy and the various other clergy, and Henry Ford and divers magnates of Big Business who are so ruthless and insistent in their effort to dry up a world incurably moistened by its Maker? The Promised Land of the children of Jacob was pictured as flowing with milk and honey. The Promised Land these agents aforesaid picture to us is one flowing with milk and water. Somehow the vision does not seem to excite the enthusiasm requisite to make it come true.

The Strain of Current Life

December, 1927

T H E newspapers have quoted Dean Inge as saying that hardly anyone now believes that democracy is the final phase of governmental progress.

Why, no! of course it isn't! If we thought heaven was run by democracy and was an illustration of popular government, we might not want to go there. The final phase of governmental progress must be sought in the invisible. So far as appears, it seems to be an autocracy. But for this world democracy may be very suitable, for the errand of persons in this world is to develop, and to gain wisdom; and the more their environment compels them to improve their own circumstances or pay the penalty, the more our life on earth makes for evolution and progress. The Dean ought to know, probably does know, that the high purpose of government is not merely to make things comfortable for the governed. It is to stimulate the governed to self-help. Democratic government is well adapted to do that service, since it is prone to rapid degeneration and needs to be nudged and prodded at frequent intervals if it is to be tolerable at all.

There are proceeding in this country flagrant examples of the propensity of governments to run down hill. Here is a very big and very rich country, and the job of according to it even the necessary minimum of government is enormous. It is a job that is profitable in a money sense only to the unscrupulous. To them it may be very profitable indeed. But the necessary minimum of government is far from satisfying the people whose hands itch to hold the reins over their fellows. What they want is just as much government as the people will endure. They want to shape it according to their own ideas of virtue or of vice. They want the spending of monies, the control of taxation, a meticulous inquiry into everybody's affairs, the ordering of private life, and the definition of crime. Dean Inge must know all that. He sees that government has got to be done by people who have the brains for the job. So he says (as reported) that *Vox populi vox Dei* is bunkum and that Lincoln's government by the people for the people is claptrap. He thinks that the theory of democracy may last in England until the end of the century, but finds it to be "in the condition of an animal less and less able to maintain itself in a state of health and vigor."

The real question about democracy is whether it is fit to produce men competent to manage government and put them into office. Every presidential election in this country is an experiment on that problem, and there is a good deal to favor the theory that such elections and the designation of candidates which precede them are determined by something more than incarnate intelligence. It is either that the invisible powers take an interest in our political concerns and get into the game we think we are playing, or else that the choice of candidates and the success of the one who wins are determined by factors too complex and obscure for our limited faculties to measure and handle. Of course the idea that Providence takes a hand in our affairs is not novel. Most of the religious people profess to believe it and make prayers based on it. Political conventions usually open with such supplications. All the same, these matters are planned beforehand and organized and worked over with all the diligence our political managers can command. They work at them just as though they could control results, thinking ahead as far as they can, pulling all the wires they can reach, and laboring faithfully and in ways often devious with all the delegates they can get hold of.

That is all right, except perhaps the devious ways; all just as it should be. If we are going to trust in Providence to pull us out of holes and give a right direction to our political courses, we must first do all we can ourselves. After that, if things go our way, it is polite at least to suggest that the Lord is on our side, and if they contradict our judgment and disappoint our efforts, we may well say that Providence is inscrutable and its ways beyond prediction.

In every mind there are underground currents not recognized even by that mind itself. Often enough we cannot predict our own actions. The job of the politician includes calculations of all these subterranean forces and, the more intent he is upon the particular things that he wants, the less qualified he is to estimate these recondite forces correctly. Very common in our political history is the story of best bets that seemed sure to win and finally lost. Very common the story of managers baffled, and a totally unexpected winner.

Our political narrative for the last four or five years has been very much the story of prosperity: how to bring it; how to keep it. Now with another political effort about to be undertaken, is that issue still going to suffice? Perhaps so, but that is a matter for discussion, and for consideration by politicians. For one of our great parties that issue is supposed to be all-sufficient. Certainly, it did well at the last election; but the other party, if it is going to make any notable performance, has got to offer something new. And what is it that can be offered as yet to American voters which will look better to them than prosperity?

Of course when prosperity cracks because the time has come for it to do so, that is a different matter. With prosperity sick abed, you might even offer virtue with some prospect of getting votes for it, but hardly when prosperity is still up and doing. Certainly we have had it in ample supply. Not perfectly distributed of course—it never is—but a vast flood of it running down to the ocean by various channels and easily diverted into private fields by persons with a gift for that exploit.

Perhaps it is being tried out. Perhaps there will be statistics about it when the flood is over, to help our judgment about its value. Florida, you may recall, had an extraordinary burst of it which more recently became modified. Perhaps earnest seekers after facts might find out something in Florida about the relation of prosperity to human happiness: how much happiness was increased when it bulged, and how much it shrunk when it waned. But we have enough going on right around us here for purposes of observation. What about it? Are we doing better than usual? Has the flood of prosperity been to our advantage? Certainly it has changed life enormously, but has it benefited it? All over the land dwellings have put out new piazzas and blown themselves to coats of paint. There has been vast material construction, and a great deal of it is good; some of it very good and likely to last a long time. All sorts of industrial plants have increased in size, and as a country we can make more things than we used to. But are people happier than they were? Is their behavior better? Are more people making true progress in human life because of prosperity than when we had less of it?

Maybe they are. As one looks about in a suburban town on his way in a motor car to the train he sees girls going to the high school (and even some boys) and admires their pretty frocks. He naturally says to himself—they must be getting something. He sees the flocks of new cars on the road, fairly cheap cars but much prettier than the cheap cars ever were before, better painted, and finds in that more evidence of prosperity. But, bless you! how filling is it? Cries for help come nowadays from a good many people who have very nice cars indeed. They are not visibly in a bad case. They have enough money, enough things, a sufficient variety of dwellings, good cars, as said; but from many people so furnished with material things proceed evidences of distress. You don't have to go to Hollywood to find them. If you show propensity as a moralist they are quite likely to come to you through the mail, and they seem to come increasingly. They carry the same burden as the old cry, "What shall I do to be saved?" Current sufferers don't word it that way. They ask, "What is the matter with this life? It does not taste good. The things we used to think important—character, manners, high thinking, modesty—don't seem so any more. Everything goes that has wheels under it." They say, "I don't like this life; what is to be done about it?"

So far as observation can guide us, prosperity seems to minister to happiness very considerably. It commands the comforts of life, and really the comforts are not so bad. The most fun in the world—or next to the most—is the exercise of one's creative energy; and in so far as prosperity promotes that, helping people to build houses, develop taste, and increase beauty, it probably does increase happiness.

But that phase of it is seldom permanent. The cries for help come from people who have passed it, people suffering apparently from spiritual or mental exhaustion, people stricken with a sense of the futility of things as they are and penetrated with a strong desire to learn the cure of life. For such people prosperity is no cure. Their "What shall I do to be saved?" means to be saved in this life and from this life. It does not necessarily betoken anxieties about the hereafter. What are you going to do with people who have enough to eat and can get a drink if necessary; who have beds to sleep in and roofs over them and no money cares, and still want to be saved from the life they lead—not a bad life, but not good enough for them? What is the cure? Nothing but love, of course; but how are they going to get it?

The cure of life is set down in the records of the great seer and teacher whose birthday we keep in December, but still the people who need the cure and know they need it and call for it have to be helped to find it. Perhaps helping them to find it is the greatest job; greater than running a steel trust or an oil company or even administering the diffusion of electrical benefits. Perhaps this job of curing lives is the most important of all, and to feel that it is may be what we are coming to when the prosperity issue wears out. The politicians are up against it. The great succeeding issue for a while may be the cure of life or how to be happy in spite of prosperity or even without it.

Perhaps something else has been going on in the United States besides this aggravation of prosperity. Perhaps we have been getting wiser as well as richer. The two advances do not often come at the same time, but they may. The enormous breaches in the habits of life have made everything more fluid than it used to be. It has really been plowing time, and prosperity has helped it by increasing the opportunities of millions of people, raising their wages, putting them on the road, making them more independent, and in many cases much more meddlesome and objectionable. Prosperity has not lulled this country into slumber. It has not spread a meringue over it. It has been a great factor in waking it up. Truth to say, it has raised hob with it. That is one reason why we get these wails from people who do not like life as it is. Their habits are all disturbed. They have to think too much; think about everything; get new programs of living; figure out the expense of them, and consider how they are going to get the money. It is very tiresome. It involves far too much bookkeeping, especially for purposes of taxation. If presently we all turn away from prosperity and run after religion it is no more than you might expect. But it won't be our grandfathers' religion except in its derivation. The interpretation of it will be ours and our descendants'. It was five years ago that an American observer wrote in a letter: "It seems to me the consolatory reflection is that all those things we were talking about to-day—both the mystical ones and the practical—would be understood and substantially agreed to by millions of persons in America (they would be incomprehensible to anyone else) and the land is being visited by a big spiritual vision of some sort. Whatever we do or say is somehow a part of it and furthers it; and the more detachedly, and as it were irresponsibly, we give way to its intimations the more we assist." Was he right that the land was being visited by a big spiritual vision of some sort? Is the visit still continuing? There are more signs of it now than there were then.

We have it on the word of eminent authority that one out of ten of the present population of this country goes first or last under treatment for nervous or mental disturbance. Also we are told that of all the hospitals in the country one-half are monopolized by patients suffering from insanity or in need of care and protection to save them from it. Governor Smith in New York State called the other day for fifty million dollars for better hospitals for the care of the insane and the treatment of deranged persons. Such a multitude of people not able to take the responsibility of their own lives and conduct is an enormous burden on the public and apparently it is steadily increasing, and that in these years which are rated as extraordinarily prosperous. Really it does look as though there was something quite serious the matter with us and our negotiation of the problem of existence; something for which increased distributions of money or mass production of commodities does not seem to be a remedy. Is it likely that we shall have an opportunity to try what healing virtues there may be in adversity? Yes, it is likely. One may say, indeed, that it is certain; certain as far as business is concerned. For business prosperity is a matter of ups and downs and adjustments spread over periods of time, and though the wealth of the world increases and holds its increase, and though our command of the resources of nature also increases constantly, and with it our capacity to create more wealth, yet there is no reason to believe that we are quit of fluctuations in prosperity. Every reaction in Wall Street brings evidence of multitudes of people who are waiting for something to drop, and their anxious expectations are not without basis.

None the less, "Take no thought for the morrow," and "Sufficient unto the day is the evil thereof" are still maxims worthy of respect. The wise course is not so much to spend one's thought in anticipating calamity and contriving means to escape it, as so to shape one's life that whether in evil days or good, we shall not fail to live profitably. In so far as we can do that, we shall escape from fear and keep out of sanitariums, but it is a spiritual achievement and implies belief and reliance on things not made by hands.

Sun Spots and Justice

November, 1927

IT may be recalled that last winter at the meeting of the American Association for the Advancement of Science, which sat at Philadelphia in the holiday season, there was read a paper of Professor Tchijevsky of Moscow about the unusual sun-spot activity that would prevail this year and next year and the disturbances that might be expected to attend it. The newspapers reported what they could about this paper—it was much too long to be given in full—but the upshot of it was, as noted in this department of this magazine last March, that all great mundane disturbances followed or attended these periods of sun-spot activity. That was the burden of the Russian professor's discourse. He said these operations in the sun followed eleven-year cycles: three years of minimum excitability of human beings; two years of increasing excitability; three years of maximum excitability, and then three years of decline to the minimum that closes the cycle. This year and until 1929, we are told, the sun-spot activity now proceeding comes to its maximum, "with resulting human activity of the highest historical importance, which may again change the political chart of the world." So said the Russian professor, and he thought the prevailing excitability would be all the livelier because the present high mark of the eleven-year cycle coincides with the maxima of sixty and thirty-five years. The Russian gentleman thinks the deportment of the sun has a great deal to do with human behavior. Another scientist, an engineer of note and an expert in violet rays, holds that it has a great deal to do with the weather and that the prevailing solar disturbances are responsible for the Mississippi floods and the wet season.

There may be something in these suggestions. Certainly we have had a curious summer both as regards the weather and the excitability of the human mind. The idea that we are creatures of circumstance is no new thought, but this suggestion that humanity at large is poignantly affected by the influence of the heavenly bodies is to this generation a good deal more novel, though ancient knowledge took notice of it and made it a factor in calculation.

At any rate, the Russian scientist in declaring that the unusually agitated condition of the sun presaged corresponding agitations in the minds of men seems to have hit it pretty accurately. We have had unusual reactions of the human mind to stimulations all through the year. The Hall-Mills case, Lindbergh and the flyers, the case of Sacco and Vanzetti, were all curious, and all very thorough jobs of widespread mental disturbance. The Hall-Mills case was bad. The immense enthusiasm over Lindbergh seems to have been useful. The Sacco and Vanzetti case was very remarkable indeed and had about it something that made people wonder whether there was not in it a revolutionary quality which made it comparable to the famous case of the diamond necklace that preceded the French Revolution.

Sacco and Vanzetti have been executed, and it may be that that is the end of it. It may also be that it is not the end of it, but on the contrary a great emphasizing fact which secures the matter against being forgotten. One thing about the case may profitably be noticed. When Governor Fuller called upon Messrs. Lowell, Stratton, and Grant to examine the trial and report on it it seemed that he had solved the problem of allaying the doubts about the fairness of the trial and that the report of those committeemen, whatever conclusion they reached, would be accepted as just and conclusive and would allay the more important part of the disturbance in the public mind. The report said the trial was all right. It found no serious fault with anybody concerned with it except it said that the Judge had been indiscreet in some things he said out of court. The report did allay the disturbance of a good many minds, of some of them permanently, of others for a day or two; but when it had been duly discussed by the opposition, the objections to the trial and to the execution of the prisoners broke out as strong as ever, and the efforts to get a new trial for the convicted men or commutation of their sentence went on impetuously to the last moment of their lives. The feeling opposed to the report was that the committeemen simply represented the established order and saw everything with its eyes and reached conclusions that were foregone, not so much from the facts of the case as from the training and the habits of the minds that considered them. The committeemen

believed one set of witnesses and disbelieved another. The assailants
of the proceedings believed some of the witnesses whom the committeemen rejected, and the committeemen refused to rate as important facts
which the assailants considered cast a shadow of doubt over the verdict.
That shadow of doubt remained in many minds, and pretty good ones
as minds go, undispersed by that report. At this writing the shadow
is still operative and is pretty sure to inspire further examination of
the facts of that case and an effort to mend the criminal procedure
in Massachusetts, with results possibly affecting criminal procedure in
all other states.

One cause to which is attributed the immense noise about this case,
and also about Lindbergh and about the Hall-Mills case, is the unprecedented efficiency for certain purposes of the contemporary publicity
machine. As a dispenser of sensations it beats any machine that we
know of. A large proportion of the strongest newspapers of the country
are in a competition for readers. This makes them primarily attentive
to such stories as the most readers will buy and inclines them sometimes
to emphasize criminal news and scandals to the partial neglect of things,
like the story of the Mississippi flood, which are much more momentous. That flood tale has only been half told, and not for the
reason that newspapers are not willing to print it, but that newspaper
readers preferred to read about something else—the something else
usually being murders, holdups, and details of crime generally. It is
nothing new that there are more readers for crime than for good behavior. There always have been. What is novel about the present times
is that facilities for giving readers what they want have been so enormously developed, and that the advertising business, which is the life
blood of current papers, depends so considerably on circulation.

Certainly some of the murders make very interesting reading, and
the more wicked and the more callous they are, the more interesting
readers find them. Mere death by accident or motor car attracts little
attention. In this morning's papers there was a heading about six men
who were killed by a current of electricity that leaked into a wire
they were working on. Will that attract attention? Scarcely any! About
seven thousand people a year are killed nowadays in the United States
by motor cars. That does attract some attention by the number, but

the individual case goes for little in the general news unless there is an element of crime connected with it. It may be, however, that these multiplied killings by accidents, which are incidental to the high speed of our mechanical civilization, help in a subtle way to undermine the respect for human life. Certain it is that homicide is appallingly common in this country at this time.

There is another thing that is increasingly common: disrespect and disregard for authority. Both of these factors were involved in the Sacco and Vanzetti case. The Italians were tried for murder. They had about as fair a trial as Massachusetts could give them and were convicted. There was only moderate interest in the killing but eventually an enormous interest in the trial. The theory grew under careful nursing that the Italians, being Reds, were being sent to the chair by the established order in Massachusetts which did not like their politics. It may be that seven years of delay used by good lawyers and an efficient publicity bureau for the diffusion of doubt about the justice of a verdict in a murder trial would destroy public confidence in any trial that was ever held. So far as that is true, the culprit in the Sacco case was the legal procedure in Massachusetts which made the long delay possible.

Most of the complaints about the Sacco and Vanzetti matter are based on the feeling that perhaps the convicted men were not guilty and that their execution was a miscarriage of justice. That feeling is set forth with unusual vehemence in some of the Radical weeklies. As to the fact of the innocence or guilt of those parties no one in sight knows absolutely; or if he does, he won't tell. There may be some persons who do know absolutely; for if five did the killing and three got away, as appears to be understood, the three who got away and have not been recovered probably know the whole story. I talked to Silas Shacklepate about this idea that so many people have that possibly these executed men were not guilty of this crime of which they were convicted. Silas is a lawyer and possibly takes a legalistic view of such matters, though he is particularly strong about the duty of resisting some laws if we do not like them. He would have nothing to do with the suggestion that maybe the men were innocent. He had read the general literature of the case, particularly the reports of Governor Fuller and of his advisors. That was enough for him. He said that these men seemed to have had a fair trial and quite a lot of it, and there was no reason for letting them off. To let them off would amount to evasion of the laws of Massachusetts by the authorities chosen to enforce them. Silas does not believe in that. If laws are going to be violated he wants it done unofficially by volunteers who take chances in that adventure. The constituted authorities he considers under obligation to enforce the laws if they can.

He told a story of two judges, one a good deal younger than the other, walking up the street in conversation on the way to the elder judge's court room. When they reached it the younger man shook hands and said: "Good-by! Go in now and do justice!" Whereupon the departing elder turned around: "Justice!" he said, "What has that got to do with my job?" Courts, said Silas, can't do justice, though they may happen to. It is not their job to do justice. Their job is to determine questions put up to them, according to the law as it exists or as they understand it. Eastern autocrats like Solomon might do justice, but imagine two women coming to one of our courts disputing over a child and one of our judges using Solomon's method to determine who was the real mother. It would not do at all. No. The great function of courts is to provide order. They do it by making decisions according to law as it exists, which they interpret to the best of their ability. Silas, being satisfied that Sacco and Vanzetti had had a fair trial as trials go, adventured with their case no father. "That is all you can do," he said. "You must not expect justice from courts. You may get it and you may not. When you come to court with a question, you get an answer. That is valuable. We could not get along without it. When a court has done its best, that is all you can ask. Take it and go."

That is a comprehensible attitude. Are you satisfied with it? Those people, not counting the Reds, who were so insistent that Sacco and Vanzetti should not be executed, were not satisfied with this point of view that Silas has. It was terrible to them to think that men should be executed about whose guilt there was a shadow of a doubt. The Eastern peoples accepted the fiats of their despots for better or worse. If they went against them, they set it down as fate. They had no newspapers to make a row in, no publicity machine; but they had to have decisions in their disputes or about their misbehaviors or the accusations made against them, and they took them as they came, and went on living if they were allowed to. That we clamor for "justice" may be a sign that we and our institutions are better than they and theirs are. I hope we are. But do the common run of us think that justice is done in court except off and on, or do we think that the man who gets it to suit him is usually the man who has the best lawyer?

Police-court justice is more like the Eastern type than that which is reached by the more elaborate proceedings in the higher courts. The police judge is more like a cadi. He takes in what is before his eyes, turns over everything in his mind, and takes action on it. But even police-court justice is liable to miscarriage. In the paper the other day there was a story of a man out of prison on probation who got a little excited with bad rum, was impressed with the fact that the streets were dirty, seized a broom from a street cleaner's kit, and began sweeping the streets. The street cleaner complained of him for stealing his broom. He was taken to a police court; some Javert in the court recognized him as a man on probation, and what happened to that unfortunate man? The papers said he was to be sent back to Clinton Prison to serve out eleven years of his sentence—and all for borrowing a broom to sweep the streets!

My gracious! Do you notice that everybody who can afford it, and who is sufficiently scared, insures nowadays against the action of the courts, particularly in accident cases? They do not dare to take chances on motor-car accidents or on accidents that may happen to people whom they employ. They think that if they do they may be ruined overnight.

No, no! Justice is hardly got by law in this world. But this order that the courts are so instrumental in keeping is extremely valuable. Life adjusts itself to what the courts do, adjusts itself particularly to the need of keeping out of them. So there is no real basis for revolution in the Sacco and Vanzetti case; there may be basis for reforms in procedure, reforms, indeed, of the laws affecting criminal cases. If we are not even getting such justice as is possible, we surely should improve our methods. The old judge of whom the tale is told above was by no means careless of doing justice. The point was that he appreciated the limitations of his power to do it.

Perhaps it is the sun spots that have made us take all these things so hard. At any rate there are proceeding in these times curious, subtle changes of mental attitude about a good many things. We have considerably lost respect for law as law, thanks quite a bit to prohibition. We know that laws do not make right and wrong, but must conform to common human judgment about those matters if they are to be any good.

Free Will, Regulation, Non-Resistance

August, 1925

WHAT is wanted in our generation with a particularly fervent desire is mass production of education. The world has been jolted pretty hard lately and a great many of the doctors have got the idea that, if people knew more, they would behave better and avoid some forms of misconduct which threaten to crack civilization. How far they are right in their supposition that education improves people and makes them more peaceable is matter for discussion. The Germans, in a way, had more education than any other people. They seemed to be the most thoroughly schooled people on earth, but it did not keep them out of the war. The great obstacle to mass production of education is not the distrust of its value but the fact that teaching has to be fitted to each individual and that no two individuals are alike. Now the parts of one Ford are just like the parts of another, and you can fit them together and the thing will go. They are all factory made, but people—especially young people—are not like that. We know they are chock full of idiosyncrasy, very individual, often obtuse in some particulars; and when you go to fitting on to them a ready-made suit of education, like as not it won't hang right. Besides being different, these creatures have inside of them a piece of clockwork called a will and that is what they run by. We are instructed by our pastors and masters—that is by some of them—that knowledge of good and evil and free will in our choice between them is the particular gift of God to us which makes the great distinction between us and the animals. Not the only distinction, of course; a good many of the animals have four legs and more sensitive perceptions in various particulars than we have, and do not bob their hair nor shave, as most of us do; but the great distinction between us and them is free will, along with which there goes doubtless a superior intellectual capacity that in truth may be for all we know, and probably is, a product of the will.

Well now, free will is valuable. How are you going to save it? It is recognized that the animals beat us in some things. They seem to have powers of sense that we have not. They have discernment of things invisible to us and apparently can see ghosts. They can smell what we can't smell and get information out of it that is quite beyond us. When we want information of that sort we go to dogs to get it. They have a sense of direction that we have lost. They can find their way out of the woods by instinctive sense of direction. The migratory birds have the same thing. They know when to start their annual journeys and in what direction to make them. Indeed the animals and their lives are very wonderful and full of mystery. There they are, living beside us! What they know we only guess. We study them and some of us who are sufficiently intelligent seem to make progress in discovering what they have and what they do with it. It is the same with the insects, big and little, down to the myriads which we see only through microscopes. So we see life going on everywhere and we know quite well that a lot of it which we do not see at all still goes on. We notice no schools for bees or ants, and nothing but parental instruction for birds and all the animals; yet we see that they get along and prosper according to their opportunity and increase or decrease according to their chances, so we conclude that what they know by the light of nature is valuable and we suspect that what is given to us and our children by nature is also valuable, and that in our educational proceedings we do well to save as much of it as we can.

Now take a modern child. A lot of trouble has been taken to produce that child. It started longer ago than anyone has been able to compute with any certainty. Put aside for the moment the evolutionary theory that we began life as seaweed or something like that, and start with man. Starting even so and avoiding discussion of the earlier methods and maneuvers of the Creator to make us, if we merely start with man we go back a long, long time that seems to grow more protracted with every significant excavation. Recorded history goes back only about ten thousand years, and that is a mere trifle in the age of man, but it is a fair length of time if one is to discuss deliberate and organized education, which has doubtless existed much longer than that. Now there have been two main ends of education—to impart knowledge, and to train the young to do as their elders thought they should. A great aim of education has been obedience. It seems very necessary in children—at least it is highly recommended in Scripture. You have to have a certain amount of it in human life or you will have more trouble than you can handle. But if it persists too long or is too fervently exacted, you lose free will and with it the greatest prerogative of man.

What does education mean anyway? It means to bring out what is in one, and that is what education ought to do. What is the greatest thing in us and the most important for education to bring out? It is free will, the capacity to choose between good and evil, between wisdom and foolishness, and to follow whichever one prefers. Without free will there is little or no permanent progress in civilization. Civilization will progress through obedience to God, but doubtfully through obedience to man. The understanding of the Divine Will is knowledge. By that men improve and develop good judgment. Not so, necessarily, by the understanding of the will of man and concurring with that. The great exercise provided for us by Almighty Wisdom for our journey through this life is the exercise of intelligence and of our wills; to meet temptation and beat it; to get as good a living as we can; not to injure or destroy our neighbors nor by them to be destroyed; to reach more and more to that understanding of the Divine Will which is knowledge and truth. That is the nature of our job here. In our childhood we need guidance, and there are only too many people who never really grow up and who need more or less guidance all their days. But those who do grow up must develop by the exercise of their own minds and their own wills, otherwise they will neither be strong nor wise. To live by rules laid down by other persons for the government of our actions is not enough. We are not machines nor made to run on rails. We don't profit, after childhood, by being told to go in when it rains or come out when it clears. We ought, ourselves, to learn about such things. If someone really knows more than we do, we should profit by his knowledge. It is not to be desired that we should be our own doctors or our own lawyers, unless indeed we know more about health than the doctors do and more about law than the lawyers, or are lucky enough to escape sickness or litigation.

We may, however, hope to know religion as well as most of the ministers do, because that is the one special subject in which we have constant training. At least some of us have it. Time was when most people had it, but that may not be true now. That does not mean that there will not be clergymen who know more about theology, men who know more about literary criticism and, indeed, about almost everything, than we do, but we may hope to get along without running to our clergy to tell us what is right or wrong.

In spite of our great need of developing each for himself our own powers of self-direction in this extraordinary country and this extraordinary time, we are afflicted with a pest of people who insist upon telling us what to do and are able to get laws through legislatures that aim to make us do it. They want to tell us, and they do tell us, what not to drink, what not to learn, what not to believe, where to send our children to school, what shows to go to, how to dress, how much to wear when we go swimming, what to do on Sunday, and to what particulars of theology to subscribe. A good deal of all that is not new in the world. It has always happened that there have been people who have thought that what they saw was all the truth there was and who insisted on imposing their conception of it on others. Prohibition is not new: insistence upon details of creed is not new, but such things have so rained upon us in recent years that really we begin to be astonished. And what is the reason? The reason is that by the working of democracy the power to regulate has gone into the hands of half-taught people whose understanding of life is imperfect and their knowledge limited. Most of them mean to do right and make right prevail, but go about it in so faulty a way that what prevails is wrong. They sow for peace and raise war. They sow for temperance and raise rebellion. They do not know what seed they scatter.

Take Mr. Bryan. Mr. Bryan supposes himself to be a Christian, and in some measure no doubt he is. He considers it essential to sound Christianity to believe in the Virgin Birth. He would not allow in the ministry of the Presbyterian Church clergymen who do not hold that belief. That is not so bad, because it affects only the Presbyterian

Church. It is not the gnats he strains at that are Mr. Bryan's real ailment but the camels he swallows. Here he is insisting on the Virgin Birth, which is difficult for some people, and running amuck through the whole philosophy of Christ's teachings of which, evidently, he has no understanding at all. Christ regulated no one; he compelled no one. As has been said of him, he had complete understanding of the psychological effect of compulsion on men, whereas the prohibitionists and the regulators by legislation seem ignorant of anything but the first and more obvious consequences of what they do. They do not seem to understand that mind is free and that all effort to compel it to accept what it does not assent to ends in hypocrisy, evasion, or resistance. They do not seem to understand that legislation makes nothing right and nothing wrong, but that our sense of right and wrong is a growth of centuries and millenniums and, that when laws conflict with it, our consciences reject them, though we may find it politic so to shape our conduct as to keep us out of trouble with the courts and avoid the attentions of the police.

The complications of the world are difficult just now, and the thoughts of many people run on the solution of them. An interesting man who has rather novel ideas on some fundamental subjects, being asked the other day what the world needs, replied: "What it needs is the gospel of Christ. Implicit faith in that will save the world. Nothing else will." His answer was interesting because of what he thought Christianity meant. The old religions, he said, stood for prohibition and punishment, but Christianity for freedom and forgiveness. His idea was altogether that Christ came to make us free; that he came to use our wills and not to suppress them; to cure the world from the inside out, not from the outside in.

Of course, it sounds like a counsel of perfection when one speaks of using the will of man to save the world and remembers that it is by the will of man that the world is imperiled. Nevertheless, that is what Christ has done and would have us do. He would save the world, not by compulsion, not be legal regulation, but by such a reshaping of the will as he had power to effect, and described as rebirth. That power undoubtedly remains in the world to this day and works in our times, and it is about the most valuable asset we have and, some day, believers think it will really be tried out and bring peace.

That, however, seems not imminent. We have to be content with much more modest deductions, as that creeds will not make belief, nor regulations make character, nor laws necessarily bring order, nor prohibition, temperance. Connected with these things are the ideas we seem to be gathering about money. The Bible says the love of money is the root of all evil, and people who go after it with energy still talk as though it was the chief end of life. But for all that, its prestige in the last quarter-century has diminished, and since the Great War we have been going through a course of silent instruction about what money really means. We have taken for granted that it was an advantage to persons who got it, albeit instances to the contrary have not been rare; but as the discussion of the war debts that Europe owes us goes on, the advantage of squeezing money out of Europe seems to grow more and more doubtful. For money is merely a form of power, a factor in compulsion. When it promotes life it is useful; when it clogs energy and impedes human intercourse, or diminishes the ardor of effort, it hinders life and does harm. Imprisonment for debt, after prevailing for centuries, passed away chiefly because it was uneconomic; because there was no sense in it; because men could not earn money to pay their debts while they were shut up in prison. So we may come in time to have sense about the war debts and cease to heckle Europe for moneys that she cannot repay without too great a strain on her resources and standards of living, and which, probably, we could not receive without serious disturbance to the working of our own delicately contrived and related economic machine. What the Great War may finally be discovered to have effected is the end of the long, long tried attempt to save the world and keep the peace by compulsion, and the beginning of an effort to do so by general consent. When the philosopher quoted above said that implicit faith in the gospel of Christ will save the world and nothing else will, something like that was what he implied.

Christ said: Resist not evil. That was one item of his counsel to his followers. It is very puzzling. Did he mean that there should be no resistance to evil? Or did he out of his profound discernment see that evil, if given its head, would breed a much more efficacious resistance than any we could provide against it? The cure for many difficult situations is to let people have their own way and face the consequences. We use that remedy often as it is, and should use it oftener if we were less combative, and were not misled by traditional valuations which rate material things too high and spiritual things too low. Our propensity to do that seems almost incurable, but we get a lot of instruction as we go along, and "Resist not evil" may not always baffle our intelligence.

NRA Me Down to Sleep

May, 1934

A doctor writes from Texas to the Easy Chair that he has been looking over *Harper's* for many a long month and has latterly become drowned or nearly so in criticisms, economics, and such like.

Is life as serious, he asks, as all this? Are we never to be joyous again? And he dismisses the idea that he cares much about the chance of a Japanese-Russian war, or has more than a casual interest in bloated bondholders, or thinks shouting of marital relations to the multitude particularly interesting. He has had to go back to Lamb, Hazlitt, and Montaigne, so he says, for acceptable reading.

Well, at this writing spring has come! For the moment the winter of our discontent does not hang around zero. It looks more as though life would go on and that our pleasure in it would find new demonstrations in the world about to be. Indeed, even in this last winter one could read in the papers of cheerful doings in Florida.

But, after all, the big things that are going on demand attention. We sit at the board, the dice are thrown, and we watch the throws and the throwers. We bet Mr. Roosevelt is right or wrong or that he will survive his mistakes. Hardly anyone bets that he won't survive them. Immense changes seem to be going on in the occupation of earth by human beings. Possibly we are fooled in thinking they are so extraordinary, but "the usual" does not seem to be happening. Nero fiddled while Rome was burning, and they say it was because he had in mind to build a better one. No objection to our Texas friend's fiddling a bit! He can't help the case by being gloomy.

A Philadelphia lawyer, busy with clients affected by new plans for the transaction of business, finds his philosophy expressed in a new version of an old petition:

> NRA me down to sleep
> I pray the Lord my codes I'll keep.
> If I should bust before I wake
> A.F.O.L. my plant will take.

That is the right spirit: cheerful resignation but not hopeless. Far from it; far from it! When we get out of the woods in a couple of years, the going, it seems, is to be smoother for some time to come. And meanwhile there is evidence that 1931 was low year, that we hit bottom at 1932, improved last year, and are moving steadily upgrade to a condition of comparative contentment.

All the same, the problem that occupies the contemporary mind to an enormous degree is how to get along on a reduced income. This very morning headlines say the President asks ten per cent rise in pay and ten per cent shorter hours of labor. Splendid, if the paymasters can find the money; but can they? Shorter hours of labor can always be produced. The President wants to cure this condition of reduced income. Reductions almost universal run all the way down from affluence to a mere competence and from enough to live on to destitution. People accustomed to living on a certain economic level and who have had means to sustain themselves socially and fiscally on that plane are notable indeed if they can maintain a philosophic attitude in a reduction that drops them from the perch they are used to. But millions of people have had or are now having that experience and, of course, the great problem of government just now is to help them out of it if possible. Those who have been used to pay their bills and find that they can't do it any longer are pretty sure to run into debt before they stop. But there is a limit to how far they can subsist on credit. Some of them will ask themselves if it is necessary to keep alive. The answer to that is, yes; they should keep alive. They should not die by their own choice, because if they do they don't know what will happen to them next, and there are abundant grounds to believe that they will not like it. It is a duty to stay alive until one's summons comes outside of his own volition.

Then what is the problem? Enough food to sustain health, life, warmth, clothing, shelter—those are the basic necessaries of the physical man. As much as that should be supplied if necessary and possible out of the public purse, and that it should be so supplied is at present the primary aim of government.

But after all, ours is not the only country in which this problem has had to be faced. Most of the others have had it in turn—Austria,

Germany, France, England, Russia, China. In a country where farmers are paid money not to plant full acreage and where the great fiscal trouble has been thought to be due to overproduction, feeding everybody ought to be comparatively easy, but it requires organization of distribution. There has to be somebody to hand out food to others, somebody to cook the food, somebody to make flour, cereals, all other things that support life. That distribution is going on at large expense, increasing the public debt. But what else is there to do?

There must be also proceeding a vast dislocation of people, from cities to the country presumably, and perhaps from cold regions to warmer ones. In the State of New York and the States near it a lot of the usual fruit seems to have been killed, the peaches, especially. We don't know yet where all that zero weather has left us. Sixty years ago and longer peaches were looked upon as a gamble, the crop depending upon the time and degree of the cold weather that they had to bear. This year it is said that even apple trees have been killed. However, that's only a detail of the problem of getting down to brass tacks and facing destitution.

Millions of people need help, many of them need it desperately. There are other millions who can get along with present strains and pinches, and a large proportion of them can do something for others if they will. Of course as taxpayers they will be the basis of what the government can do except that the government—that is, the Federal Government—has much more credit than anybody else and can run deeply into debt without submerging. But beyond that and between individuals, money is ceasing to be money and becoming food, clothes, warmth, and such things which pass from hand to hand without creating obligation.

Our greater newspapers are confronted by a highly diversified collection of readers. The more startling news of the day, whatever it is, appeals to pretty much everyone, and you have it on the front page. If something remarkable has happened, as when the good King Albert fell and died, or the big storm held up railroad traffic, everyone is interested. There is a volume of normal news that gets general attention because it is generally interesting. Beyond that on the inside pages there are, of course, the advertisements, to which all well-wishers of newspapers take off their hats; an assortment of news for different groups of readers; the foreign news—what the Nazis are doing—what the Austrians are doing—whether the prospects of a war in Asia are brighter or less so; the columns of lighter remarks; the sporting news, the theatrical news, the book news, the stock market news, the real estate market news, and the editorial page. A large company will read the stock-exchange reports; another will read about sports and another about the theater, still another about books, and selected groups of readers will read codes and the details of the efforts of the administration to make all things work together for good. All that means that you have to skip a lot in a newspaper in order to get along with it at all. Probably everybody skips the codes except persons affected by them, and so with all the other departments. Persons interested in foreign affairs and finance could skip the theaters, the movies, and sports.

One observes that pictures are an increasingly notable detail of the news. They are very informing, easy to read, can be looked at quickly, tell more in the same space of time than most of the print does. And perhaps it is because they count for so much that so many papers print so many pictures of the domestic fluctuations of the movie people, the attachments they form and the detachments that eventuate pretty regularly. One may ask what do these girls and these fellows matter? In their private lives how many of them have any characters, how many of them have any particular reputation? Those that have reputation as orderly persons, are they careful of it? Consider Douglas Fairbanks mixed up with the British nobility and considerably speckled as a result of it. One could have spared those headlines and many others. The bandit, bank-robber, kidnaping, and jail-breaking stories are better reading. Detective stories from current life run nowadays in every issue of every newspaper, and they are not bad reading and not unwholesome.

To another line of popular literature there is more objection. The newsstands have been cleaned up. So far as they were concerned March came in like a lion. Stimulated by Father McCaffrey, Chaplain of the Police Department; and back of him by Mons. Lavelle, Vicar General of the R. C. Diocese of New York and rector of St. Patrick's Cathedral;

and back of him by Cardinal Hayes in a pastoral letter against immoral publications, and back of him by the Holy Father in Rome, Paul Moss, Commissioner of Licenses, prohibited the sale and display of fifty-nine magazines and illustrated papers from licensed newsstands, and Police Commissioner O'Ryan instructed Chief Inspector Valentine to see that the prohibition is carried out.

Oh, well! Quite likely the newsstands will be none the worse for some deflation though some of the publishers of banished magazines object. If the cleansing goes too far it can doubtless be abated sufficiently. Whether it will do any good or not is another matter. Literature can be sold in Paris that cannot be openly sold in New York, and one would hardly say that Paris is any better off for the increased freedom in the matter. And there is Judge Woolsey to fall back on if the strings here are drawn too tight.

The clean-up is probably timely and is likely to be useful, but evidently it proceeds from the celibate mind, and the celibate mind in these matters that concern sex can hardly be regarded as sufficiently up to date to be trusted with the police power. Consider, for instance, Mons. Lavelle, Rector of St. Patrick's, as before said, who is quoted as saying that he made a trip to Boston to learn how it was that censorship of books could be enforced there. He probably discovered, though he does not say so, by calling on Cardinal O'Connell, who would be apt to know.

A very successful book in current literature is *Anthony Adverse,* which has sold something over three hundred thousand copies and is still selling. Mons. Lavelle has read it, so he says, and calls it the rottenest book he ever handled. He sent his copy to be burned in the furnace. It will be news to persons who have not read it that this very popular story is so objectionable, and many new readers may want to see what ails it. Father Lavelle was quoted as saying, "There was no kind of wickedness that Anthony Adverse did not investigate." Perhaps that is why it has sold so big. People good and bad have always been interested in wickedness. There is a lot about it in the Bible and full candor in narrating cases, and the Bible is the leading best seller of all time.

In the matter of clothes there has been something approaching a revolution. In the 19th century clothes were not only well thought of and bountifully provided but looked upon as necessary to propriety, particularly for women. To go round half naked was something that was not done. People felt about it much the same as doubtless Father Lavelle does now. This writer also, being born about the middle of the 19th century, shudders a bit at the degree of nakedness that goes on, and though interested is not unaffected by a feeling that he ought not to be. The younger generation are growing up with very different traditions from Father Lavelle and the present writer. See the daily paper pictures of what the young ladies of high fashion wear or don't wear on the sun-beaches of Florida. Amazing! But, after all, the youngsters may be right. Among the publications to be removed from the newsstands was the monthly publication of the Nudists. Now there is nothing bad about that except that the Nudists go naked. The old notion that clothes were part of the Christian religion has weakened a great deal. It has been discovered that it is more a matter of climate than of piety, and that in some climates the natives are healthier, cleaner, and just as good if they go naked. Missionaries have made this discovery. Clothes are a convention but, of course, they are related to climate and to style. They are not going to pass out of use, not in this climate, but they have diminished for women from two-thirds to three-quarters in the last fifty years and most of the change has been good. The Greeks were more or less indifferent to clothes. The Japanese were very indifferent to nakedness, perhaps are still so unless they have been corrupted by Western manners. That seems nearer to the ideal state than too much reverence for clothes, but still, for us at least, nudity will continue to have limits. The textile interests will hope so.

V/Bernard DeVoto

1935-1955

At one time before I became editor of *Harper's Magazine* I was in charge of the trade book department of Harper & Brothers, the department that published fiction and nonfiction for the general reader, as distinguished from text books and others in such specialized fields as medicine and religion. When I took it over, I was appalled to find that the department had to write off many thousands of dollars a year in unpaid advances. It was customary, then as now, for a publisher to make an advance payment to an author at the time he signed his contract, with the expectation that it would be repaid out of his royalties after the book came out. Such advances ranged from $500 to six figures. All too often, alas, they were never repaid—because the writer was unable to finish the book, or it turned out to be unpublishable, or it failed to sell enough copies to cover the advance.

Consequently, I undertook a study to see whether there might be some way to identify ahead of time those authors who were likely to earn their advances and those who were not. Talent was not the answer. Some of the most brilliant writers were also the most erratic; they would deliver their manuscripts years behind schedule, or they would follow a splendidly realized novel with another that was totally unsalable. Neither did sex nor age nor education seem to offer any reliable clue. In the end, I was able to discover only one common factor among those authors who always paid off: it was sheer animal vitality. John Gunther, who was built like a football line backer, and Thornton Wilder, who was slight and wiry, resembled each other in only one respect. Both had extraordinary reserves of energy. So did writers as diverse as Joyce Cary, Peter Drucker, and Bruce Catton. On the other hand, I could name a dozen authors of undeniable talent but low metabolism who turned out to be bad bets for their publishers.

Bernard DeVoto was a prime example of this rule. He was moody, vulnerable to fits of depression, and something of a hypochondriac; once he told me that he must have Dutch elm disease, because he felt awful even though the doctors could find nothing wrong with him. Yet no matter how bad he felt, he was a prodigious worker, and his physical presence radiated energy like a Franklin stove. This was fortunate for him and his family, since anyone who hopes to earn a living by free-lance writing has to turn out an unremitting stream of copy. His lifetime literary output, like Howells's and Curtis's, ran to millions of words; his bibliography fills eighty-nine closely printed pages. Although he never attempted to write a play, he was a competent journeyman in every other literary form and in two of them, history and the essay, he was superb. In my view, the columns he contributed to the Easy Chair have a consistent quality that has never been surpassed before or since—and as my editorial colleagues will testify, I am not afflicted with modesty, false or otherwise.

He was born in Ogden, Utah, in 1897, and his growing up there endowed him with a permanent love-hate relationship with the West. He loved the country, and hated those predators—cattle and sheep raisers, miners, lumbermen, and real estate speculators—who were trying to ruin it. As a historian, the exploration of the West and the character of its people was his dominant theme. From his parents—''an apostate Catholic and an apostate Mormon,'' as he put it—he acquired an abiding distrust of all revealed truths, dogmas, and established institutions, from the modern corporation to the Communist party; hence the sturdy skepticism which echoes through nearly everything he wrote.

For one year DeVoto attended the University of Utah and helped found a chapter of the Intercollegiate Socialist Society. When the administration disbanded it, and fired a handful of unorthodox professors to boot, DeVoto left in wrath and enrolled at Harvard. His education there was interrupted by a two-year stint of army duty during World War I. He never got overseas, because he was too good with a rifle; his superiors decided he would be most useful as a marksmanship instructor in training camps.

After his graduation from Harvard, he taught English for a few years at Northwestern University, where he married the brightest freshman in his class. He also began writing articles, mostly for Mencken's *American Mercury;* and by 1927 he felt confident enough to abandon teaching, move to Cambridge, Massachusetts, and embark on the career of a free-lance writer. He stuck with it for the rest of his life—except for a brief and unhappy term in the mid-thirties as editor of the *Saturday Review of Literature*—and his family never starved, an achievement that can't be fully appreciated except by those who have tried it.

It is not my business here (nor am I competent) to venture an appraisal of his work as historian, critic, and novelist; Wallace Stegner presumably will take care of that in his forthcoming DeVoto biography. His talents as an essayist the reader can judge for himself from the sampling that follows. But there are two aspects of his career about which I have some personal knowledge, and both seem to me worth recording.

As a journalist he was the complete professional. During the twenty years he wrote the Easy Chair, he turned his copy in to three editors of widely differing outlook and temperament: Lee Hartman, Frederick Lewis Allen, and myself. All thought themselves immeasurably fortunate to have him as a regular contributor, not only because his copy was so good, but because he was so *regular*. Never once did he miss a column. Never did a manuscript arrive late. Never, so far as I know, did he make a mistake in a major fact, and blessed few in minor ones. His copy was clean; the spelling and syntax were correct; the length was right; his pages could go direct to the printer with virtually no editing and no anxious editorial afterthoughts. Such professionalism has always been rare, and on some grim days I suspect that it may have disappeared with Benny.

Even more rare was his sense of obligation, to his country and his craft. Writers commonly tend to be more self-centered than most people, with scant concern for anything—the public weal, other authors, sometimes even their families—that distracts them from their work. Not Benny. Somehow he always managed to find time, in an impossibly crowded schedule, to do more than his share as a citizen, both of the United States and of the Republic of Letters.

He taught fledgling authors at the Bread Loaf Writers' Conferences. He advised and encouraged countless young novelists and historians— among them Arthur Schlesinger, Jr. He read and commented on hundreds of manuscripts (mostly hopeless) sent to him by friends and occasionally by complete strangers. He spent long evenings with editors and publishers, analyzing their products and conspiring to jack up the level of American literature. Apparently he was never too tired or busy to recommend a young talent to a university, or an editor, or a foundation.

So too he devoted a generous share of his energies to public service—as advisor to the Interior Department, counselor to members of Congress, policy consultant to Adlai Stevenson, and always-available crusader for the environment. Time after time he interrupted work on a book "to go to Washington and save the nation some more. . . ."

He did save quite a lot of it. Shortly after his death I wrote a column in which I tried to suggest that his example—now being followed by millions—might be the most enduring part of his life work. Here, rather than in the last section of the book, seems the right place to reprint it.

May, 1956

Remembrance in a High Valley

A little later this spring, when the snow melts in the passes of the Bitterroot mountains, the ashes of Bernard DeVoto will be scattered along the Lochsa River near the border between Idaho and Montana. He loved the American land—all of it—with a passion which channeled the whole course of his life; he knew it from one coast to another as few Americans ever have; and this was the stretch of country he loved best.

It is a rough, lonely place, majestic with history. Here Lewis and Clark came closest to disaster, in what one member of their party called "the most terrible mountains I ever beheld." Here they finally stumbled upon the Lolo Trail, which led them across the continent— and thus stretched the nation to the Pacific. Through this maze of timbered ridges DeVoto traced their path, mile by mile, as he did his field work for the classic history of the greatest of American explorations. Here he found his "days of well-being and content . . . on the Lolo and the Lochsa which since fate vouchsafed them to you it can never take away." One of his last wishes was that his ashes should be brought back to this valley; they have been waiting for the spring, in a Forest Service vault in Ogden, Utah, where he was born.

Today this stretch of wilderness lies within the Clearwater National Forest. One of his friends who traveled it with him—Senator Richard Neuberger of Oregon—has asked Congress to change its name to the Bernard DeVoto National Forest. Already his suggestion has encountered angry opposition.

For DeVoto was, in Neuberger's phrase, "the most illustrious conservationist who has lived in modern times." For twenty years he waged his battle—in these pages and elsewhere—to save the remnants of our national heritage. Time and again he blocked the schemes of greedy men to seize and despoil the forests, parks, game refuges, and wilderness areas which belong to all of us, and which give our country its unique grandeur.

So he made enemies. Many of them call themselves "conservatives"—a curious abuse of language, since it is they who want to change and destroy; and they could not recognize in DeVoto the true conservative: the man who wanted to conserve not only the primeval loveliness of American land, but also the American spirit which needs such places to survive. (He believed, with the Old Testament, that the soul shrivels when it is crowded in noise and ugliness, and that patriots grow best where it is open and green and quiet.) Even in Congress there are men—Senator Herman Welker of Idaho is one of them—who detest the idea of a memorial to any conservationist, and especially to DeVoto. This would have delighted DeVoto: he thought a man could be measured by the kind of enemies he makes.

Since his death last November many readers of *Harper's* have asked how they could best express their affection and sense of loss. Senator Neuberger has offered one opportunity. Perhaps such friends will want to let their own Senators and Congressmen know how they feel about the proposal to designate DeVoto's favorite national forest as his memorial.

But they can do another thing which Bernard DeVoto would have valued far more.

Bill Johnston, editor of the Lewiston, Idaho, *Morning Tribune,* summed it up like this:

"DeVoto loved the sound of the rushing Lochsa more than the sound of his own name. He was more interested in the forest itself than in its nomenclature. . . . He worked and fought for principles, not for money or fame. He was not as concerned about what people thought of him as he was about what they thought of National Forests and National Parks."

And Mr. Johnston set down his personal pledge "to the memory of a dedicated man" to "fight as he did for the forest itself."

That kind of enlistment is the remembrance which DeVoto would have appreciated most. The fight isn't over. There are still people, plenty of them, who believe that beauty is waste . . . that a tree is

worthless until it is chopped down and converted, for cash, into comic
books and beer cartons . . . that it is foolish sentimentality to try
to save a piece of America for the generations yet to come. So long
as they infest the land, the battle for conservation will have to go
on, and recruits for the DeVoto Memorial Battalion will still be needed.

Come as you are. The nice thing about this particular scrap is that
you can pitch into it any time, any place. Chances are that in your
own town, at this very hour, somebody is getting ready to bulldoze
away one of the few remaining meadows or patches of woods. They
will do it in the name of Progress—a convenient word to cover the
prefabricated slums-of-tomorrow, the asphalt parking lots, the endless
concrete scabs of the new highways. They can nearly always prove—to
the satisfaction of the City Council, dominated as it usually is by real-
estate men—that we can't afford to leave a little open space here and
there. Nobody can make a dime out of "idle" land; so a strip of
greenery is a luxury the taxpayers will never stand for. After all, nobody will ever enjoy it except the taxpayers, and their children, and
their grandchildren.

The end result of this variety of Progress is the Bronx. It is nearly
all of eastern New Jersey. It is the West Side of Chicago. It is Ham-
tramck. It is U.S. 1 between Baltimore and Washington. It is the
cut-over slopes of the Cascades, and the stinking, septic rivers of Ohio
and Pennsylvania. It is Lake George and Joliet and Gary, Indiana.
It is the hundreds of square miles of flaking stucco shanties which
disfigure Southern California. It is the hideous eczema, creeping out
like a Wave of the Future, from every metropolitan center—what De-
Voto once described as "an uninterrupted eyesore of drive-ins, diners,
souvenir stands, purulent amusement parks, cheapjack restaurants
. . . a jerry-built, neon-lighted, overpopulated slum."

Give us a few more decades, and most of the United States accessible

137

Bernard DeVoto

by auto quite possibly will look the same way—and by that time the ruination of a once-splendid continent will have gone so far that no remedy is possible. If you don't want to live in that kind of America—if you are not willing to hand the country over to your grandchildren in that shape—then you are a conservationist; and you have your work cut out for you.

It is not pleasant work. It requires you to make a nuisance of yourself before the Board of Aldermen and the Zoning Commission. It will mean quarrels with respectable citizens of your own community who want to make a quick buck—and can't understand why it is any of your business where they put up their billboards and tourist cabins and juke joints. It means interference with the private use of private property—something most Americans approach with sensible reluctance, even when the welfare of the whole community is at issue. It calls for lots of patient missionary work in civic associations, women's clubs, and local political organizations. Sometimes it may involve a head-on collision with powerful business interests, and often it means higher taxes (including your own) to pay for that bit of potential park land which the city has to buy now or lose forever.

But the Lord's work is never easy, or the good citizen's either. And it has been an article of faith in this republic from the time of the Plymouth Colony that the man who plants a tree, or saves one, is serving both God and his country.

Flood in the Desert

Many of DeVoto's columns on conservation and the environment dealt with specific issues—notably the efforts of the sheep and cattle raisers' lobby to weaken federal protection of forest and grazing land, and to seize public lands for themselves. More than any other single person, he was responsible for the defeat of these efforts. For the time being at least, the lobby is quiescent; and DeVoto's columns dealing with its raids in Congress now sound like reports on battles of long ago.

But the following column could serve as a living text for today's environmentalists. Like so much that he wrote, it was far ahead of its time.

August, 1952

IN the mountain West last winter's snowfall was one of the heaviest of which there is any record. It was the heaviest on record in the Sierra Nevada, which always gets much snow, as the whole country learned when a great streamliner was marooned for three days in Donner Pass. When I visited the Pass early in May most of the snow was gone, though in sheltered places you could find drifts up to twenty feet deep. The runoff, however, had been gradual; the rivers of the western slope seemed unlikely to flood. The floods I kept hearing about while I was in California were to the eastward. They were in Utah, and that did not make sense.

For the typical Utah flood occurs not in the spring but after midsummer, and it is produced not by melting snow but by a cloudburst. In the past thirty years many such floods have taken the form of mud-rock flows. A cloudburst does not last long but at its greatest intensity the rain may fall at the rate of three, four, even six inches an hour. When such a weight of water strikes an area on a mountainside that has been denuded of vegetation it may sweep an enormous mass of soil into the flooding creek of a canyon. A torent of mud rushes out of the canyon, taking with it gravel and rocks and boulders that may weigh two hundred tons or more. It damages or destroys whatever buildings, roads, and orchards may be in its path, and spreads over villages and fields, sometimes to a depth of many feet. In the late nineteen-twenties such flows threatened to ruin the richest farming region in Utah, Davis County, which lies at the western foot of the Wasatch Mountains. I once described in the Easy Chair the project, directed by the Forest Service and manned chiefly by CCC workers, which rehabilitated the watersheds, saved Davis County, and made it extremely unlikely, in fact almost impossible, that such floods will occur there again. Knowing how seriously impaired many Utah watersheds are, I assumed that their bad condition was responsible for the floods I kept reading about. Indeed for some years conservationists have been predicting serious floods for Salt Lake City, where the newspapers said the worst of them now were.

When I got to Utah, however, I found that my assumption had been wrong. Most of the rivers of the Wasatch front were in flood. The three largest Utah cities, Salt Lake City, Ogden, and Provo, had suffered considerable damage; so had many smaller communities. Sizable creeks were rushing down some of the streets of Salt Lake City, whose appalled citizens were building sandbag barricades like those I had seen three weeks earlier at Council Bluffs. On the flat land along the rivers thousands of acres had been inundated. But the Forest Service scientists assured me that the impairment of the watersheds was not responsible for the floods. True, most of the silt they carried had been deposited in the rivers by previous summer cloudbursts, which were also responsible for the deeply gouged riverbeds that made excellent storage receptacles for it. But the floods occurred because of the unprecedented snowfall of last winter and because a period of unseasonable summer heat interspersed with heavy rains melted the snow with unprecedented speed. That combination would have produced floods regardless of the condition of the watersheds. There can be no dissent from the finding of the Forest Service experts, and yet there remains a phenomenon which it does not cover. Some of the canyons above Salt Lake City where trouble had been predicted were in flood. Just north of the city Davis County begins and I drove across it, across the region which twenty-odd years ago was experiencing those catastrophic mudrock flows. The Davis County creeks are precisely like those at Salt Lake City and they come down from the same mountains, which presumably had a fairly uniform snowfall throughout; the only difference is that their watersheds have been protected for twenty years. Every one of them was now well within its banks and was flowing beautifully clear water, not the chocolate-colored stuff that was depositing silt in Salt Lake City basements.

Davis County ends where the Weber River comes out of Weber Canyon into the pleasant little valley of Uinta. And the Weber was incredible, at least to one who remembered it as a small and shallow stream only a dozen yards wide in summer. It was a quarter of a mile wide, had cut a new channel in Uinta valley, was flowing dark brown water with the velocity of a rocket. It had washed out many long stretches of highway; it was undercutting the Union Pacific roadbed; upstream towns and villages were furiously building levees against it. And eight miles north of it, the Ogden River was pouring a similar and only slightly smaller flood over roads and summer houses and the flat land below the city.

The Davis County creeks, whose watersheds had been rehabilitated, were not in flood; other Wasatch creeks just north and south of them were. So I went on to the Logan River, which flows through one of the most beautiful canyons in the Wasatch before coming out on the benchland where the fourth largest city in Utah stands. There was no flood here; nothing had been damaged, no one was sandbagging streets or houses. The Logan was well within its banks; its water was clear; it was the healthiest stream I had seen in Utah. Now it is true that this watershed being in great part limestone country is somewhat more stable geologically than those to the south, but there is something else that I cannot ignore. Long ago the Logan watershed was very seriously damaged by excessive timber-cutting and by what is the curse of the entire West, prolonged overgrazing by stock, but the people of the region took action in time. At their insistence the Cache National Forest was established to repair and protect it. This was about 1906, so that the watershed has had nearly fifty years of proper management. It has restored itself, producing an ever-increasing yield of timber and ample forage for the stock that graze it—and producing no floods or waste of water. Add to this the one canyon in Davis County that made no trouble during the disastrous years. The people there also recognized the danger in time, prohibited grazing on the denuded parts, properly regulated the grazing elsewhere, and thus protected the watershed till it restored itself. That creek was safe and stable following cloudbursts that produced serious floods in creeks no more than three miles away.

In the next few days I traversed much of Utah by plane and automobile. The experience dramatized what I already knew by heart: the rigorous conditions of life, the inexorable problems, and the pressing dangers of Utah, which are typical of the whole mountain West, though sometimes more extreme. It is a beautiful country and it is a desert. Of its 85,000 square miles only 3 per cent is arable or, in any but the most limited sense, habitable. Basically it is a farming and stock-growing economy, but farming and stock-growing are possible only where there is water. They can never develop much past their present level; allow for the greatest conceivable advance in scientific agriculture and in the reclamation of now unirrigated land, and still there can be but little gain. If Utah is to have any considerable increase in population (already it is exporting much of its annual crop of college graduates), or any sizable increase in wealth, or any general rise in its standard of living, they must come from new industries. And industry is absolutely limited by the amount of available water and absolutely dependent on the production of water. And the ability of this region to produce water has been badly impaired by the denudation of its watersheds.

What happens in Utah, in all the arid West, depends on elevations of 8,000 feet and more. The minimum annual rainfall necessary to produce crops without irrigation is generalized at twenty inches. At the foot of the Wasatch, where the magnificent fields and orchards are, the rainfall is fifteen inches, five less than the minimum. Fifty miles farther west it falls off to four or five inches, to absolute desert, and the average across the state is about seven inches. But on the peaks it averages between forty and fifty inches. Winter snows above 8,000 feet make possible the crops of Utah (of all the West), the towns and cities, and all industry present and to come. Mr. Reed Bailey of the Forest Service has found the right phrase for the mountains: they are humid islands in a desert.

The plane I took from Portland to Salt Lake City landed in a dust storm; another one was making the sun a sickly pale-green disk the afternoon I left Utah. Popular belief attributes these dust storms to the atomic explosions in Nevada, but it is wrong; they were occurring when I was a child in Utah. In some more nearly flat parts of the West they are usually due to improper methods of cultivation, such as failure to plow on the contours, and especially to the cultivation of soil so unstable that it should never have been plowed but used only as grazing range. But in Utah they are due primarily to unwise and excessive grazing of the mountain, foothill, and desert range. Wherever I went it was the same story, and a hideously visible one. Most of the range in the West has been or is being overgrazed; only on ranges administered by the Forest Service is effective rehabilitation being done, and it is not being done on all of them, and on some of them it is not being done fast enough. The dust that hides the sun in Salt Lake Valley comes from ranges, most of them in the desert, where the plant cover has been exhausted.

But dust storms are the least of it. The same dislodged soil is the silt that gives the flooding streams their chocolate color. It increasingly chokes the irrigation systems that are the arteries of Utah. It is steadily filling up the reservoirs that store the water on which wealth and even life depend, and just as steadily it is rendering the big dams and the little ones less useful. (Practically all the dams in the West but especially the most famous ones. Year by year such mammoths as Boulder Dam pile up the sediment that makes their reservoirs shallower, and engineers must plan other, probably less efficient, certainly more expensive dams to replace them.) And as the soil that should stay in place becomes dust storms and silt and sediment, water that should sink into the ground where it would be available for use runs off in floods. There is always less water for city and rural life, less water for the industries that might transform the state.

You see it unmistakably from a plane: mountainsides bare from unwise logging, from the burning of brush for a variety of mistaken reasons, from forest fires and brush fires that got out of control, from grazing on slopes that should not have been grazed at all, from excessive grazing where a moderate amount would have been safe. Almost at the tips of peaks, gullies have formed and are joining in a web; great bare patches carry the scars of landslides. Brooks, creeks, and rivers that should be as clear as Logan River are tan or brown; they

carry long, dark stripes into the still water of reservoirs that only gradually become green and then blue. You can see it on the ground.
Forage plants are "pedestaled," the soil has washed or blown from
their root systems; Russian thistle and similarly worthless weeds are
everywhere (the dreaded halogeton has not yet invaded the parts of
Utah I saw, but it will); sheep have fed as high as they could reach
on the desert juniper. Bare patches are spreading; so are the gullies
that carry away soil with the runoff. And figures rise in one's mind:
with more than twice as many people as it had fifty years ago, the
state is able to raise fewer cattle and sheep than it did then.

This is true of all the arid West but the process has gone farther
in Utah than in most other states and is more ominous there. And
there is poignancy in the fact that the very virtues of the people, of
the tremendously successful social experiment of Mormonism, have
helped to accelerate the process. Probably no one but the farseeing
genius Brigham Young could have built a society in Utah, and he
could not have built one except with the industrious, obedient, cooperative Mormon people. Relinquishing the region's great mineral wealth
to the Gentiles, he founded his society on an agricultural base, to
maintain the vigor of family life, of rural communities, of mutually
helpful enterprise. Practically all the arable and irrigable land in Utah,
and the water, came into Mormon hands. But farms or ranches adequate
for single families, and ranges adequate for small communities of
ranchers, were not adequate for the families of the sons that grew
up round them and for the communities thus enlarged. So in order
to bolster the patriarchal family, pressure went on the land, and the
long process of degrading it originated in the most estimable motives.
Now the unforeseeable has come about: in order to progress further,
Utah must industrialize—but cannot unless it repairs the injured land,
saves the water it now loses, and finds ways of utilizing to the utmost
the land's potential ability to produce water. And as in Utah, so to
some degree in all the West.

In the Dixie National Forest I saw the biggest range-reseeding project in the world, 40,000 acres where in only four years an exhausted
land has been brought back almost to maximum productivity, erosion
has been halted, the soil anchored in place, the stock business stabilized.

Far too few people have learned its lesson and the cost of reseeding is high, but the time is at hand when we must all master the lesson and will count the cost trivial. Even more impressive, to me, was the Forest Service's Desert Experimental Range. The entire staff here for research, experiment, and management has usually been a director, a part-time assistant, and occasionally some part-time laborers—but the results are staggering at once to the eye and to the imagination. Put it simply: in a seriously impaired desert range some small plots and some large plots have been fenced off, and bands of sheep have been grazed on them to the extent proved safe by experiment. These plots, that is, have been grazed properly, in the right numbers and herded in the right ways. In most places, proper grazing has turned out to be two-thirds of that to which the eroded range had been subjected. And the fenced plots have restored themselves unassisted; the range outside them, continuing to be overgrazed, has continued to deteriorate.

For a few feet inside the fence the noxious and unpalatable plants still grow; then the healthy, useful growth chokes them out. The "upward succession," the progress from less to more desirable plants, goes on smoothly. Gullies, checked and filled by new growth, are disappearing. The land is producing a maximum crop of forage. And the Station has found that it will improve as fast under proper grazing as it will when not grazed at all. Whereas outside the fence, weeds choke off forage plants, gullies and bare patches multiply, and the soil is washed away to settle eventually in storage reservoirs or on dinner tables in Salt Lake City. And the stockmen who use the regulated plots, though they graze a third fewer sheep, make more money than they did before. At a smaller overhead they get more wool and meat and they lose far fewer lambs.

Here the land has been healed by no more than wisdom. This is desert range and in the West there are forty million acres like it, grazed now by half a million cattle and between four and five million sheep—and deteriorating with terrifying rapidity. That vast area is now producing between a third and a half of its potential usable forage; it can produce no more because it has been so viciously abused. With proper grazing practices it could be restored to full productivity; the profits of those who use it would be doubled and, what counts more, the erosion that is steadily reducing the West's water supply could be stopped. Stockmen who use the fenced allotments at the Desert Experimental Range have learned the lesson it makes clear. But Utah and the West in general have not, and I was shocked to learn there that other bureaus of the government which are concerned with grazing have manifested no interest in it.

It has taken a long time to work out the principles of the scientific management of timber land and range land, of watersheds. But enough is known now so that the steady destruction of the West's principal resource could be halted and reversed; the rest must wait on public realization, acceptance, and support. Meanwhile the West clamors for the industry that would emancipate and enrich it—and the water runs off in floods, the water table falls, the reservoirs silt up, and dust clouds shut out the sun. A flight down the principal valley of the Wasatch is a symbol of a million square miles. At your left hand are the peaks, the givers of life and wealth; below you is the narrow strip of fecund land, the orchards and fields and towns; and always crowding close at your right hand is the desert. Utah is caught between millstones, between public education and the arrest of its promise; between, it may be, public education and disaster. So is the future of the whole West.

Due Notice to the FBI

Criticism of the Federal Bureau of Investigation is commonplace today, but in 1949 it was almost unheard of. Anyone who questioned the methods or motives of J. Edgar Hoover and his heroic agents invited a cloud burst of denunciation as a Communist, blasphemer, and enemy of the Republic. Just such a storm broke over DeVoto and *Harper's* when they published the following column. It expresses one of DeVoto's abiding passions—the defense of American rights and liberties—and it remains as pertinent today as it was in 1949.

October, 1949

THE quietly dressed man at your door shows you credentials that identify him as Mr. Charles Craig of the Bureau of Internal Revenue. He says he would like to ask you a few questions about one of your neighbors. The Harry S. Deweys are friends of yours, aren't they? Yes, you tell him. How long have you known them? Ever since they moved to Garden Acres eight or nine years ago—or was it seven?—no, thirteen. Mr. Craig says the Deweys moved into their house June 1, 1935, which makes it fourteen years. By the way, have they got a mortgage on it? Sure, you say, we all have. Harry didn't buy till about eight years ago. He is paying it off on a monthly basis; must be down to a couple of thousand by now.

Mr. Dewey's older son graduated from Yale this spring? Mr. Craig asks. Yes, you say. The daughter—she's at Vassar? Yes, she's a sophomore. And the other boy?—Exeter? Yes, first form. Mr. Dewey bought a new car last year, a Buick? Yes, he'd driven that Chevrolet for nine years. Who is his tailor? Gummidge? Pretty high-priced firm. Does Mrs. Dewey spend a lot on clothes? The trash barrels were on the curb when Mr. Craig came by and he noticed several empty Black and White bottles—do the Deweys drink a lot? Didn't they have Zimmerman, the caterer, for that big party last April?—Zimmerman comes high. Have you noticed their garbage—pretty rich stuff? What labels have you seen? Bellows & Co., maybe, or Charles & Co., Inc.? Do you happen to know what Mr. Dewey's income is?

By this time you are, I hope, plenty mad. You say, for God's sake, it's none of my business. Mr. Craig explains. Investigation by the Bureau of Internal Revenue does not necessarily mean that the person being investigated is under suspicion. These checks are routine in certain kinds of cases. Orders to make them come from above; the local echelons do not initiate inquiries, they simply find out what they can. Then back in Washington the information thus gathered is evaluated. No improper use is made of anything and of course the evaluators know that most of the stuff sent in is mixed, idle, or untrue—they simply go through the vast chaff in order to find an occasional grain of wheat. The Bureau, Mr. Craig points out, is part of the United States government. It conducts its inquiries with entire legality and under rigid safeguards. The duty of a citizen is to assist his government when he is asked to.

So you say, look, Harry is district manager of the Interstate Gas Furnace Corporation and everybody knows that IGF pays district managers fifteen thousand a year. Yes, Mr. Craig says, IGF pays him fifteen thousand but one wonders whether he hasn't got other sources of income. How can he send three children to prep school and college, buy a house and a new Buick, and patronize Gummidge and Zimmerman on fifteen thousand? And he belongs to the City Club and the Garden Acres Country Club. He took Mrs. Dewey to Bermuda last winter. He has heavy insurance premiums to pay. He had a new roof put on the house last fall and this spring Mrs. Dewey had the whole second floor repainted and repapered. How come? Does it make sense? Where's he getting it from?

Does Harry S. Dewey belong to the Wine and Food Society? The Friends of Escoffier? Has he ever attended a meeting of either group? Does he associate with members of either? Has he ever been present at a meeting of any kind, or at a party, at which a member of either was also present? Has he ever read Brillat-Savarin's *The Physiology of Taste?* Does he associate with people who have read it? Has he ever been present at a meeting or a party at which anyone who has read it was also present? Does he subscribe to or read *Daily Racing Form?* Has he ever made a bet on a horse race? A dog race? A football game? Does he play poker or shoot craps? Has he ever been present at a meeting or a party at which anyone who makes bets or plays poker was also present? Does he play the market? Do you know whether Harry puts any cash into diamonds? Does he associate with people who own diamonds? Does he know any millionaires, or people who own cabin cruisers, or people who have accounts in more than one bank? Has he ever attended meetings of such persons? Has he ever been present at a meeting or a party at which such persons were also present? Does he read the *Wall Street Journal?* Has he ever been present at a cocktail party at which anyone who does read it was present? Is it true that Harry gave his secretary half a dozen pairs of nylon stockings for Christmas? Could she be fronting or dummying for business deals that are really his? What kind of girl is she? Does she always leave the office at five o'clock? Whom does she associate with?

Where does Harry stand on the Bureau of Internal Revenue and the income tax laws? Have you ever heard him say that the income tax laws ought to be changed or the Bureau reorganized or abolished? Have you ever heard him damn the income tax? Does he associate with people who damn it? Has he ever been present at a meeting or a party where people who want to abolish the Bureau or revise the tax laws were also present?

Let us assume that you remember nothing which indicates that Harry S. Dewey is a tax-dodger or a crook. But Mr. Craig goes a few doors down the street and interviews Frances Perkins Green, who is a prohibitionist and has suffered from nervous indigestion for many years. She has seen truffles and artichokes and caviar in the Dewey garbage. The Deweys' maid has told Mrs. Green that they have porterhouses much oftener than frankforts, that they always have cocktails and frequently have wine, that sometimes cherries and peaches come all the way from Oregon by mail. Mrs. Green has seen many suspicious-looking characters come to the Dewey house. She doesn't know who they are but it's striking that mostly they don't come till after dark, seven o'clock or later. Some of them, she says, are staggering when they leave at midnight. So Mr. Craig tries the next house and finds Henry Cabot White at home. Cabot is doing all right now but he had tough going for a couple of years after Harry Dewey fired him. Everyone in Garden Acres is familiar with the neighborhood feud and would tend to discount Cabot's revelation to Mr. Craig that Harry's secretary used to work as a cashier at a race track. He confirms the nylons but says there were a dozen pairs. Sure Harry is sleeping with her—Cabot has seen them lunching together several times. Matter of fact Harry only took Mrs. Dewey to Bermuda because she blew up about the girl. Yes, and do you know who was on that boat? Gooks McGonigle—you remember, he runs the numbers racket and they almost got him for wire-tapping. Cabot wouldn't like to say anything either way, but Harry took the same boat and Harry manages to lay his hands on money when he needs it.

I have hung this fantasy on the Bureau of Internal Revenue precisely because it does NOT *operate in this way.* When it suspects that someone is making false tax returns its investigators go to the suspect's books, his bank, the regular channels of his business, and similar focal point where factual evidence can be uncovered and made good. If Harry S. Dewey reads Brillat-Savarin or serves Stilton with the cocktails, the Bureau is not interested. It does not ask his friends or enemies to report on his wife's visits to the hairdresser as a patriotic duty.

But if it did, would you be surprised? In fact, would you be surprised if any government bureau sent round its Mr. Craig to ask you if Harry Dewey reads the *New Republic* or has ever gone swimming in the nude at Bay View? I think you wouldn't be surprised. What is worse, I think that for a moment Mr. Craig and his questions would seem quite natural to you. And this feeling that the interrogation of private citizens about other citizens is natural and justified is something new to American life. As little as ten years ago we would have considered it about on a par with prohibition snooping, night-riding, and blackmail. A single decade has come close to making us a nation of common informers.

It began with the war. Candidates for commission in the services or for jobs in non-military agencies had to be investigated. If enormous asininities resulted, if enormous injustice was done, they were inevitable, part of the cost of war. They are not inevitable now. But several branches of the government are acting as if they were. Several branches of the government and far too many of us private citizens are acting as if they didn't matter.

True, we have occasional qualms. The Committee on Un-American Activities blasts several score reputations by releasing a new batch of gossip. Or a senator emits some hearsay and officially unaccused persons lose their jobs without recourse. Or another senator blackens the name of a dead man and then rejoices in his good deed, though the people he claimed to be quoting announce that they didn't say what he said they did. Or some atrocious indignity inflicted on a government employee by a loyalty board comes to light. Or we find out that the FBI has put at the disposal of this or that body a hash of gossip, rumor, slander, backbiting, malice, and drunken invention which, when it makes the headlines, shatters the reputations of innocent and harmless people and of people who our laws say are innocent until someone proves them guilty in court. We are shocked. Sometimes we are scared. Sometimes we are sickened. We know that the thing stinks to heaven, that it is an avalanching danger to our society. But we don't do anything about it.

Do you think the questions I have put in Mr. Craig's mouth are absurd? They are exactly like the questions that are asked of every government employee about whom a casual derogatory remark has been unearthed, even if that remark was made twenty years ago, even if a fool or an aspirant to the employee's job made it. They are exactly like the questions asked of anyone who is presumed to know anything about him, whether casual acquaintance, grudgeholder, or habitual enemy. They are exactly like the questions asked about anyone outside the government of whom anyone else has reported that he has radical sympathies. Have you (has he) ever studied Karl Marx? Have you (has he) ever been present at a meeting or a party where anyone sympathetic to Communism was also present? Did you (did he) belong to the Liberal Club in college? Did you (did he) escort to a dance a girl who has read Lenin or is interested in abstract painting? Have you (has he) recommended the *Progressive* to a friend? Those questions and scores like them, or worse, have been asked of and about millions of American citizens.

The FBI—to name only one agency that asks such questions—tells us that everything is properly safeguarded. The investigators gather up what they can and send it in, but trained specialists evaluate it, and whatever is idle, untrue, false, malicious, or vicious is winnowed out. So the FBI says. But we are never told who does the evaluating and we have seen little evidence that anyone does it. Along comes the Coplon case, for instance, and we find out that a sack has simply been emptied on the table. The contents are obviously in great part idle and false, in great part gossip and rumor, in great part unverifiable—and unverified. Investigator K-7 reports that Witness S-17 (for we have to cover up for our agents and our spies) said that Harry S. Dewey is a member of the Party, or wants to make the revolution, or knows some fellow-travelers, or once advised someone to read Marx, or spent a weekend at a summer resort where there were members of an organization on the Attorney-General's list. If K-7 is only two degrees better than half-witted, if S-17 is a psychopath or a pathological liar or Harry's divorced wife, no matter. And also, no one can be held accountable. If the same sack has previously emptied for the loyalty board of any government department nobody can be held responsible for that act, either, and Harry Dewey has no recourse. He will never know and neither will you and I. We will never learn who K-7 or S-17 is, in what circumstance the information was given, whether or not it is true or deliberate falsehood, how far it has been spread or by whom.

In the Coplon trial the government did its utmost to keep from the public view certain information which it was using and which had been gathered by the FBI. That was a sagacious effort. For when the judge ruled that it must be made public some of it turned out to be as irresponsible as the chatter of somewhat retarded children: it would have been farcical if it had not been vicious. For instance, some S-17 had given some K-7 a list of people whom he considered Communists or Communist-sympathizers. One of them was the president of a large university. In all candor, he is not continentally celebrated for intelligence but his economic and political ideas are a hundred miles to the right of Chester A. Arthur. He is a man of unquestionable patriotism, loyalty, integrity, and probity, incapable of any kind of behavior with which the FBI is authorized to concern itself. But it was the privilege of someone—perhaps a fool, a personal enemy, a boy who had flunked out, a maniac—to lodge in the FBI's files a declaration that he is a Red.

Well, the university president will not suffer in public esteem. But his university may be damaged in many ways, now, next week, ten years hence. And Senator Mundt or Congressman Dondero or any public official with the gleam of a headline in his eye can denounce the university, its students, and all who have acquired their guilt by contagion—on the basis of a remark which may have been made by an imbecile and for which no one can be held to account. And that remark remains permanently indexed in the FBI files. And what about humbler names on that list? How many people have been fired? How many are having their reading, their recreation, and their personal associations secretly investigated? Against how many of them are neighbors with grudges or senile dementia testifying to some Mr. Craig, hereafter and alias K-7? What redress have they got? What redress has anyone got whom anyone at all has named to the FBI or any other corps of investigators as a Communist, a Communist-sympathizer, a fellow-traveler, a bemused dupe, or just a person who happened to be in the bar at the New Willard when a subscriber to the *Nation* was buying a drink?

I say it has gone too far. We are dividing into the hunted and the hunters. There is loose in the United States today the same evil that once split Salem Village between the bewitched and the accused and stole men's reason quite away. We are informers to the secret police. Honest men are spying on their neighbors for patriotism's sake. We may be sure that for every honest man two dishonest ones are spying for personal advancement today and ten will be spying for pay next year.

None of us can know how much of this inquiry into the private lives of American citizens and government employees is necessary. Some of it is necessary—but we have no way of knowing which, when, or where. We have seen enough to know for sure that a great deal of it is altogether irresponsible. Well, there is a way making it all responsible, of fixing responsibility. As one citizen of the United States, I intend to take that way, myself, from now on.

Representatives of the FBI and of other official investigating bodies have questioned me, in the past, about a number of people and I have answered their questions. That's over. From now on any representative of the government, properly identified, can count on a drink and perhaps informed talk about the Red (but non-Communist) Sox at my house. But if he wants information from me about anyone whomsoever, no soap. If it is my duty as citizen to tell what I know about someone, I will perform that duty under subpoena, in open court, before that person and his attorney. This notice is posted in the courthouse square: I will not discuss anyone in private with any government investigator.

I like a country where it's nobody's damned business what magazines anyone reads, what he thinks, whom he has cocktails with. I like a country where we do not have to stuff the chimney against listening ears and where what we say does not go into the FBI files along with a note from S-17 that I may have another wife in California. I like a country where no college-trained flatfeet collect memoranda about us and ask judicial protection for them, a country where when someone makes statements about us to officials he can be held to account. We had that kind of country only a little while ago and I'm for getting it back. It was a lot less sacred than the one we've got now. It slept sound no matter how many people joined Communist reading circles and it put common scolds to the ducking stool. Let's rip off the gingerbread and restore the original paneling.

Crusade Resumed

As Ralph Nader will recognize, this column was an early precurser of his crusade and of the whole Consumer Movement. It had two results:

1. It is now possible, though not easy, to find in most hardware stores a carbon steel kitchen knife that actually will hold an edge.

2. When Julia Child read the column, she sent DeVoto such a knife from Paris, where they have always been readily available. This led to correspondence, and then to close friendship between Julia Child and the DeVotos. Both of them, but especially Avis DeVoto, herself an accomplished cook, encouraged Mrs. Child to write a book about French cooking, an art she had been studying and teaching for years. The upshot was her two-volume work, *Mastering the Art of French Cooking,* the famous Julia Child programs on National Educational Television, and a revolution in American eating habits.

In the first volume Mrs. Child acknowledged the help of Mrs. DeVoto, "our foster mother, wet nurse, guide, and mentor. She provided encouragement for our first steps, some ten years ago, as we came tottering out of the kitchen with the gleam of authorship lighting our innocent faces." Mrs. DeVoto is still, at this writing, helping Mrs. Childs with her literary and television enterprises.

November, 1951

IF I publish a book, within two months up to a hundred and fifty people, in newspaper and magazine space allotted to them for the purpose, will tell the public how bad they may think it is. Everyone who publishes ideas and everyone who practices one of the arts has to submit to criticism. The appraisal of ideas, books, art, and skill is considered to be in the public interest and so the freedom of criticism has been buttressed by many safeguards. A writer, for instance, can make it hard or impossible for you to quote from his book unless you are quoting for the purpose of criticism but he can do nothing about that. As for what you say about the book, or within the laws of personal libel what you say about him as the author of it, he cannot restrain you at all. The same holds for painters, musicians, actors, vaudeville performers, philosophers, college professors, and politicians. So long as you are appraising their products of performances, society sanctions you to say whatever you may choose to. It does not even require what you say to be true, or for that matter honest; better to risk a certain amount of error, bias, and dishonesty than restrict criticism.

Thinkers, writers, and artists expect public criticism of their work; they regard it as a necessary accompaniment of their job. Being a robust folk besides, they are always amused by a type of business man who is too timorous and sissified to take criticism. He is usually a manufacturer or a retailer of consumers' goods. He regards it as his right, granted by God and protected by the Constitution, to sell anything he can induce the public to buy and to offer it for sale in full immunity from criticism.

If his shirts go to pieces at the third washing, if his hairbrushes break off the ends of women's hair and force them to take expensive treatments at the beauty parlor, if this year's model of his radio sets differs from last year's only in that it distorts musical tones 50 per cent more and costs twice as much—society must restrain anyone who wants to tell the public so. Society in fact has got to treat this sensitive thing a good deal more tenderly than that. It must license him to lie about his product as much as he sees fit. If he wants to advertise that his hairbrush, far from damaging women's hair, repairs any damage which age, climate, and accident may have done up to now and will protect it from all such damage hereafter, his advertisement must not be exposed to the brutality of literary criticism. It would be morally wrong, un-American, and an offense to nature to tell the public that his stuff is lousy and that he lies about it.

This does not alarm me. (Though I am willing to suggest to Mr. John Chamberlain that it may be one reason why, as he has been complaining lately, writers tend to picture business men as unable to take it.) Rather, I find it endlessly fascinating. Which is another reason why I periodically return to the only mission I have ever set myself, that of trying to get for the American housewife a kitchen knife she can cut something with.

Last spring the editors of a magazine invited me to examine in their columns some aspects of business which, it was clear, had failed to inspire my admiration. So I described some tribal magic of the advertising business and speculated about the motives of certain manufacturers who hired the magicians. Did they or didn't they believe that the ads they paid for told the truth, and what did the answer suggest about on the one hand their intelligence or on the other their ethics? I also described the poor quality of certain manufactured goods, including the kitchen knife, and wondered aloud whether some businesses might not be systematically degrading their goods as a matter of policy.

The results were as usual, howls of anguish and protestations of purity that would have got the howlers a universal horse laugh in the comparatively uneffeminate world of literature. There was only one novelty worth mentioning. In Canada, where business men must be either self-confident or blind, a national advertising association invited me to address its annual convention. On this side of the line there was no such dalliance with evil. Instead an officer of a national advertising association buckled down to his duty. He wrote to the magazine in which my piece had appeared, demurring to the editorial note which had described me as "obviously no Leftist." He advised them forthwith to take a gander at page 350 of the Fourth Report on Un-American Activities in California. California had the dope on me: on that page I was "listed as being associated with some others who are definitely known as Leftists . . . as [he meant 'in'] denouncing the Thomas Committee investigating un-American activities in America." Possibly I was all right, he said, "but association with such activities would leave this [open?] to question."

So far this was routine; time was when to allege a flaw in business was only morally revolting but for some years now it has been clear proof of treason. The novelty came when the hurt but game pantywaist ran off a number of copies of his letter and sent them to places where they might do some good, including the offices of *Harper's*. The *Harper's* official he picked out was the business manager.

Let's look this over. I had said that some kinds of advertising were full of fallacies, as on occasion reviewers have been known to assert that books of mine were. Thereupon an officer of a presumably powerful advertising association sent to my employers, choosing the man who sells advertising space, an imputation made on the letterhead of his organization (but phrased so as not to be actionable) that I am a Communist or a fellow-traveler. He was saying: we are in a position to control a lot of advertising contracts, better watch out what your columnist does. In short, I had criticized a sacred institution and maybe he could get me fired. A nice try but since it was documentary it comes within my immunity as a literary critic and I may add that it was silly, classified him, and stank.

To resume my mission. Presently the magazine which had published my piece ran a couple of others that undertook to refute it. One was by an officer of a big advertising agency, who said that I could probably have made a fortune writing advertising copy. Since even on the rack I believe in complete freedom of criticism, I took that in silence. The other was by the head of an organization which I greatly admire. It was a good piece but had some holes in it. Thus when he got round to kitchen knives he said that I was altogether wrong. Very fine knives, he said, are available at all good stores. Today's knives are a lot better than those we used to get. In his organization, as in all other good ones, there is an unvarying relationship between the price asked and the value given, and no knife is sold till it has passed severely scientific tests in the firm's laboratory. Finally, just so that I would have to eat my words, but with the privilege of first cutting them to convenient size, he was sending me a selection of kitchen knives from his own stock.

The case of the housewife and the kitchen knife is simple. It is true that she can get good knives. If she has a friend with the right skill and equipment, she can have him forge and turn her one from any available piece of good steel, say an old rasp. For a good paring knife she can go to a store that sells cobblers' supplies and buy the kind of knife that is used to cut sole-leather; or, since the handle of a cobbler's knife may be too thick for her hand, she can go to a school-supply store and buy the kind that is used for cutting stencils. Neither costs more than firesale junk and both are incomparably better than anything sold as a paring knife. If she wants a good butcher knife, she can frequent auctions and second-hand stores till one turns up, which is what her butcher probably does, or she can wait till the butcher retires and buy one from him. If she wants a good carving knife, the best idea is to inherit one. Or she can pay outrageous prices for imported English or Swedish knives, though good English cutlery is getting increasingly hard to find.

What she can't do is go into a hardware store in the expectation that the price asked for American-made knives will have any relationship to their quality, or that at any price she can buy a really good American-made knife. Chisels, planes, scalpels, yes; kitchen knives, no. She will be offered knives of ingenious and somewhat bewildering shapes, knives with handles painted or stained any color to match the woodwork or her apron, knives with blades as shiny as her trustful eyes. They look wonderful but they won't cut anything. They are made of what is, inaccurately, called stainless steel, an admirable material for many things but never used in cutting instruments that have to be sharp, the chisels and scalpels I have mentioned, say, or the guillotine with which the copy of *Harper's* you are reading was trimmed. The chromium that makes them shiny and retards the rate at which they stain makes them incapable of holding an edge. If there were enough to make them stainproof they would not take an edge to begin with.

That he was sending me some knives showed that the executive was a kindly man as well as a lover of truth, but it was clear that top-level problems of management took all his time and had necessitated his taking the firm's testing rooms on faith. Whereas years of the crusade have made me and my family experts on kitchen cutlery. I felt a little sad but the truth must prevail and I intended to turn his gift over to a housewife whose sentiments about some sectors of American business make mine seem old-issue Republican.

The three knives I received were beautiful. Two of them had been designed by someone who had studied abstractions at the Museum of Modern Art. As artifacts they were so pleasing that you would have been willing to hang them on the living-room wall. The blades were so shiny that they could have been used to shave by, though not with. But functionally neither of these two was a knife. One, which I find sells locally for about $1.25, had no edge. If the testing room had made sure that the children couldn't get lead-poisoning from the handle, the home-safety board would have certified it as a toy.

I succeeded in giving it an edge but only as you wave to the engineer, for I had to sharpen it again every time it was used. The other, which sells for about $3.50 here, had an edge but declined to keep it. Slice a meat loaf and retire to the oilstone and steel. We have lent them to butchers for use and comment and they always cause quite a stir. Everybody in the shop gathers round and there is a period of silence and awe before the comment begins. I am unable to report the comment; the anti-obscenity laws forbid. It adds up to this: in the judgment of men who have to have good knives, these are worthless. Hardware dealers whom I have consulted as a check say the same.

I myself would not go quite so far. I judge that they are worth up to fifty cents apiece as stage properties to someone who wants an art photograph of the kitchen. But let's be fair. The Easy Chair classification of manufactured goods recognizes three categories: those that are made to be used, those that are made to be sold, and those that are made to be replaced. These knives are in the second category, not the third.

The third knife surprised me. The accompanying printed matter said it was made of that advertising specialty, a new, secret material developed by our own scientists, and was manufactured by our secret process with a security check at the factory gate. Research has failed to reveal to me what the material and process are but I find that the scientists of another manufacturer are secretly producing identical knives. It is a pretty good knife, the first one with a "stainless" blade I have ever seen. You can cut celery or butter or beef with it and find that the edge has not turned. It had an edge when it arrived and kept it for what is these days a phenomenally long time. True, if I had paid for it myself I should have been entitled to my money back fifty-seven months before the accompanying bond expired, but these days a knife that needs only a few licks with the steel amounts to an industrial miracle. It sells here for $3.50 and my butchers, my hardware dealers, and I agree that in comparison with the other two it is worth every cent it costs. We figure that it is fully half as good as a knife that would sell for $1.25 (bearing the inflation in mind) if manufacturers went back to using carbon steel as they did in a happier day, as manufacturers of edged tools, still do.

This knife has reawakened my congenital optimism. It may be that if the scientists of enough manufacturers make enough secret experiments, ten years and fifty million knives from now the industry will be able to circle back to 1900. With, of course, the customer paying for the experiments, and provided that advertising theory does not forbid.

When the housewife in question reported to the donor the results of our home testing-laboratory, he abandoned the position he had taken in public about my article. His new position was that though she might want a knife that would cut, her desire was eccentric, for the American housewife in general assuredly did not, and that the sacred obligation of American business was to provide the customer with what he wanted. Women wanted, he said, just such knives as with dedication that matched its ingenuity business was selling them.

There is much in what he says, though there is less in it than he believes, as is attested by the number of women with blood in their eye who curse the business system in language that defies the Committee on Un-American Activities. I'm sure that there is a big demand for shiny knives that are functionally worthless. But I'm sure too that the demand has been created by economically wasteful advertising. You develop new selling points: stainlessness, color in the kitchen, modern design, secret processes, caste prestige, and whatever else your advertising agency can dream up. You bludgeon the customer with them in advertising campaigns till you have convinced her that those are the attributes knives should have. Naturally you sell a lot more knives. Though the selling points you have given the product are factitious there are a lot of them, whereas apart from them a knife can have only one, that it is a good instrument for cutting. Meanwhile producing a more salable knife has made it impossible for you to produce a good one.

At a later time this seminar will take up in detail the economics of "Hell, we sell more, don't we?" Let's glance now at the odd way in which production for nonfunctional use, or to be precise production for sales, works out. You will recall the fearful damage that has been done since 1932 by the paternalism of our government. It has undermined the sturdy old American virtues. It has destroyed self-reliance, initiative, personal enterprise. It has robbed our people of the precious privilege of doing things for themselves and given them a decadent desire to have more and more done for them. And as a consequence it has forced them to conform to the rigidities of a bureaucratic system against which the will and self-help that were once our greatness break in vain.

Well, business makes a bread knife that sells fast but won't cut bread. So the baker has to cut it, with a machine that has no stainless steel in it, before he packages it and the advertising agency thinks up the glorious word "pre-sliced." Business goes on to make a butcher knife that won't cut meat; so the butcher has to pre-cut chops, pot roasts, and for those who can afford them steaks. Continuing its inspired policy, business makes a great variety of knives that rank as bijouterie but won't cut anything; so more and more food has to be pre-cut. If the sturdy American housewife has ideas of her own about the size, shape, thickness, or weight of chops or any other food, she is simply out of luck. She will damn well take what a paternalistic business system that is undermining initiative and individuality sees fit to give her. By now precutting has opened up a big new demand for cellophane, so there is additional reason to poison her mind with socialistic visions of ease. Propaganda campaigns, paid for by the consumer, celebrate the enervating vision of security—excuse me of convenience, labor-saving, and an increase in leisure that may be used for personal development. Small wonder if, a helpless victim of bureaucratic philosophy, the housewife repudiates the personal responsibility that once made the American home sacred and increasingly demands food she does not need to cut and knives that need not be sharp since there is nothing to use them on. I direct the attention of the Un-American Activities Committee to manufacturers of kitchen knives and the advertising agencies they subsidize. They may not be Communists but association with such activities would leave this (open) to question.

Strange Fruit

This column and the two that follow provide a fair indication of DeVoto's dominant ideas about literature and the people who produce it.

He had no use for "pure" criticism. Always he viewed literature in the context of history, and the urgent issues of the times in which it was written. His volumes on Mark Twain, for example, are as much history as they are criticism; and often, as in these columns, he used a literary subject as a point of attack on a political issue.

DeVoto also was profoundly distrustful of "the literary mind," because he believed that most novelists, professional critics, and teachers of literature were too insulated from the facts of American life and the real feelings of its people. These views were unpopular, then as now, and he was frequently berated for them by other critics.

As they originally appeared in *Harper's,* these columns were untitled, for reasons unknown to me; I have supplied titles which seem to me appropriate.

May, 1944

L E T me summarize some ideas about the South which we tend to believe in Boston. We understand that the South is culturally backward. We know that many Southerners are well-bred, well-educated people—cosmopolitan, of liberal minds, tolerant, interested in ideas, cultivated in the arts and occasionally adept at them. We think of them, however, as a minority which is made impotent by the surrounding illiteracy, ignorance, and prejudice, and by a social myth which looks back to a romanticized, unreal past and has kept the Southern mind from adjusting to the modern world. We understand that educational standards in the South are low and though we concede that this is due in part to poverty we believe that it is also due to traditions which set no great value on education. Moreover, a primitive form of Christianity, economic discrimination against Negroes, economic medievalism, fear of miscegenation, and a defensive psychology which goes back to defeat in the Civil War and back of that to the necessity of defending slavery—such additional matters, we tolerantly realize, have helped to make the Southerner bigoted, emotional, and reactionary. His prejudices are violent, his defensiveness makes him aggressive, he cannot permit the objective discussion of ideas that is one of the marks of a civilized man, he settles all questions by force.

We do not, in Boston, expect much from Southern civilization, and especially we do not expect liberality. We have, for instance, been trying to solve the Negro problem for well over a century, and for well over a century what has prevented us from solving it is Southern prejudice, Southern passion, and Southern intolerance. Naturally we do not expect much devotion to the arts down South. Liberal thinking and artistic thinking require a kind of cultural leadership which the South lacks. We realize that even cultivated Southerners are too indelibly stained with the prejudices of the section to provide that kind of leadership. It follows that we do not expect a mature literature from the South. The soil is unfavorable, and even if one should germinate in it, Southern intolerance would stamp it out.

A Southern woman has lately published a novel about the South. It is both a courageous novel and a good one, serious, mature, wise, excellently written. It may be something of a landmark, but all these facts are irrelevant. It contains some words which were certain to arouse the bigotry of the South's primitive backwoods religion. Worse still, its theme is the most inflammatory of all themes down South, miscegenation. That is a topic on which no Southerner can hold an objective opinion. It strikes home to his deepest fears and taboos, he cannot tolerate any discussion of it, he cannot permit anyone to express an opinion about it. It was easy enough to predict that this novel, Miss Lillian Smith's *Strange Fruit,* would be suppressed by a culturally backward society, illegally but with complete social assent, in the distorted violence and prejudice which animate such a society. And that in fact has occurred.

It has not occurred, however, exactly as predicted. *Strange Fruit* is being sold freely in for example Atlanta and Birmingham, as freely as in more advanced cultures like Oshkosh, Davenport, and Three Rivers. It is being sold just as freely in those ominous little Southern towns which we Bostonians recognize as socially sick and from which we fear an American fascism may emerge sometime. It is being discussed intelligently, temperately, and frequently with high praise in the Southern press which we have learned to regard as one of the most dangerous bulwarks of Southern prejudice. The mobbing of *Strange Fruit* did not take place down South. It took place in Boston.

That reversal may momentarily disconcert outlanders who do not understand Boston, and I feel that a decent respect to the opinions of mankind requires me to explain my home town.

To begin with, you must understand that the suppression was in fact a mobbing. It occurred, that is, outside the law—so far outside that both the official and the unofficial suppressors are announcing that no suppression has occurred. As yet—I sent this to the press on March 25th—the book has not been subjected to review by any official board or any socially accountable officer whomsoever. The truth is, we learned better than that long ago. There was a time when the police used to proceed against books which they thought Bostonians ought not to read. We did not object to the assumption of such authority by the police but we found that their exercise of it exposed us to ridicule, to the ridicule of even backward cultures. Furthermore it proved profitable to publishers. They inserted "Banned in Boston" in their advertising and readers soon came to understand that if Boston suppressed a book, that book was a serious treatment of an important subject by a writer of considerable skill—for exceedingly few books of any other kind were ever suppressed here. So we resorted to an ingenious expedient.

Many of us in Boston are Republicans and many more are anti-New Deal Democrats. As such we realize that one of the most dangerous threats to our institutions is government by fiat. Executive commissions and similar agencies which are not restrained by statutory law and are not accountable to elected representatives of the people, we have proclaimed, are despotic, essentially totalitarian, and incompatible with democracy. We believe in a government of laws, not men. With that principle in mind we have set up a committee of the Board of Trade of Boston Book Merchants. Whenever that committee thinks that a book may be prosecuted by the police, it notifies the booksellers that that book has been withdrawn from sale—withdrawn, that is, by the stores represented on the committee. That notification suffices. No Boston bookseller sells that book, knowing that if the police should prosecute him the Board of Trade would not come to his defense. (He is perfectly free to do what he likes, the head of the committee explained to me, but the committee has done its part.) Everyone is happy. The affair has been conducted in complete privacy, free alike of official dictation and social control. There has been no official censorship, no one has received any objectionable publicity, the police are tranquil and the booksellers safe, and if any freedom of any Bostonian or any author has been infringed, Boston does not give a damn.

Next you must realize that literature is not important in Boston. It has been seventy-five years since there was any general respect for literature hereabout and fully fifty years since there was any general interest in it. Books which make a lot of money are respected, of course, and it remains possible for a writer to be respected and even admired if he achieves eminence as a fisherman or a skier, if he makes money on the stock market, or if his collection of porcelains or even his love affairs create newspaper publicity, which is fully appreciated in Boston. But it is inconceivable that literature could be made a public issue here. There was a time when men like Ralph Waldo Emerson and Henry Thoreau could summon public opinion to the defense of such obscenity as Whitman's *Leaves of Grass,* but that was many years ago.

Again, you must understand that *Strange Fruit* was not mobbed because of its inflammatory theme. It is true that racial tensions are increasing in Boston, as I shall report in a later Easy Chair, but we are extremely tolerant about discussions of the Negro problem at a distance. In holding this attitude we are living up to our traditions. The typical Boston reformer was a factory owner who felt deeply about slavery in Georgia, as Thoreau said, or a corporation lawyer who longed to bestow economic justice on the Filipinos, as Thoreau would have said if he had lived long enough. The cause of this suppression was not at all the theme of the book, miscegenation, it was sex. It was in fact three lines of sexual phraseology. The head of the booksellers' committee has told me that he assured the publisher that the book could be sold in Boston if the author would make deletions amounting to no more than three lines. (I asked him if he did not consider this suggestion an insult to the author. He said no. I asked him if he did not consider it an insult to me as a writer, a buyer of books, and a citizen of Massachusetts. He said no.)

Here it must be made clear that Boston is not uninterested in sex, afraid of sex, or opposed to the portrayal, representation, or exploitation of sex. All we have ever objected to is an honest, decent, or artistic treatment of sex. In the name of righteousness and for our taste's sake we insist that sex be treated with a leer and a snigger. Pornography circulates as freely in Boston as in any other city, as any casual visitor may determine. Boston is a town where strip-teasers flourish but the ballet must wear tights, where sexual and homosexual humor in night clubs is immune from prosecution provided only that it is kept vulgar enough, but three frank lines will get a novel lynched provided only that it is a decent and serious novel. Burlesque shows do a rousing business and we are the best town on the road for revues, but *Strange Interlude* cannot play here at all. You may freely patronize any kind of pornography in Boston, but the local standards of taste and morality, which the booksellers' committee accurately translates, will see to it that you cannot buy distinguished books which treat sex seriously. The much-repeated allegation that we are over-squeamish about indecency is a libel: we object only to decency.

True, Massachusetts has an anti-obscenity statute rather more idiotic than most such laws. Right here one is supposed to stop talking out loud and to whisper, as several who say they have been outraged by this latest suppression have whispered to me, that nothing can be done to attack that statute because it is supported by the Catholic Church. Protestant Bostonians tend to speak about the Catholic Church in whispers and one of them lately put it to me this way, "The cops run straight to the Cardinal." As one reared in and shaped by the Catholic Church, I deny both the statement and the implication. Both are a comforting alibi for Bostonians; they enable the timorous to excuse themselves from taking action. Certainly, though the Catholic Church has not officially backed the statute and though a very great many Catholics are opposed to it, certainly it has Catholic support. Also it has the support of the Watch and Ward Society (yes, that really is its name), which is Protestant, and of several queer remnants of Puritan heresies—Puritanism was never to my knowledge Catholic. Even an alliance between Catholic bigotry and Protestant bigotry, however, could not have put this statute on the books and enforced it (as the experience of New York, for one instance, shows) if that alliance were not supported by still a third group. Actually it is made effective by a third group, the well-born, the rich, the cultivated, the heirs of the old ruling class, from whom social and cultural leadership would normally be expected. It is made effective because this group —generalize them as the Harvard alumni—will not accept social responsibility or exercise leadership.

For many years Boston has been unable to buy good books legally because this group has refused to act—from indifference, the profit motive, or simple cowardice. These people do not believe in suppression or approve of the anti-obscenity statute, they denounce it in private, they know that the situation is ridiculous and dangerous, but they will do nothing about it. Why? Well, literature is not important in the Boston culture and neither are civil rights. Not important enough, certainly, to make a fight for them. Boston will not defend a writer in the exercise of his freedom. And if either a bigot or a committee which has no legal status chooses to infringe Boston's own freedoms, that is perfectly all right with Boston.

You may suggest that a determined stand by anyone, even a bookseller, would certainly overturn the statute and restore literature to a respectable status in Boston and Boston to a decent respect in the opinions of mankind. That is true. The Society for the Suppression of Vice, for instance, can no longer successfully attack a decent book in New York—it no longer even tries to. The fight for freedom of expression in literature has been won everywhere except in Boston because it has been made everywhere except in Boston. You may think that the mere existence and still more the public toleration of a socially uncontrolled and irresponsible body like the booksellers' committee—which deprives both writers and readers of a basic freedom without any process of law whatever—you may think that its existence and public toleration are considerably more important than an absurd law or the suppression of a few books. You fail to understand how repugnant that idea is to the committee. It sees its motives as pure beyond expression and is proud of the fact that its activities assure every Boston bookseller who acts on its warnings that he will never go to jail, at least not for obscenity. It cannot see that any other issue is involved. And you must understand that it accurately expresses Boston's point of view. Boston does not mind being under the subjection of bigotry and it sees no reason to make a fight against either intolerance or the infringement of personal liberty.

You may keep coming back to that self-evident fact, after thinking over the history of censorship in Boston. You may end by deciding that there probably is in Boston a minority of liberal, tolerant people who are interested in ideas, cultivated in the arts, and occasionally adept at them. But that minority, you may decide, appears to be made impotent either by an absurd social myth which looks backward to an unreal past or by the ignorance and prejudices of the society that surrounds it. For the Bostonian, you observe, has violent prejudices, they make him aggressive, he will not permit the objective, detached discussion of ideas that is one of the marks of a civilized man. Boston, you may decide, must be a backward culture.

It seems possible that the mobbing in Boston of one more serious, decent novel may suggest such conclusions to you. This sort of suppression is routine in Boston, it happens every once in a while, and you are forced to make two observations about it. The suppression is not even legal, and it is done with complete public assent—with only the most scattered and perfunctory protest. Not only a backward culture, you may think, but something else as well. For in this comfortable acceptance of the intolerable, beginning moreover in the area of civil rights where early decay is always significant, you catch a whiff of something sick and dangerous.

The Literary Fallacy

A glance at the make-up sheet for this issue shows that world problems are being amply taken care of by other hands. I suppose you will not mind, therefore, if I take a couple of my colleagues aside and exhort them to repent.

We begin with Mr. C. Hartley Grattan's article about literature in last month's *Harper's*. Mr. Grattan usually confines himself to social analysis, an area in which his ideas command immediate respect. He has held only retired rank as a literary critic in recent years, but he proved last month that he is still entitled to a union card. He revealed the skilled professional's ability to discuss a part in the solemn pretense that it is the whole and to read immense significance into stuff which, on normal mornings when he was practicing social analysis, he would have recognized as ephemeral.

Nothing could be more professional, for example, than what he says about me. The text of my book, *The Literary Fallacy,* he says, is "Look around you, boys, and the state of the nation will exalt you." That is what the pros said when the book came out and it is quite unimportant—for criticism—that the book not only does not say that, but never touches on any subject that would make it relevant. Criticism has little interest in what a book actually says. A pro prefers to deal with what he knows better than the author it meant to say, or on what it ought to have said if the author had been bright enough to see the implications of what he was not writing about. Mr. Grattan knows what I meant to say or ought to have said, and so the hell with what I actually said. I am not objecting: I carry a union card and know the standard operating procedure. I merely call your attention to the trade practice because it leads to Mr. Grattan's results.

Mr. Grattan is writing about what he calls *tendenz* literature and about the painful collapse of its most conspicuous recent coterie. He builds up to a forecast of the literature we are going to get hereafter, as the world moves into a peace which is sure to be less than utopian. He lists varieties of books, or categories of literature, which may be called the package goods: there is always a demand for them and writers satisfy it without regard to period or tendency. But then he names four kinds of books which, he says, we are going to get because that last tendency did in fact collapse. (The tendency was economically and politically radical, oriented from the Russian Revolution, and progressively more Stalinist as time went on.) Let's skip the first one for a moment. The other three are: books which are essentially religious (for Mr. Grattan sees that many intellectuals are looking for a new faith to replace the lost revolution and thinks that some will find it on the gospel train), books of nihilism and disenchantment which portray life as a futile horror (because some, having seen one set of dogmas collapse, are never going to embrace another), and books which undertake to be glad, happy, and full of eager expectation.

Mr. Grattan is betting on a lead-pipe cinch but I can't see that he has got hold of the operative cause. What has all this got to do with the late belief of many literary men that the world uprising of the proletariat was about to take place, with their late hope that Russia would lead us into the world society, or with their late disillusionment by the treaty of nonaggression between Russia and Germany? Mr. Grattan has been around as long as I have and the same histories are open to us both. I wish he would name one period during the past three hundred years (I leave earlier times to specialists) when most literature could not have been classified in the three categories he differentiates. Writers did not wait for the collapse of the late tendency to write books of faith, hope, and despair. Mr. T. S. Eliot's conversion to the faith of *Ash Wednesday,* following an extreme disenchantment which had nothing to do with revolution, did not stem from the collapse of the neo-Marxian hope of a better world which, among literary folk, occurred ten years after his poem was written. Look as long as you like at the failure of the dictatorship of the proletariat to establish itself by 1940—and still that was not what made a Catholic of G. K. Chesterton in 1920, of half the *fin de siècle* English writers twenty years earlier, or of half the symbolists twenty years before that. It was not the 1930's that made Catholics of Orestes Brownson (our first proletarian writer) and Isaac Hecker long before the Civil War.

It was not the 1930's that made Transcendentalists of half their contemporaries and spiritualists, Buddhists, and positivists of another third.

The discovery that Utopia is not going to be ushered in this year was not made for the first time in 1939. Writers, like vulgar people, have always been barking their shins on the evils and insufficiencies of this world, have always been abandoning beliefs which they could not square with reality, have always tried to find new ones. There has never been a time when religion was not a refuge from reality for some and a stay and sustenance for others. Hope, cynicism, despair—they happen alike to writers and the humble and for due cause. But just where is the spot news and just how in this *tendenz* literature?

Mr. Grattan's remaining category is books of social criticism. Even before 1930 travelers had reported an occasional specimen of the type, but Mr. Grattan predicts that social criticism is going to be less leftish from here on than it was during the thirties and is going to have less "optimistic single-mindedness." The last is an inspiring prophecy but I produce my union card and predict that a lot of it is going to be as single-minded as possible—for a lot of writers, especially those of the seeking-and-believing type, tend to be single-minded. Mr. Grattan thinks the collapse of literary Marxism taught writers a lot. I pay my dues to the union and I say no.

In fact, I demur to his assumption that what we used to call proletarian literature, with its immediate expectation of a brave new world, defined the hopes and beliefs of American writers and spoke for a whole period of American life. I thought otherwise at the time, I frequently said so in this magazine and elsewhere, and now, looking back on it, I can see no more than some writers, some hopes and beliefs, and some fashions. I cherish in my files an article in which a dozen and a half of the writers Mr. Grattan is talking about set down, in 1932, the dates on which they expected the proletarian revolution to break out in the United States. The most distant of those dates is now four years in the past and at some proper time I am going to reprint the prophecies. I didn't think in 1932, or in any other year, that the proletarian revolution was due to break out in the United States at any foreseeable date, but that it was soon to do so became an article of faith for a literary coterie—and gave me a slant on that coterie. The coterie did not and does not seem to me to have produced the most important literature of the time. Mr. Grattan is perfectly free to consider that it produced the most significant; I prefer to say, most revealing. But certainly it did not speak for the generality of nonliterary Americans. Mr. Grattan announces the collapse of a tendency. No, just the passing of a coterie. Let us not, as criticism does, seize on a part and mistake it for the whole. Mr. Grattan has been committing the literary fallacy. The heart of literature is not broken; it's just that some writers have heartburn.

In the larger field which Mr. Grattan customarily works he would never venture to employ so simple an analysis. Outside literary criticism he knows that variables must be allowed for, that some variables are exceedingly complex, that generalizations are no good unless they account for all the data, and especially that when you set out to interpret a fact you must first make sure just what the fact is.

That, however, is outside literary criticism; and so let us now move on to Mr. Edmund Wilson.

My respect for Mr. Wilson is on record (see for example *Minority Report,* 169 ff.) and extends to nearly any kind of opinion he may see fit to express but not, it has been revealed to me, every kind of opinion. For Mr. Wilson recently found himself obliged to discuss detective stories. The mood in which he approached them might seem to a censorious eye, which I do not profess to have, a trifle lofty, patronizing, and academic. Be that as it may, the standard operating procedure plunged him deep into irrelevance, his professional imperatives threw him out of orientation with his subject, and he brought in a cosmic finding that was almost cosmically cockeyed. I'm sorry, his piece was so wrong that there is nothing to do but correct him and explain what this form of literature is and how we who read it feel about it.

First, Jacques Futrelle belongs to what Mr. Lewis Mumford, if he reads detective stories, calls the paleotechnic age. For first-rate stuff by contemporaries of Futrelle who managed to transcend their time (as Coleridge and Mallarmé did) he should have looked up Frederick Irving Anderson and Melville Davisson Post. As for Poe, he was not even eotechnic. Sherlock Holmes was right when he remarked that M. Dupin's "ratiocinative intensity" was nonsense, and if Mr. Wilson will read Poe's ratiocinative stories without regard to the imposing

but irrelevant fact that Poe was a precursor of the symbolists, he will
see that those precursors of the detective story are pretty godawful.
Moreover, though we revere Conan Doyle as a kind of Tubal Cain
we do not think too highly of his stories. When Mr. Wilson finds
"wit and fairy-tale poetry" in them he finds something which a critical
tradition says is there but which we cannot uncover. The Baker Street
Irregulars (I do not belong) and their rituals ought not to impose
on Mr. Wilson. The point is that the detective story, as a literary
form, has developed with great rapidity, that its techniques have advanced far beyond Doyle, and that to compare Rex Stout with Doyle
is equivalent to comparing *Ulysses* with, say, *Rosalind*. Finally, Doyle
did not invent "the Sherlock Holmes formula" nor does Rex Stout
use it any more intensively than Poe did.

When Mr. Wilson complains about bad writing in mysteries his
scale and comparisons trouble me. I too think that Mr. Stout writes
better prose than Mr. Hammett but I cannot agree that Mr. Cain is
better still. Besides, is there not a question of function? If distinguished
prose as such is what Mr. Wilson wants, let him try Mr. Raymond
Chandler. In fact, let him try Mr. Chandler on any ground, for he
is one of the best mystery writers now practicing, has carried the
Hammett subspecies to a distinction its originator never attained, and
in a recent movie greatly improved on Mr. Cain's dialogue. Mr. Carter
Dickson and Mr. Dickson Carr writes (the verb is correct) excellent
prose, so does H. C. Bailey, so do Margery Allingham and Ngaio
Marsh and Dorothy Sayers, so do many others. But though good prose
as such is a virtue in mystery stories it is by no means indispensable.
The mysteries of Erle Stanley Gardner and A. A. Fair are among
the very best there are, but the prose is commonplace; some first-rate
mysteries are written in tolerably bad prose. Mr. Wilson is accustomed
to a similar phenomenon in novels and would hardly require Theodore
Dreiser to write gracefully or forbid Scott Fitzgerald to be rhetorical.
In mysteries, as in impure forms of fiction, good writing is not
exclusively or even fundamentally good prose. Writing is a means
to an end; it is good writing when it furthers that end.

And will Mr. Wilson be so good as to stop asking Mr. Stout to
be Proust? Will he please stop applying to mystery stories critical cri-

teria which, when applied to them, produce nonsense? He complains that he cannot go slow enough to read Agatha Christie for values because she forces him to hurry on and find out how the puzzle is solved. Yes, and Thomas Nashe's "In Time of Plague" is also excellently achieved in its own terms. He complains that Mr. Stout does not provide sufficient psychological subtlety to absorb his interest, and reduces me to awe and reverence by saying that Mr. Hammett "lacks the ability to bring the story to imaginative life."

See here. Some of us mystery fans, like Woodrow Wilson, have quite liberal ideas; some of us, like W. B. Yeats, are widely acquainted with literature; some of us, like me, know how to use the jargon of literary criticism. But it happens, and without derogation of Proust or of ourselves, that there come times when we don't feel like reading Proust. Live and let live, in the house of literature there are many mansions, and let us be no more magisterial than the context requires. There are many kinds of mysteries.

Some of us don't like some of the kinds; some of us like all kinds; few of us suppose that our preferences represent a law of nature or an imperative of taste. Some like the kind which Mr. Wilson would apparently favor if he liked any kind, those which employ an "ingenious or picturesque or amusing" criminal device. I like a plain shooting, myself, though my enthusiasm Mr. Stout has used a bushmaster and a hoked-up golf club, my enthusiasm Mr. Dickson likes a room locked on the inside and produced one of his corpses with a crossbow, and one of the best of all mystery stories employed a burning-glass. Some of us like them simple, some complicated; some like an additional ingredient of battery or romance or horseplay; some like the mystery undiluted. I suppose we fall into two great classes, those who insist on the puzzle being airtight and rigorous and those who are willing to accept a somewhat less than perfect puzzle if the story is good enough. But all of us insist on a murder, the events that led up to it and those that followed it, and a solution of the mystery it caused.

Well, sinners, no writer who gives us that is going to be able to give us Charlus too. For what he must give us to satisfy our demand is, to get back to the jargon, story. We can have Charlus or we can have story but we can't have both. A writer who is engaged in telling us objectively what happened and in what sequence and why, in constructing a coherent and accelerating narrative, in giving us both drama and puzzle, is quite unable to be Proust at the same time. Furthermore, it is a principle of fiction that if we had Charlus we would be so deeply engrossed with him that we could not bear to have him killed, by crossbow or Army .45, in Chapter Two.

So that Mr. Wilson, to explain the cult of mystery stories, need not have developed the psycho-metaphysical theory which makes him conclude that the anarchy and especially the insecurity of our time are responsible. It is simpler than that. For nearly a century now the scope of the novel has been widening to include things never dreamed of by Fielding or Smollett: dissection of motive, exploration of psychological states, social analysis and criticism, economic theorizing, every conceivable variety of thesis and crusade. All this has greatly enriched the novel but also it has steadily diminished the element of narrative, of pure story, diminished and sometimes threatened to destroy it. But the element of narrative, which first brought the novel into existence, is indestructible. It expresses a deep and everlasting need which many people bring to literature, and if you heave it out the door it always comes back in through the window.

Coming back in through the window, it has produced the detective story. The detective story, or rather the mystery story (which is the inclusive term), is a thoroughly legitimate form of fiction and it is so popular right now because it is the only current form of fiction that is pure story. Mr. Wilson is under no obligation to enjoy the form but his dislike of it is not a disparagement—he need not suppose that because he is virtuous there will be no more Archie Goodwins or tolerably cultivated people to enjoy them. But if he does not like detective stories, the trade in which he holds a union card nevertheless requires him to understand the form better than he has understood it so far. Let him begin by realizing that it takes a considerable expertness at the art of fiction to write a good one.

Literary Men and the Common Man

April, 1944

YOU may remember the Lost Generation. It was primarily a literary phenomenon, an invention of novelists. It was a myth cultivated because it gave fine effects in prose. The Lost Generation was supposed to consist of men whose souls had been so maimed by the ugliness of war that they saw quite through life's hollow shams, and of women who caught the contagion from them, presumably as the supreme benignity of love. The phrase itself was an invention of Miss Gertrude Stein, whose art had no connection whatever with life or death, love or hate, rejoicing or grief, success or failure, belief or doubt, any other emotion of mankind, any experience of anyone, or any of the values that enable people to live together—an art which floated freely in a medium of pure caprice sustained by nothing except its awareness of its own inner wondrousness. The literary development of the phrase was almost exclusively American, and its first, perhaps its greatest prophet was Mr. Ernest Hemingway, who has lived to recant. Mr. Hemingway epitomized the entire meaning of his time in symbols of sexual impotence. He believed with a full heart that the symbols were altogether tragic, though a sounder judgment would be that they expressed a first-rate literary criticism.

The idea of the Lost Generation was sickly and unclean. No one has ever known how many soldiers of the last war, or how many contemporaries of theirs who had not known war at first hand, identified themselves with it. I do not think that many did. In the variety, vigor, and optimism of the American people following the last war there is no evidence that any considerable number thought of themselves as lost, and literature is far less able to persuade people to imitate it than writers like to believe. It may be, however, that literary praise of a moral depletion said to have been induced by the ugliness of war persuaded some people to act on it. If so, I suggest that we may include among the problems of reconversion a study of therapeutic and even preventive measures. If it is possible it is certainly desirable to dispense with a Lost Generation altogether this time, both in literature and in the populace at large.

Military physicians and psychiatrists have lately issued to the general public some suggestions concerning attitudes toward crippled veterans. We are advised—wholly for the sake of the crippled—to avoid expressing excessive sympathy. We are told to ignore their handicaps, to make as little fuss as possible, to treat them as a matter of course so far as we can. In this way, the Medical Corps says, we shall be helping them to acquire a sense of reality and, by helping them to be casual toward themselves, shall be helping them to triumph over their handicaps. If that is good therapeutics for the wounded, it is also an excellent attitude to adopt toward veterans who have not been crippled. Certainly it is an excellent attitude for them to adopt toward themselves.

What I say implies no failure to understand that the debt which the United States owes its defenders, crippled or whole, is beyond payment. Even the hastiest reader will understand that I am not proposing any skimping of our obligations to those who have been physically or mentally wounded in the service of the country. For the incapacitated everything possible must be done. For the wounded everything must be done that can heal their wounds, help them to overcome their handicaps, and so far as possible make up to them for the satisfactions and achievements which their wounds may have denied them. And those who emerge whole will have an imperative claim on the nation for whatever education, training, or guidance can enable them to resume life in the commonwealth on the most favorable terms. No compensation could be enough for the strain, hardship, and suffering undergone, the time lost, the dreams and ambitions forfeited, the sacrifice made in our service.

Nevertheless, if a tough-minded realism is essential to the soldier in war, it is equally essential to the ex-soldier in peace. The hard decree of nature is that he has got to live his life out to the end. Either he is going to make as much as he can of that life or something is going to frustrate him, and the easiest possible frustration is a paralysis of will engendered by self-pity. Certainly it is too bad that he was not permitted to make what he could of his personality and capacities, as the years of peace promised he would be able to. Certainly it is too bad that the years of his youth were spent in a war he never asked for, that the fulfillment of his promise has been delayed or quite forbidden, that he has had to experience horror and brutality and filth. But in peace as well as in war, time and chance happeneth to them all, the conditions of life are not what any of us would choose. It is too bad that we grow old, too bad that we prove less admirable than we thought, too bad that love fails, ambition peters out, friends die, dreams come to nothing. Given only omnipotence, any of us could create a world more kindly than the one we have to live in, but man must live in the world that is. He has always had to live in it, and he will have to live in it henceforth whether or not he has gone to war. He will live in it more successfully if he will understand that he has no claim on its tenderness, that none of its rigors will be relaxed for him because he has been a soldier.

I say nothing about the compensations which are any soldier's. They certainly exist—self-mastery, the knowledge that one has met and passed the ultimate test, the knowledge of dedication and sacrifice, the fellowship of men fighting in contempt of death—and in every war there have been some who counted them worth more than all the rest. But, disregarding them, there is no realistic philosophy for the ex-soldier except a recognition that fortune turned out the way it did. On him happened to fall the sternest obligation of citizenship as it fell on other Americans in three major and three minor wars. That turn of the wheel may have been, if you will, hard luck. It was hard luck that war prevented him from being the garage mechanic, radio announcer, or physician that he designed to be. It was hard luck that he had to serve a term in hell. It remains hard luck that memories of unspeakable horror will abide with him, that he has lost more than he can regain, that part of his life has been, in private terms, wasted. But it is hard luck in the peacetime world that we accomplish less than we hoped to, that a wife or a child dies, that our personalities erode, that we deal less than magnificently with the assigned task. Like the civilian, the soldier and the ex-soldier have had hard luck

—and that is that. The waste or failure of any individual does not mean that God had it in for him, and no private pain in the bowels proves that the world is evil.

The Lost Generation mistake was to generalize individual failure into a law of God and to suppose that a private pain in the bowels revealed the nature of reality. Every soldier has to learn a personal discipline of courage for war. The ex-soldier has got to learn an identical discipline for peace, since the inexorable condition is that the world's work will go on. Either he will take such a part in it as he best can or he will get in its way and be run over. Either war is an interruption of it or else we are all fools—and no fool greater than the soldier. War was not gentle with him; peace will not try to be.

Literature would do well to clarify its understanding. Following the last war it gave us, and gave us worshipfully, the image of a hero crying into his gin because he had seen more than he could bear. A hero sneering at fools who tried to make something of their lives because he had come to understand that there is no use in effort, the mourners go about the streets, and desire must fail. It gave us, that is, the image of a hero who was either a craven fool or a desperately sick soul. It gave us this image, either base or diseased, and bade us not pity but admire. Well, one thinks of the returning doughboy of 1919 who had no time for tears because he was too busy trying to get his job back and pick up where he had left off. One thinks of an earlier war that had more victims than Mr. Hemingway's, a war much more comparable to this one. Of a man making his way homeward from Appomattox in ragged and stinking shoddy and without shoes, to get the field plowed, the kids fed, and the shattered South rebuilt. Or making his way homeward to Vermont or Iowa with the best years of his youth devoured by war, no fine thing done, no fine thing possible in the time remaining. Both had known lice and the fire of dysentery in the bowels, hunger and panic, the private filth and public feculence of war. Both had seen friends blown to bloody shreds beside them. Both were items of helplessness, victims of the evil fate which twists the lives of men quite irresponsibly. War had left neither of them any intelligent choice except to recognize that they were lost, to renounce effort, and to rise superior to the illusions of labor and free will. So they went out and sowed the crops, repaired the bar, begot children, served on the school board, and sat with their shoes off at the end of a hard day. They broke the prairies, dug the mines, occupied the West, built the railroads, manned the industry that remade the world, tugged the United States to the forefront of civilization, and laid up the wealth that was later to support literature while it found all this an illusion. A defect in them was that they offered prose too little chance for exquisite effects. That was also a defect in their grandsons who came back from Château-Thierry and the Argonne with a feeling that they had done an unpleasant job rather creditably, and straightway got to work as near as possible to the place where they had left off. Coarseness of soul, economic Puritanism, or mere vitality prevented them from understanding that they were lost.

The Lost Generation, that is, was a cliché, one of the formulas, superstitions, or stereotypes which the pressure of literary fashion is apt to substitute for ideas. This time it would be wise for writers to avoid thinking of the returning soldier as lost. And there are other components of that old cliché which it will be desirable not to repeat. As, for instance, thinking of the returning soldier as a dupe. We went to war in 1917 to defeat a threat to our national existence—to crush institutions, even conceptions of mankind, that were a mortal danger to our own. But after the war was won it became strangely fashionable to believe that we had gone to war to secure the principal of Mr. Morgan's loans to Great Britain or (this with no apparent sense of incongruity) to earn profits for the death merchants, the makers of armament who were above nationality. If that were true, then the returning soldiers had indeed been dupes. The logic was unimpeachable—only the premise was wrong. At the present moment it seems impossible that anyone outside the fools' paradise of Peace Now will ever be able to persuade anyone that we went to war in 1941 for anyone's bonds or anyone's profits. Too many, one thinks, will remember the years we lived through on the way to war. Too many will remember the rising of the flood, the onrush of Nazism, the ghastly summer of 1940, the stunned hours following Pearl Harbor. But though quite as many could remember the autumn of 1914 and the early spring of 1917, the cliché of stupidity and betrayal formed never-theless. This time we ought to do what we can to prevent its forming. We are supposed to learn from experience.

We are supposed, I repeat, to learn from experience. In the literature of the Lost Generation it was orthodox to deride such attributes as patriotism, courage, loyalty, self-sacrifice, and the resolution to die in defense of values greater than oneself. Such virtues were sternly shown to be snares, traps, or tricks of illusion by which unscrupulous, clever persons were able to manipulate the stupid to their private gain. John Doe was an uncritical fool whom an international banker or a merchant of death could delude into dying gallantly for his profit balance. As time went on this exalted understanding changed somewhat and it became evident that John Doe lacked gallantry altogether. Back in the world's lost springtime there had perhaps been such virtues as courage and self-sacrifice, but clearly they did not exist now, not at least in the brutish citizen of everyday life. The modern world had brutalized John Doe, coarsened his soul, softened his nature; he was scum and a menace, incapable of greatness. Only a little while ago, so recently that every bystander remembers it, the manipulators of these clichés woke with a shock that verged on panic to the dilemma which the outbreak of war horribly unmasked. The virtues of patrio-tism, courage, and self-sacrifice, which had lately seemed fetishes proper to inferior people only, were essential to the survival even of the literary cliché, and there was no possible place where they could be sought except among the people who had lately been proved to have no capac-ity for them at all.

Read your morning newspaper. The chronicle of patriotism, courage, fortitude, loyalty, self-sacrifice, and willingness to die for matters greater than oneself—the chronicle of ordinary, unpretentious heroism has no end. Apparently such virtues are the ordinary endowment of people everywhere, apparently they are attributes of the human race, and we may assume that they cannot be inspired by literature or even implanted by a crisis. John Doe has always had them. He is a different person from the literary portrayal of him in the Lost Generation, and he always was. For the time being literary thinking is admitting as much. It describes him with a nauseous phrase, a phrase that reeks of condescension, the Common Man. But, reading its morning news-paper, it is willing to concede that the Common Man is endowed by nature with heroic virtues.

Precisely that amendment of opinion must be remembered in the period of reconversion. The day will come when the graveyard shift can check out for the last time, writers can retool, and literature turn to examine an ended war. Hopeful new ideas will bud and glistening new clichés begin to form. So, if there should be another impulse to portray the ex-soldier as a fool duped by cleverer men, if it begins to appear once more that the run-of-the-mill citizen is a boor and a craven enemy of all good things—let us remember that literature formally decided otherwise while the heat was on. We may be able to forestall or discredit another literature of the Lost Generation.

John Doe can remember too, when as an ex-soldier he takes up citizenship again. He has had the empirical proof. When the heat went on he found that he possessed courage, fortitude, loyalty, self-sacrifice, and all the rest. He found that they sufficed for war and may intelligently decide that they will suffice for peace. If he reaches that decision his generation will not be lost.

All Quiet along the Huron

When the following column was written, isolationist feelings were still strong throughout the United States; Hitler had conquered Western Europe; an invasion of England seemed imminent; and this country was woefully unprepared for the war which DeVoto thought inevitable.

November, 1940

B Y the diagnosis of a gentleman in Michigan, the Easy Chair needs medical attention. Hysteria. The evidence is that, reaching Santa Fe just when the House of Brabant saved itself by enslaving its people, just when the Nazi tanks and bombers began the attack that was to enslave France, the Easy Chair wrote that these things were a danger to America, that they threatened the gentleman's home town. That made the gentleman in Michigan mad and, with a number of others, he said so. He called the Easy Chair an agent of the hysterical East. He said that the Easy Chair ought to get away from the East oftener and seek the quiet of the West.

He like that phrase, "the quiet of the West," for he repeated it. The West, understand, was quiet in that the death of Europe did not disturb it. It saw no portents; it wasn't sacred. Maybe the Nazis were making a new earth under a new heaven, but let's take that in our stride—it was only Europe after all, and the Western pulse was calm. The world we grew up to know and count on had been blown to hell by *Panzer* divisions, and the world we hoped our children might inherit had become a broken and fantastic dream—but water was flowing down the Huron in the old untroubled way. There was a hand on our throat, but no matter, why make a noise about it? The future of America had become very much what the future of a house under construction becomes when a flood sweeps the foundation away, but the West was quiet. The gentleman from Michigan enjoyed that quiet and he resented a voice from the hysterial East shouting that the dam was out and the waters on their way down the valley.

I have a certain snobbery. I grew up in the Rocky Mountains, and so I have always objected to the carelessness of Middle Westerners who call their section the West. And you're wrong, brother, it wasn't the West that was quiet when Europe died. I found the West, where the conditions of life, so much harder than those you're used to in Michigan, make people realistic—I found the West just as disturbed as I was by those trivial events overseas, just as certain that America was in ghastly danger. The West wasn't quiet. It was the Middle West that was quiet—people like you in places like Michigan. So, since we can all be diagnosticians, I'm going to explain your disease.

I'm pretty scared, brother, but you're scared far worse. Do you know that hysteria is the mind's retreat from what it dares not face? A crisis can get through your instinctive defenses and make you, for a moment, see things plain. During those days when the French army was being pushed always farther back, while France was opening along the seams, you hung over the radio, desperate for each new bulletin. You kept asking yourself and everyone who would listen, When will Weygand counter-attack? You clung to your friends and the clerk in the cigar store and strangers on the street, trying to understand what was going on, trying to master your alarm, trying to find some intelligent defense against it. You read Dorothy Thompson and Walter Lippmann and other people who were telling you that the catastrophe of France was an American catastrophe too. You understood that, you agreed with them, you kept asking Why doesn't someone *do* something? Maybe you sent some wires to your good, gray Senator Vandenberg telling him he was blind and obsolete. There was a healthy quiver of fear in your stomach, quiver enough to make you amenable to thought and capable of action but not enough to stampede you. This was while the crisis was at its height, while every headline and every broadcast beat its urgency over your head, while the tension of life in a crumbling world was at its tightest stretch.

Then the tension got too great and snapped; France fell, the head-lines had so long overloaded the sensory nerves that no further sensation could get through; there came a lull which was just exhausted emotions, the crisis—as we playfully put it—was over. At once you went into what is correctly diagnosed as traumatic shock. Dorothy Thompson and Walter Lippmann went on pointing the moral of what had happened, but suddenly you couldn't take it. Instead of feverishly absorbing every word they wrote, you found yourself unable to absorb or even read them any more. You began to feel that they were dangers to America, which means that you felt them as dangerous to you. Probably you wrote to them saying they were suffering from hysteria: that's what you wrote to me when I remarked that you were in danger. Panic had laid hold of you. Panic assured you that these events in Europe could not possibly affect you. Panic told you that everything would be all right if only people would shut up. Panic told you that quiet was best. It was panic that made you quiet, that made the Middle West quiet, hysterial panic. Hysteria, remember, is the mind's retreat from what it dares not face. That's what happened to you, that's why your home town is serene. Of course you're quiet; anyone is quiet who is sacred stiff. There is such a thing as coma.

You'll come out of that quiet every time events go into the crescendo of another crisis. You'll hang over the radio again, and read Walter Lippmann like a starving man seeking bread. Each time, however, you'll come out of it not quite so far; you'll scurry back faster into the amniotic waters; you'll demand quiet more desperately and find it more easily. You'll get madder at anyone who seems likely to disturb you. You'll yell at them always more loudly: Oh, for God's sake leave me alone, peace at any price, we've got to live in the same world with Hitler, haven't we? it's not our war, America has its own problems to solve, and shut up, shut up, shut up, I've got to have my sleep.

Do you know that you're a set-up, brother? They count on you, overseas. You're in all the books. You know that phrase, the war of nerves, you use it glibly. It's aimed at you. They know about your nerves and how to work on them, how to make you panicky, how to induce their quiet in the Middle West. They've said they needn't bother to spend money or risk lives invading America, for America is a soft, timorous, peace-loving, hysterial nation that can be handled ever so easily. America, they say, will be a pushover. They're talking about you, and your quiet town.

Catatonia. A forced flight into sleep because the waking world is too terrible to be faced. You need the treatment given people who have taken an overdose of some hypnotic. We must keep you walking the floor no matter how drowsy you may be, feed you all the black coffee you can take, subject you to endlessly repeated stimuli, stimuli so simple that the numbed mind cannot misinterpret them, repeated so frequently that it gets no time to harden its defense.

Have you got a car? Of course you have, you live in Michigan. Probably it's a Buick, for your printed letterhead shows that you are comfortably placed, and Flint, where Buicks are made, is just an hour's drive east of your quiet town. Do you count on turning it in next year, on a new one? Maybe you won't. When the time comes to turn it in you may oddly find yourself unable to afford a new car. There will have been a queer but very quiet erosion; it will have taken part of your bank account away. They are building other machines besides automobiles in Flint; whether asleep or awake you'll be paying for them. That is one thing that Mr. Lippmann has been talking about, the new car you won't be able to afford.

Have you got a house? Of course you have. You belong to the well-upholstered middle class; you've done well for yourself even during these past ten years when it hasn't been so easy to do well for oneself as it used to be. It's a fine house too, a new one, no doubt a better one than you could have managed if it hadn't been for the twenty-year amortization plan that the FHA and the banks worked out. You're proud of that house, you love it profoundly, it symbolizes the deepest part of you and your expectation of America. Maybe you aren't going to pay off that mortgage. Maybe you're going to lose that house. That too is what Miss Thompson and Mr. Lippmann are talking about, the collapse in America of your house and the organization that enabled you to build it, under the weight of the events abroad that you don't want to hear about. You like a bit of butter on your bread, just like Christopher Robin's king, and that house is a bit of butter. Some of your butter is going to be turned into guns no matter what happens; American guns if you and your quiet towns get the point in time, or German guns if you don't—and if German guns, why, then, all your butter. While you sleep quietly, shingle by shingle that house of yours is blowing down the wind. Better not sleep too long.

Have you got children? It was the children I was talking about. Your dreams for them are the best of you. All these years you have hoped to start them off on their own a little more favorably than you started. You've wanted them to have sound bodies, good health, skills and training, poised and disciplined minds. You've wanted to fit them to grapple with the unknowable future. Millions of fathers have shared that desire; it is the health and the promise of our middle class; the trite phrase for it is "the American dream." And while everything stays quiet in your home town, bit by bit that expectation is being vetoed. A bomb falling on Dover has hit your children's school. The War Department must order some more planes, and so your daughter won't be going to that summer camp you had in mind. The Nazis seize Rumania, and so you won't be able to send your son to a professional school; maybe even college will prove to be quite out of the question. You've got to accept a lesser expectation for them, in detail, in the whole, and for their children too. You won't like that. They won't like it either.

During these past years that dream of yours has sometimes been displaced by a nightmare. You have had brief, paralyzing phantasies of your son unable to find work during the years of his vigor—your son, impotently idle—on Relief. They have been a sharp agony, and so how do you like the picture of your son sucked into the aimless rioting of the dispossessed as jobs get fewer, as business and society progressively break down, as the framework of American life caves in? Or, alternatively, how do you like the picture of him with a bland smile on a vacant face, goose-stepping in one of the youth-pulverizing battalions that the Nazis know how to organize, all the personality and individuality you've labored to give him systematically destroyed? I'm not talking about some foreigners pictured in *Life;* I'm talking about your son in the quiet Middle West.

Your house is on fire and your children will burn. Your country will burn—that pleasant town in Michigan, an hour west of Flint. *Life* shows you some Dorniers and Messerschmitts flying across the English Channel. What you're too scared to see is that they're flying across Lake Huron too. You boast of the quiet there in Michigan. But, you see, that's yesterday. Placid in yesterday, you've watched Europe go down; for over a year you've seen tanks and planes blasting their way across it. Because they haven't blasted their way across America you think they haven't moved across it; but they have. The world has changed forever; America's place in it has changed; with every beat of your pulse America is becoming something different—pounded into a different shape by the detonations which you think of as merely sound-effects in a newsreel. It really is a pleasant town—I know for I drove through it a month or so before you wrote to me—but it won't be pleasant very long now unless you wake up. Even if you do wake up it will never again be the town you've lived in up to now—but you can keep it a good town.

If you wake up. This angry protest of yours comes out of sleep; it is a sleeper's defense against realities that would shatter his dream. When the world is dangerous sleep is so much better than waking, dream is so much easier than courage. But sleep and dreaming are death just now, and that is why you must be waked and kept awake no matter how angrily you may resent the voices that get through to you. I didn't know that I was writing to you personally when I sent that letter from Santa Fe, but it turns out that I was—to you. About your house, your car, your school system, your children—about the United States and you and your home town. We have still got a chance to control events, to bring America and your son through the storm in such a way that the promise of both of them can still be fulfilled. Oh, not at all in the way you and I hoped for, perhaps not in any way that we can understand just now, but certainly in some way that will preserve the worth and use the talents of both, some way that will save their freedom. Our chance to do it is still a good chance, the odds are still in our favor—if we stand on our feet and face things, if we keep our nerve, if you come out of the coma that is pure panic.

You know the Burma Shave signs. Our highways ought to be lined with similar sequences that you would have to read, sequences of simple, plain, bitter truths. Still shorter and plainer ones ought to be set up at every stop light, and over the entrance to your office building, and on the counter where you buy tobacco. Little slogans which would pound the nerve that winced when you read my piece. Skywriters ought to smear them in mile-long letters above your golf course. Every radio program ought to plug them at the beginning and at the end and half-way through. They ought to leap out at you from billboards; sound trucks should blare them all evening long in the street before your fine new house. Because, you see, this desperate drowsiness resists them with the full strength of your panic. If that panic wins we lose—you lose.

What ought they to say? Simple, elementary, readily understandable things. The things that you dread most and so deny most vehemently. Just that the world is on fire. That America will be burned up unless you come awake and do something. That time is passing. That the quiet of your home town, which you boast about, is the quiet of a slumber that is settling toward the quiet of death.

For the Wayward and Beguiled

Probably the most widely reprinted of DeVoto's columns is his essay on the martini. Together with other columns on American drinking habits, expanded and revised, it was published in book form by Houghton, Mifflin under the title *The Hour*.

December, 1949

THROUGH the fifteen years of my ministry I have kept the Easy Chair almost entirely free from controversy. If I now venture into a field where no one can say anything without being violently attacked—and attacked by virtuous men who err only through ignorance, not sin—it is in austere dedication to American culture. One of the greatest of our arts is in danger. The worst is, the threat comes from schismatics and heretics within the too small band of true believers who should be of one united heart to hold our frontiers against the heathen. Error stalks the streets and disputation has brought darkness over the land. I am not one to withhold the light. I know how many enraged fanatics will jam the offices of Western Union as soon as this issue of *Harper's* hits the newsstands. But I know too that sometimes wisdom has its victories. To recall to wisdom some who have strayed from it and to discover wisdom to some who have sought but not found it, I proceed to explain the philosophy of the martini cocktail.

First we must understand what, functionally, a cocktail is. I will inquire into no man's reasons for taking a drink at any hour except 6:00 P.M. They are his affair and he has a rich variety of liquors to choose from according to his whim or need; may they reward him according to his deserts and well beyond. But when evening quickens in the street, comes a pause in the day's occupations that is known as the cocktail hour. It is the lifeward turn. The heart wakens from coma and its dyspnea ends. Its strengthening pulse is to cross over into campground, to believe that the world has not been altogether lost or, if lost, then not altogether in vain. But it cannot make the grade alone. It needs help; it needs, my brethren, all the help it can get. It needs a wife of similar impulse and equal impatience and maybe two or three friends, but no more than two or three. These gathered together in a softly lighted room and, with them, what it needs most of all, the bounty of alcohol. Hence the cocktail. After dinner you may, if you like, spend an hour or so sipping a jigger of whiskey diluted to the tenth attenuation with soda or branch water—though at my age you have probably learned that after-dinner study or meditation will assure you a smoother morning. But at 6:00 P.M. we must have action. When we summon life to reveal forgotten benisons and give us ourselves again, we do so peremptorily. Confirm that hope, set the beacon burning, and be quick about it. So no water.

There are only two cocktails. The bar manuals and the women's pages of the daily press, I know, print formulas for scores of messes to which they give that honorable name. They are not cocktails, they are slops. They are fit to be drunk only in the barbarian marches and mostly are drunk there, by the barbarians. It is a fact of great sadness that, as well, a few of them are drunk by people of good-will, people fit for our fellowship. We will labor to bring them out of the darkness they wander in, but we will charitably believe that they wander there as victims of history. Our forebears were a tough people; nothing so clearly proves it as that they survived the fearful mixtures they drank. A defect of their qualities, I suspect, led them into abomination. They had the restless mind, the instinct to experiment and make combinations that produces inventions. We got radar from that instinct, and Congress, and the Hearst press, and many other marvelous or mysterious works. And we got, four generations ago, mixtures of all the known ferments and distillates in every combination that whim, malice, or mathematics could devise. When the instinct reached an apex of genius, we must remember, it flowered into the martini. But it bequeathed us too a sore heritage of slops, and as the twentieth century came on the most ominous of these was probably the Bronx.

For the Bronx was fashionable. The gay dogs of the Murray Hill Age drank it, the boulevardiers who wore boaters with a string to the left lapel and winked at Gibson Girls as far up Fifth Avenue

as 59th Street. It had the kind of cachet that Maxim's had, or Del-
monico's, or say the splendid Richard Harding Davis at the Knicker-
bocker bar, or O. Henry in his cellar restaurant, or the bearded (or
Van Dyke-ed) critics of Park Row. And the Bronx had orange juice
in it. Then, swiftly, came the Plague and the rush of the barbarians
in its wake, and all the juices of the orchard went into cocktails. Now,
bathtub gin was not a good liquor—though, gentlemen, there have
been worse and still are. But it was not bathtub gin that came close
to destroying the American stomach, nervous system, and aspiration
toward a subtler life. Not the gin but the fruit juices so basely mixed
with it: all pestilential, all gangrenous, and all vile. A cocktail does
not contain fruit juice.

In that sudden roar the word you make out is "Daiquiri." Yes,
yes, I know. As a historian, I give rum its due. It gave us political
freedom and Negro slavery. It got ships built and sailed, forests felled,
iron smelted, and commercial freight carried from place to place by
men who, if their primordial capitalist bosses had not given it to them,
would have done something to get their wages raised. In both cheapness
and effectiveness it proved the best liquor for Indian traders to debauch
their customers with. People without taste buds can enjoy it now,
though the head that follows it is enormous, and sentimentalists such
as the seadogs of small sailing craft can believe they do. But mainly
it is drunk as all sweet liquors are, in a regressive fantasy, a sad hope
of regaining childhood's joy at the soda fountain. No believer could
drink it straight or gentled at the fastidious and hopeful hour. No
one should drink it with a corrosive added, which is the formula of
the Daiquiri.

There are only two cocktails. One can be described straightforwardly.
It is a slug of whiskey and it is an honest drink. Those who hold
by it at 6:00 P.M. offend no canon of our fellowship. Scotch, Irish,
rye, bourbon at your will, but of itself alone. Whiskey and vermouth
cannot meet as friends and the Manhattan is an offense against piety.
With dry vermouth it is disreputable, with sweet vermouth disgusting.
It signifies that the drinker, if male, has no spiritual dignity and would
really prefer white mule; if female, a banana split.

To make a slug of whiskey, you pour some whiskey on some ice.
(This year's fashionables are saying "whiskey on the rocks"; suffer

them patiently.) It is functional; its lines are clean. Perhaps the friend for whom you make it will want two or three drops of bitters. Fine; there is no harm in bitters, so long as they are Angostura—all others are condiments for a tea-shoppe cookbook. If he wants fruit salad in it, remind him that cocktails are drunk, not eaten, but go along with him as far as a thin halfslice of orange or, better, one of lemon peel. Deny him pineapple, cherries, and such truck as you would cyanide. If he asks for sugar, tell him you put it in to begin with, and thereafter be wary in your dealings with him. For sugar means that he is backsliding and will soon cross the frontier to join the heathen, with bottles of grenadine and almond extract in his pack. But before you give a slug of whiskey to anyone be sure that it is cold. Cocktails are cold.

With the other cocktail we reach a fine and noble art, and we reach too the wars over the gospel that have parted brothers, wrecked marriages, and made enemies of friends. It is here that heresies bourgeon and the schismatics bay. I suppose it is natural enough. Those who seek the perfect thing must have intense natures; there are many roads for them to take, all difficult, none lighted more than fitfully. No wonder if they mistake marsh fires for light, or when they find a light believe it is the only one. From their love comes their tirelessness to defend and praise their love—tenaciously, arrogantly, intolerantly, vindictively. We may understand how cults form with the martini as with all arts, how rituals develop, how superstitious or even sorcerous beliefs and practices betray a faith that is passionate and pure but runs easily to fanaticism. But if we understand these matters we must not be lenient toward them, for they divide the fellowship. Always remember that differences among ourselves will give arms to the heathen. Frighten a woman with a bit of ritual and you may produce a hostess who will serve Manhattans. Affront a man with cultish snobbery and you may turn him, God forbid, to rum.

For instance there is a widespread notion that women cannot make martinis, just as some islanders believe that they cast an evil spell on the tribal fishnets. This is a vagrant item of male egotism: the art of the martini is not a sex-linked character. Of men and women alike it requires only intelligence and care—oh, perhaps some additional inborn spiritual fineness, some feeling for artistic form which, if it isn't genius, will do quite as well. Or take the superstition, for I cannot dignify it as heresy, that the martini must not be shaken. Nonsense. This perfect thing is made of gin and vermouth. They are self-reliant liquors, stable, of stout heart; we do not have to treat them as if they were plover's eggs. It does not matter in the least whether you shake a martini or stir it. It does matter if splinters of ice get into the cocktail glass, and I suppose this small seed of fact is what grew into the absurdity that we must not "bruise the gin." The gin will take all that you are capable of giving it, and so will the vermouth. An old hand will probably use a simple glass pitcher, as convenient and functional; it has no top and so cannot readily be shaken. But if a friend has given you a shaker, there are bar-strainers in the world and you need have no ice-splinters in your martinis.

A martini, I repeat, is made of gin and vermouth. Dry vermouth. Besides many bad vermouths, French, Italian, and domestic, there are many good ones. With a devoted spirit keep looking for one that will go harmoniously with the gin of your choice and is dependably uniform in taste. You have found a friend: stay with it. Stay with them both, store them in quantity lest mischance or sudden want over-take you, and in a world of change you will be able to count on your martinis from season unto season, year to year.

It is heresies more vicious than these that make us home-loving people. We have proved our friends, but anyone else's invitation to a cocktail party or casual suggestion that we stop by for a drink may take us into a house where martinis are made of sweet vermouth or of sweet mixed with dry. It is a grievous betrayal of trust; the bottles should not even be kept on neighboring shelves, still less brought near the martini-pitcher. And, I suppose, nothing can be done with people who put olives in martinis, presumably because in some desolate childhood hour someone refused them a dill pickle and so they go through life lusting for the taste of brine. Something can be done with people who put pickled onions in: strangulation seems best. But there is a deadlier enemy to the good hour than these, the man who mixes his martinis beforehand and keeps them in the refrigerator till cocktail time. You can no more keep a martini in the refrigerator than you can keep a kiss there. The proper union of gin and vermouth is a great and sudden glory; it is one of the shortest-lived. The fragile tie of ecstacy is broken in a few minutes, and thereafter there can be no remarriage. The beforehander has not understood that what is left, though it was once a martini, can never be one again. He has sinned as seriously as the man who leaves some in the pitcher to drown.

A voice from the floor reminds me that there may be dire emergencies. True, though not in your own home; they usually come when some hostess whose favorite drink is green mint mixed with whipping cream asks you to make martinis. Well, if she has sweet vermouth, make the proportion practically unthinkable, say seven to one—and remind your companions that the product has a high muzzle velocity. If she has sherry you will be much better off. Govern the proportions according to its sweetness; about five to one will do if it is dry, and put a pinch of common table salt into the pitcher. These drinks are not martinis, they are only understudies, but they damn no souls. They are incomparably better than Manhattans, marshmallows, or rum.

Sound practice begins with ice. There must be a lot of it, much more than the catechumen dreams, so much that the gin smokes when you pour it in. A friend of mine has said it for all time; his formula ends, "and five hundred pounds of ice." Fill the pitcher with ice, whirl it till dew forms on the glass, pour out the melt, put in another handful of ice. Then as swiftly as possible pour in the gin and vermouth, at once bring the mixture as close to freezing point of alcohol as can be reached outside the laboratory, and pour out the martinis. You must be unhurried but you must work fast, for a diluted martini would be a contradiction in terms, a violation of nature's order. That is why the art requires so much ice and why the artist will never mix more than a single round at a time, counting noses.

And, I'm sorry, you are not a bartender. There are cultists whose pride is to achieve the right proportion by instinct, innate talent, the color of the mixture, or what Aunt Fanny said about born cooks. They are the extreme fanatics and would almost as soon drink an Alexander as measure out their wares. I honor a great many of them who have served me sound martinis made with what they thought of as perfected skill. I honor them—but the martinis vary from round to round, and one or another must fall short of perfected skill. Serenely accept the cultist's scorn and measure your quantities with an extra glass. There is a point where the marriage of gin and vermouth is consummated. It varies a little with the constituents, but for a gin of 95 proof and a harmonious vermouth it may be generalized as about 3.7 to one. And that is not only the proper proportion but the critical one; if you use less gin it is a marriage in name only and the name is not martini. You get a drinkable and even pleasurable result, but not art's sunburst of imagined delight becoming real. Happily, the upper limit is not so fixed; you may make it four to one or a little more than that, which is a comfort if you cannot do fractions in your head and an assurance when you must use an unfamiliar gin. But not much more. This is the violet hour, the hour of hush and wonder, when the affections glow again and valor is reborn, when the shadows deepen magically along the edge of the forest and we believe that, if we watch carefully, at any moment we may see the unicorn. But it would not be a martini if we should see him.

So made, the martini is only one brushstroke short of the perfect thing, and I will rebuke no one who likes to leave it there. But the final brush-stroke is a few drops of oil squeezed from lemon rind on the surface of each cocktail. Some drop the squeezed bit into the glass; I do not favor the practice and caution you to make it rind, not peel, if you do, and, of course, you will use cocktail glasses, not cups of silver or any other metal, and they will have stems so that heat will not pass from your hand to the martini. Purists chill them before the first round. If any of that round is left in the pitcher, throw it away.

The goal is purification and that will begin after the first round has been poured, so I see no need for preliminary spiritual exercises. But it is best approached with a tranquil mind, lest the necessary speed become haste. Tranquillity ought normally to come with sight of the familiar bottles. If it doesn't, feel free to hum some simple tune as you go about your preparations; it should be nostalgic but not sentimental, neither barbershop nor jazz, between the choir and the glee club. Do not whistle, for your companions are sinking into the quiet of expectation. And you need not sing, for presently there will be singing in your heart.

VI/John Fischer
1955-

Crime, as defined by Oxford University, led to my association with
Harper's.

After my graduation from the University of Oklahoma in 1932
I went to work for the *Daily Oklahoman* as night police reporter
for $25 a week, an enviable wage in those Depression times. About
a year later a friend on the university faculty called to suggest that
I apply for a Rhodes scholarship, since the state did not have any
promising undergraduate candidates just then. I did, and to my considerable astonishment found myself a few months later in Oxford.

In those days the Oxford colleges locked their gates at midnight,
and any student who was not inside when the key turned was liable
to severe discipline. This irked me, since I then regarded myself as
a pretty worldly fellow, well equipped to run at large at all hours.
After all, in the preceding year I had covered fifty violent deaths—
counting murders, suicides, and an execution—plus bank robberies,
rapes, knifings, raids on bawdy houses, and the kidnapping of an oil
millionaire. It was probably inevitable, therefore, that one night when
I was out on a promising date I should ignore the curfew, and attempt
the most ambitious athletic feat of my life. At 3 A.M. I clambered
over a fifteen-foot wall topped with nine-inch spikes. Miraculously,
I neither broke my neck nor got impaled; but I did tear my coat
and get a good deal of mortar on my shoes. This damning evidence
was discovered by the college servant who looked after my rooms,
and duly reported to the dean. Result: a twenty-pound fine.

Because that took all the funds I was depending on for food and
lodging during the coming vacation, I had to make some money fast.
I wrote an article about the British Labour Party—a subject I knew
fairly well, since I was then editing a quarterly for the undergraduate
Socialist club—and sent it off to *Harper's,* the magazine I respected
most. To my surprise, it was accepted. Ever since then I have been
connected with the magazine and its sister-enterprise, Harper & Broth-

ers (later Harper & Row) as both writer and editor, although I did not become a full-time member of the staff until 1944.

At other times, before Oxford and afterward, I have worked for four dailies in the Southwest, for press associations in Europe and Washington, for a wartime intelligence organization in London and the China-Burma-India theater, for a postwar relief organization in Russia, and for Adlai Stevenson and John F. Kennedy as a speech writer. Incidental ventures have taken me into other fields, ranging from wheat-raising to ward heeling for the Democratic party. I mention all this simply because a writer needs as broad a spectrum of experience as he can get. In my case it has provided material for four books, articles for many magazines, and seventeen years in the Easy Chair.

Many of my columns, like DeVoto's and Curtis's, have dealt with political issues which were, in their nature, ephemeral. In the following selections I have included only two that make points about federal and local government which—I hope—are still pertinent. One of the others is partly autobiographical. The rest deal with those subjects that have interested me most intensely during recent decades—the environment, American education, and the restructuring of social institutions. I have chosen these particular columns partly because they evoked an unusually lively response from magazine readers, and partly because I enjoyed writing them and hope therefore that at least some readers may enjoy them too.

Survival U: Prospectus for a Really Relevant University

October, 1969

It gets pretty depressing to watch what is going on in the world and realize that your education is not equipping you to do anything about it.

—*From a letter by a University of California senior.*

S H E is not a radical, and has never taken part in any demonstration. She will graduate with honors, and profound disillusionment. From listening to her—and a good many like-minded students at California and East Coast campuses—I think I am beginning to understand what they mean when they say that a liberal-arts education isn't relevant.

They mean it is incoherent. It doesn't cohere. It consists of bits and pieces which don't stick together, and have no common purpose. One of our leading Negro educators, Arthur Lewis of Princeton, recently summed it up better than I can. America is the only country, he said, where youngsters are required "to fritter away their precious years in meaningless peregrination from subject to subject . . . spending twelve weeks getting some tidbits of religion, twelve weeks learning French, twelve weeks seeing whether the history professor is stimulating, twelve weeks seeking entertainment from the economics professor, twelve weeks confirming that one is not going to be able to master calculus."

These fragments are meaningless because they are not organized around any central purpose, or vision of the world. The typical liberal-arts college has no clearly defined goals. It merely offers a smorgasbord of courses, in hopes that if a student nibbles at a few dishes from the humanities table, plus a snack of science, and a garnish of art or anthropology, he may emerge as "a cultivated man"—whatever that means. Except for a few surviving church schools, no university even pretends to have a unifying philosophy. Individual teachers may have personal ideologies—but since they are likely to range, on any given campus, from Marxism to worship of the scientific method to exaltation of the irrational (*à la* Norman O. Brown), they don't cohere either. They often leave a student convinced at the end of four years that any given idea is probably about as valid as any other—and that none of them has much relationship to the others, or to the decisions he is going to have to make the day after graduation.

Education was not always like that. The earliest European universities had a precise purpose: to train an elite for the service of the Church. Everything they taught was focused to that end. Thomas Aquinas had spelled it all out: what subjects had to be mastered, how each connected with every other, and what meaning they had for man and God.

Later, for a span of several centuries, Oxford and Cambridge had an equally clear function: to train administrators to run an empire. So too did Harvard and Yale at the time they were founded; their job was to produce the clergymen, lawyers, and doctors that a new country needed. In each case, the curriculum was rigidly prescribed. A student learned what he needed, to prepare himself to be a competent priest, district officer, or surgeon. He had no doubts about the relevance of his courses—and no time to fret about expanding his consciousness or currying his sensual awareness.

This is still true of our professional schools. I have yet to hear an engineering or medical student complain that his education is meaningless. Only in the liberal-arts colleges—which boast that "we are not trade schools"—do the youngsters get that feeling that they are drowning in a cloud of feathers.

For a long while some of our less complacent academics have been trying to restore coherence to American education. When Robert Hutchins was at Chicago, he tried to use the Great Books to build a comprehensible framework for the main ideas of civilized man. His experiment is still being carried on, with some modifications, at St. John's—but it has not proved irresistibly contagious. Sure, the thoughts of Plato and Machiavelli are still pertinent, so far as they go—but somehow they don't seem quite enough armor for a world beset with splitting atoms, urban guerrillas, nineteen varieties of psychotherapists, amplified guitars, napalm, computers, astronauts, and an atmosphere polluted simultaneously with auto exhaust and TV commercials.

Another strategy for linking together the bits-and-pieces has been attempted at Harvard and at a number of other universities. They require their students to take at least two years of survey courses, known variously as core studies, general education, or world civilization. These too have been something less than triumphantly successful. Most faculty members don't like to teach them, regarding them as superficial and synthetic. (And right they are, since no survey course that I know of has a strong unifying concept to give it focus.) Moreover, the senior professors shun such courses in favor of their own narrow specialties. Consequently, the core studies which are meant to place all human experience—well, at least the brightest nuggets—into One Big Picture usually end up in the perfunctory hands of resentful junior teachers. Naturally the undergraduates don't take them seriously either.

Any successful reform of American education, I am now convinced, will have to be far more revolutionary than anything yet attempted. At a minimum, it should be:

1. Founded on a single guiding concept—an idea capable of knotting together all strands of study, thus giving them both coherence and visible purpose.

2. Capable of equipping young people to do something about "what is going on in the world"—notably the things which bother them most, including war, injustice, racial conflict, and the quality of life.

Maybe it isn't possible. Perhaps knowledge is proliferating so fast, and in so many directions, that it can never again be ordered into a coherent whole, so that molecular biology, Robert Lowell's poetry, and highway engineering will seem relevant to each other and to the lives of ordinary people. Quite possibly the knowledge explosion, as Peter F. Drucker has called it, dooms us to scholarship which grows steadily more specialized, fragmented, and incomprehensible.

The Soviet experience is hardly encouraging. Russian education is built on what is meant to be a unifying ideology: Marxism-Leninism. In theory, it provides an organizing principle for all scholarly activity—whether history, literature, genetics, or military science. Its purpose is explicit: to train a Communist elite for the greater power and glory of the Soviet state, just as the medieval universities trained a priesthood to serve the Church.

Yet according to all accounts that I have seen, it doesn't work very well. Soviet intellectuals apparently are almost as restless and unhappy as our own. Increasing numbers of them are finding Marxism-Leninism too simplistic, too narrowly doctrinaire, too oppressive; the bravest are risking prison in order to pursue their own heretical visions of reality.

Is it conceivable, then, that we might hit upon another idea which could serve as the organizing principle for many fields of scholarly inquiry; which is relevant to the urgent needs of our time; and which would not, on the other hand, impose an ideological strait jacket, as both ecclesiastical and Marxist education attempted to do?

Just possibly it could be done. For the last two or three years I have been probing around among professors, college administrators, and students—and so far I have come up with only one idea which might fit the specifications. It is simply the idea of survival.

For the first time in history, the future of the human race is now in serious question. This fact is hard to believe, or even think about—yet it is the message which a growing number of scientists are trying, almost frantically, to get across to us. Listen, for example, to Professor Richard A. Falk of Princeton and of the Center for Advanced Study in the Behavioral Sciences:

> The planet and mankind are in grave danger of irreversible catastrophe . . . Man may be skeptical about following the flight of the dodo into extinction, but the evidence points increasingly to just such a pursuit. . . . There are four interconnected threats to the planet—wars of mass destruction, overpopulation, pollution, and the depletion of resources. They have a cumulative effect. A problem in one area renders it more difficult to solve the problems in any other area. . . . The basis of all four problems is the inadequacy of the sovereign states to manage the affairs of mankind in the twentieth century.

Similar warnings could be quoted from a long list of other social scientists, biologists, and physicists, among them such distinguished thinkers as Rene Dubos, Buckminster Fuller, Loren Eiseley, George Wald, and Barry Commoner. They are not hopeless. Most of them believe that we still have a chance to bring our weapons, our population growth, and the destruction of our environment under control before it is too late. But the time is short, and so far there is no evidence that enough people are taking them seriously.

That would be the prime aim of the experimental university I'm suggesting here: to look seriously at the interlinking threats to human existence, and to learn what we can do to fight them off.

Let's call it Survival U. It will not be a multiversity, offering courses in every conceivable field. Its motto—emblazoned on a life jacket rampant—will be: "What must we do to be saved?" If a course does not help to answer that question, it will not be taught here. Students interested in musicology, junk sculpture, the Theater of the Absurd, and the literary *dicta* of Leslie Fiedler can go somewhere else.

Neither will our professors be detached, dispassionate scholars. To get hired, each will have to demonstrate an emotional commitment to our cause. Moreover, he will be expected to be a moralist; for this generation of students, like no other in my lifetime, is hungering and thirsting after righteousness. What it wants is a moral system it can believe in—and that is what our university will try to provide. In every class it will preach the primordial ethic of survival.

The biology department, for example, will point out that it is sinful for anybody to have more than two children. It has long since become glaringly evident that unless the earth's cancerous growth of population can be halted, all other problems—poverty, war, racial strife, uninhabitable cities, and the rest—are beyond solution. So the department naturally will teach all known methods of birth control, and much of its research will be aimed at perfecting cheaper and better ones.

Its second lesson in biological morality will be: "Nobody has a right to poison the environment we live in." This maxim will be illustrated by a list of public enemies. At the top will stand the politicians, scientists, and military men—of whatever country—who make and deploy atomic weapons; for if these are ever used, even in so-called defensive systems like the ABM, the atmosphere will be so contaminated with strontium 90 and other radioactive isotopes that human survival seems most unlikely. Also on the list will be anybody who makes or tests chemical and biological weapons—or who even attempts to get rid of obsolete nerve gas, as our Army recently proposed, by dumping the stuff in the sea.

Only slightly less wicked, our biology profs will indicate, is the farmer who drenches his land with DDT. Such insecticides remain virulent indefinitely, and as they wash into the streams and oceans they poison fish, water fowl, and eventually the people who eat them. Worse yet—as John Hay noted in his recently published *In Defense of Nature*—"The original small, diluted concentrations of these chemicals tend to build up in a food chain so as to end in a concentration that may be thousands of times as strong." It is rapidly spreading throughout the globe. DDT already has been found in the tissues of Eskimos and of Antarctic penguins, so it seems probable that similar deposits are gradually building up in your body and mine. The minimum fatal dosage is still unknown.

Before he finishes this course, a student may begin to feel twinges of conscience himself. Is his motorcycle exhaust adding carbon monoxide to the smog we breathe? Is his sewage polluting the nearest river? If so, he will be reminded of two proverbs. From Jesus: "Let him who is without sin among you cast the first stone." From Pogo: "We have met the enemy and he is us."

In like fashion, our engineering students will learn not only how to build dams and highways, but where *not* to build them. Unless they understand that it is immoral to flood the Grand Canyon or destroy the Everglades with a jetport, they will never pass the final exam. Indeed, our engineering graduates will be trained to ask a key question about every contract offered them: "What will be its effect on human life?" That obviously will lead to other questions which every engineer ought to comprehend as thoroughly as his slide rule. Is this new highway really necessary? Would it be wiser to use the money for mass transit—or to decongest traffic by building a new city somewhere else? Is an offshore oil well really a good idea, in view of what happened to Santa Barbara?

Our engineering faculty also will specialize in training men for a new growth industry: garbage disposal. Americans already are spending $4.5 billion a year to collect and get rid of the garbage which we produce more profusely than any other people (more than five pounds a day for each of us). But unless we are resigned to stifling in our own trash, we are going to have to come up with at least an additional $835 million a year.[1] Any industry with a growth rate of 18 per cent offers obvious attractions to a bright young man—and if he can figure out a new way to get rid of our offal, his fortune will be unlimited.

Because the old ways no longer work. Every big city in the United States is running out of dumping grounds. Burning won't do either, since the air is dangerously polluted already—and in any case, 75 per cent of the incinerators in use are inadequate. For some 150 years Californians happily piled their garbage into San Francisco Bay, but they can't much longer. Dump-and-fill operations already have reduced it to half its original size, and in a few more decades it would be possible to walk dry-shod from Oakland to the Embarcadero. Consequently San Francisco is now planning to ship garbage 375 miles to the yet-uncluttered deserts of Lassen County by special train—known locally as "The Twentieth Stenchery Limited" and "The Excess Express." The city may actually get away with this scheme, since hardly anybody lives in Lassen County except Indians, and who cares about them? But what is the answer for the metropolis that doesn't have an unspoiled desert handy?

A few ingenious notions are cropping up here and there. The Japanese are experimenting with a machine which compacts garbage, under great heat and pressure, into building blocks. A New York businessman is thinking of building a garbage mountain somewhere upstate, and equipping it with ski runs to amortize the cost. An aluminum company plans to collect and reprocess used aluminum cans—which, unlike the old-fashioned tin can, will not rust away. Our engineering department will try to Think Big along these lines. That way lies not only new careers, but salvation.

Survival U's Department of Earth Sciences will be headed—if we are lucky—by Dr. Charles F. Park, Jr., now professor of geology and mineral engineering at Stanford. He knows as well as anybody how

---

1. According to Richard D. Vaughn, chief of the Solid Wastes Program of HEW, in his recent horror story entitled "1968 Survey of Community Solid Waste Practices."

fast mankind is using up the world's supply of raw materials. In a paper written for the American Geographical Society he punctured one of America's most engaging (and pernicious) myths: our belief that an ever-expanding economy can keep living standards rising indefinitely.

It won't happen; because, as Dr. Park demonstrates, the tonnage of metal in the earth's crust won't last indefinitely. Already we are running short of silver, mercury, tin, and cobalt—all in growing demand by the high-technology industries. Even the commoner metals may soon be in short supply. The United States alone is consuming one ton of iron and eighteen pounds of copper every year, for each of its inhabitants. Poorer countries, struggling to industrialize, hope to raise their consumption of these two key materials to something like that level. If they should succeed—and if the globe's population doubles in the next forty years, as it will at present growth rates—then the world will have to produce, somehow, *twelve times* as much iron and copper every year as it does now. Dr. Parks sees little hope that such production levels can ever be reached, much less sustained indefinitely. The same thing, of course—doubled in spades—goes for other raw materials: timber, oil, natural gas, and water, to note only a few.

Survival U, therefore, will prepare its students to consume less. This does not necessarily mean an immediate drop in living standards—perhaps only a change in the yardstick by which we measure them. Conceivably Americans might be happier with fewer automobiles, neon signs, beer cans, supersonic jets, barbecue grills, and similar metallic fluff. But happy or not, our students had better learn how to live The Simpler Life, because that is what most of them are likely to have before they reach middle age.

To help them understand how very precious resources really are, out mathematics department will teach a new kind of bookkeeping: social accounting. It will train people to analyze budgets—both government and corporate—with an eye not merely to immediate dollar costs, but to the long-range costs to society.

By conventional bookkeeping methods, for example, the coal companies strip-mining away the hillsides of Kentucky and West Virginia show a handsome profit. Their ledgers, however, show only a fraction of the true cost of their operations. They take no account of destroyed land which can never bear another crop; of rivers poisoned by mud and seeping acid from the spoil banks; of floods which sweep over farms and towns downstream, because the ravaged slopes can no longer hold the rainfall. Although these costs are not borne by the mining firms, they are nevertheless real. They fall mostly on the taxpayers, who have to pay for disaster relief, flood-control levees, and the resettlement of Appalachian farm families forced off the land. As soon as our students (the taxpayers of tomorrow) learn to read a social balance sheet, they obviously will throw the strip miners into bankruptcy.

Another case study will analyze the proposal of the Inhuman Real Estate Corporation to build a fifty-story skyscraper in the most congested area of midtown Manhattan. If 90 per cent of the office space can be rented at $12 per square foot, it looks like a sound investment, according to antique accounting methods. To uncover the truth, however, our students will investigate the cost of moving 12,000 additional workers in and out of midtown during rush hours. The first (and least) item is $8 million worth of new city buses. When they are crammed into the already clogged avenues, the daily loss of manhours in traffic jams may run to a couple of million more. The fumes from their diesel engines will cause an estimated 9 per cent increase in New York's incidence of emphysema and lung cancer: this requires the construction of three new hospitals. To supply them, plus the new building, with water—already perilously short in the city—a new reservoir has to be built on the headwaters of the Delaware River, 140 miles away. Some of the dairy farmers pushed out of the drowned valley will move promptly into the Bronx and go on relief. The subtraction of their milk output from the city's supply leads to a price increase of two cents a quart. For a Harlem mother with seven hungry children, that is the last straw. She summons her neighbors to join her in riot, seven blocks go up in flames, and the Mayor demands higher taxes to hire more police. . . .

Instead of a sound investment, Inhuman Towers now looks like criminal folly, which would be forbidden by any sensible government. Our students will keep that in mind when they walk across campus to their government class.

Its main goal will be to discover why our institutions have done so badly in their efforts (as Dr. Falk put it) "to manage the affairs of mankind in the twentieth century." This will be a compulsory course for all freshmen, taught by professors who are capable of looking critically at every political artifact, from the Constitution to the local county council. They will start by pointing out that we are living in a state of near-anarchy, because we have no government capable of dealing effectively with public problems.

Instead we have a hodgepodge of 80,000 local governments—villages, townships, counties, cities, port authorities, sewer districts, and special purpose agencies. Their authority is so limited, and their jurisdictions so confused and overlapping, that most of them are virtually impotent. The states, which in theory could put this mess into some sort of order, usually have shown little interest and less competence. When Washington is called to help out—as it increasingly has been for the last thirty-five years—it often has proved ham-handed and entangled in its own archaic bureaucracy. The end result is that nobody in authority has been able to take care of the country's mounting needs. Our welfare rolls keep growing, our air and water get dirtier, housing gets scarcer, airports jam up, road traffic clots, railways fall apart, prices rise, ghettos burn, schools turn out more illiterates every year, and a war nobody wants drags on and on. Small wonder that so many young people are losing confidence in American institutions. In their present state, they don't deserve much confidence.

The advanced students of government at Survival U will try to find out whether these institutions can be renewed and rebuilt. They will take a hard look at the few places—Jacksonville, Minnesota, Nashville, Appalachia—which are creating new forms of government. Will these work any better, and if so, how can they be duplicated elsewhere? Can the states be brought to life, or should we start thinking about an entirely different kind of arrangement? Ten regional prefectures, perhaps, to replace the fifty states? Or should we take seriously Norman Mailer's suggestion for a new kind of city-state to govern our great metropolises? (He merely called for New York City to secede from its state; but that isn't radical enough. To be truly governable, the new Republic of New York City ought to include chunks of New Jersey and Connecticut as well.) Alternatively, can we find some way to break up Megalopolis, and spread our population into smaller and more livable communities throughout the continent? Why should we keep 70 per cent of out people crowded into less than 2 per cent of our land area, anyway?

Looking beyond our borders, our students will be encouraged to ask even harder questions. Are nation-states actually feasible, now that they have power to destroy each other in a single afternoon? Can we agree on something else to take their place, before the balance of terror becomes unstable? What price would most people be willing to pay for a more durable kind of human organization—more taxes, giving up national flags, perhaps the sacrifice of some of our hard-won liberties?

All these courses (and everything else taught at Survival U) are really branches of a single science. Human ecology is one of the youngest disciplines, and probably the most important. It is the study of the relationship between man and his environment, both natural and technological. It teaches us to understand the consequences of our actions—how sulfur-laden fuel oil burned in England produces an acid rain that damages the forests of Scandinavia, why a well-meant farm subsidy can force millions of Negro tenants off the land and lead to Watts and Hough. A graduate who comprehends ecology will know how to look at "what is going on in the world," and he will be equipped to do something about it. Whether he ends up as a city planner, a politician, an enlightened engineer, a teacher, or a reporter, he will have had a relevant education. All of its parts will hang together in a coherent whole.

And if we can get enough such graduates, man and his environment may survive a while longer, against all the odds.

How I Got Radicalized: The Making of an Agitator for Zero

April, 1970

To my astonishment, the political convictions that I had cherished for most of my life have suddenly deserted me. Like my children, these were convictions I loved dearly and had nurtured at considerable expense. When last seen they were—like all of us—somewhat battered by the events of the last decade, but they looked durable enough to last out my time. So I was disconcerted when I found that somehow, during the past winter, they sort of melted away, without my consent and while I was looking somewhere else.

Their place has been usurped by a new set of convictions so radical that they alarm me. If the opposite kind of thing had happened, I would have felt a little melancholy but not surprised, since people traditionally grow more conservative as they get older. But to discover that one has suddenly turned into a militant subversive is downright embarrassing; at times I wonder whether it signals the onset of second childhood.

Except that I seem to be a lot more radical than the children. Those SDS youngsters who go around breaking windows and clubbing policemen now merely depress me with their frivolous irrelevance. So do most other varieties of New Leftists, such as the Women's Liberation movement; if some dire accident should, God forbid, throw one of those ladies into my clutches, she can be sure of instant liberation. I am equally out of tune with those old fogies, the Communists. The differences between capitalism and Communism no longer seem to me worth fighting about, or even arguing, since they are both wrong and beside the point. Or so it seems to me, since the New Vision hit me on my own small road to Damascus.

Let me make it plain that none of this was my doing. I feel as Charles Darwin must have felt during the last leg of his voyage on the *Beagle*. When he embarked he had been a conventional (if slightly lackadaisical) Christian, who took the literal truth of Genesis for granted. He had been raised in that faith, as I was raised a Brass Collar Democrat, and had no thought of forsaking it. Only gradually, while he examined fossil shellfish high in the Andes and measured the growth of coral deposits and the bills of Galapagos finches, did he begin to doubt that the earth and all its inhabitants had been created in six days of October, 4004 B.C., according to the pious calculations of Archbishop James Ussher. By the time he got back to England, he found himself a reluctant evolutionist, soon to be damned as a heretic and underminer of the Established Church. This was not his fault. It was the fault of those damned finches.

Recently I too have been looking at finches, so to speak, although mine are mostly statistical and not nearly as pretty as Darwin's. His gave him a hint about the way the earth's creatures came into being; mine, to my terror, seem to hint at the way they may go out. While I am by no means an uncritical admirer of the human race, I have become rather fond of it, and would hate to see it disappear. Finding ways to save it—if we are not too late already—now strikes me as the political issue which takes precedence over all others.

One of the events which led to my conversion was my unexpected appointment to a committee set up by Governor John Dempsey of Connecticut to work out an environmental policy for our state. Now I had been fretting for quite a while about what is happening to our environment—who hasn't?—but until the work of the committee forced me into systematic study, I had not realized that my political convictions were in danger. Then after looking at certain hairy facts for a few months, I found myself convinced that the Democratic party, and most of our institutions of government, and even the American Way of Life are no damned good. In their present forms, at least, they will have to go. Either that, or everybody goes—and sooner than we think.

To begin with, look at the American Way of Life. Its essence is a belief in growth. Every Chamber of Commerce is bent on making its Podunk grow into the Biggest Little City in the country. Wall Street is dedicated to its search for growth stocks, so that Xerox has become the American ideal—superseding George Washington, who expressed *his* faith in growth by speculating in land. Each year Detroit prays for a bigger car market. Businessmen spend their lives in pursuit of an annual increase in sales, assets, and net profits. All housewives—except for a few slatterns without ambition—yearn for bigger houses, bigger cars, and bigger salary checks. The one national goal that everybody agrees on is an ever-growing Gross National Product. Our modern priesthood—the economists who reassure us that our mystic impulses are moral and holy—recently announced that the GNP would reach a trillion dollars early in this decade. I don't really understand what a trillion is, but when I read the news I rejoiced, along with everybody else. Surely that means that we were in sight of ending poverty, for the first time in human history, so that nobody would ever again need to go hungry or live in a slum.

Now I know better. In these past months I have come to understand that a zooming Gross National Product leads not to salvation, but to suicide. So does a continuing growth in population, highway mileage, kilowatts, plane travel, steel tonnage, or anything else you care to name.

The most important lesson of my life—learned shamefully late—was that nonstop growth just isn't possible, for Americans or anybody else. For we live in what I've learned to recognize as a tight ecological system: a smallish planet with a strictly limited supply of everything, including air, water, and places to dump sewage. There is no conceivable way in which it can be made bigger. If Homo sapiens insists on constant growth, within this system's inelastic walls, something has to pop, or smother. Already the United States is an overpopulated country: not so hopelessly overcrowded as Japan or India, of course, but well beyond the limits which would make a good life attainable for everybody. Stewart Udall, former Secretary of Interior and now a practicing ecologist, has estimated that the optimum population for America would be about 100 million, or half of our present numbers. And unless we do something, drastic and fast, we can expect another 100 million within the next thirty years.

So our prime national goal, I am now convinced, should be to reach Zero Growth Rate as soon as possible. Zero growth in people, in GNP, and in our consumption of everything. That is the only hope of attaining a stable ecology: that is, of halting the deterioration of the environment on which our lives depend.

This of course is a profoundly subversive notion. It runs squarely against the grain of both capitalism and the American dream. It is equally subversive of Communism, since the Communists are just as hooked on the idea of perpetual growth as any American businessman. Indeed, when Khrushchev was top man in the Kremlin, he proclaimed that 1970 would be the year in which the Rusians would surpass the United States in output of goods. They didn't make it: a fact for which their future generations may be grateful, because their environment is just as fragile as ours, and as easily damaged by headlong expansion. If you think the Hudson River and Lake Erie are unique examples of pollution, take a look at the Volga and Lake Baikal.

No political party, here or abroad, has yet even considered adopting Zero Growth Rate as the chief plank in its platform. Neither has any politician dared to speak out loud about what "protection of the environment" really means—although practically all of them seem to have realized, all of a sudden, that it is becoming an issue they can't ignore. So far, most of them have tried to handle it with gingerly platitudes, while keeping their eyes tightly closed to the implications of what they say. In his January State of the Union message, for instance, President Nixon made the customary noises about pollution; but he never even mentioned the population explosion, and he specifically denied that there is any "fundamental contradiction between economic growth and the quality of life." He sounded about as convincing as a doctor telling a cancer patient not to worry about the growth of his tumor.

The Democrats are no better. I have not heard any of them demanding a halt to all immigration, or a steeply progressive income tax on each child beyond two, or an annual bounty to every woman between the ages of fifteen and forty-five who gets through the year without becoming pregnant. Neither Ted Sorensen nor any of the other Kennedy henchmen has yet suggested that a politician with a big family is a space-hog and a hypocrite, unworthy of public trust. No Democrat, to my knowledge, has ever endorsed the views of Dr. René Dubos of Rockefeller University, one of the truly wise men of our time. In an editorial in the November 14, 1969, issue of *Science* he predicted that in order to survive, "mankind will have to develop what might be called a steady state . . . a nearly closed system" in which most materials from tin cans to sewage would be "recycled instead of discarded." His conclusion—that a viable future depends on the creation of "social and economic systems different from the ones in which we live today"—apparently is too radical for any politician I know.

Consequently I feel a little lonesome in my newfound political convictions. The only organization which seems to share them is a tiny one, founded only a few months ago: Zero Population Growth, Inc., with headquarters at 367 State Street, Los Altos, California 94022. Yet I have a hunch that I may not be lonesome for long. Among college students a concern with ecology has become, almost overnight, nearly as popular as sideburns. On many campuses it seems to be succeeding civil rights and Vietnam as The Movement. For example, when the University of Oregon announced last January a new course, "Can Man Survive?", it drew six thousand students, the biggest class in the university's history. They had to meet in the basketball court because no classroom would hold them.

Who knows? Maybe we agitators for Zero may yet turn out to be the wave of the future.

At the same time I was losing my faith in the virtues of growth, I began to doubt two other articles of the American credo.

One of them is the belief that technology can fix anything. Like most of us, I had always taken it for granted that any problem could be solved if we just applied enough science, money, and good old American know-how. Is the world's population outrunning its food supply? Well, then, let's put the laboratories to work inventing high-yield strains of rice and wheat, better fertilizers, way to harvest seaweed, hydroponic methods for growing food without soil. If the air is becoming unbreathable, surely the technologists can find ways to clean it up. If our transportation system is a national disgrace, all we have to do is call in the miracle men who built a shuttle service to the moon; certainly they should be able to figure out some way to get a train from New York to New Haven on time.

I was in East Haddam, Connecticut, looking at an atomic power plant, when I began to suspect that technology might not be the answer after all. While I can't go along with the young Luddites who have decided that science is evil and that all inventions since the wheel ought to be destroyed, I am persuaded that technology is a servant of only limited usefulness, and highly unreliable. When it does solve a problem, it often creates two new ones—and their side effects are usually hard to foresee.

One of the things that brought me to East Haddam was curiosity about the automobile. Since the gasoline engine is the main polluter of the air, maybe it should be replaced with some kind of electric motor? That of course would require an immense increase in our production of electric power, in order to recharge ten million batteries every night. Where would it come from? Virtually all waterpower sites already are in use. More coal- and oil-fired power stations don't sound like a good idea, since they too pour smoke into the atmosphere—and coal mining already has ruined countless streams and hundreds of thousands of acres of irreplaceable land. Atomic power, then?

At first glance, the East Haddam plant, which is fairly typical of the new technology, looked encouraging. It is not as painful an eyesore as coal-burning stations, and not a wisp of smoke was in sight. When I began to ask questions, however, the company's public-relations man admitted that there are a few little problems. For one thing, the plant's innards are cooled with water pumped out of the Connecticut River. When it flows back in, this water raises the river's temperature by about twenty degrees, for a considerable distance. Apparently this has not yet done any serious damage to the shad, the only fish kept under careful surveillance; but its effect on other fish and algae, fish eggs, microorganisms, and the general ecology of the river is substantial though still unmeasured.

It would be possible, though expensive, for the company to build cooling towers, where the water would trickle over a series of baffles before returning to the river. In the process it would lose its heat to the atmosphere. But this, in turn, threatens climatic changes, such as banks of artificial fog rolling eastward over Long Island Sound, and serious wastage of water through evaporation from a river system where water already is in precarious supply. Moreover, neither this process nor any other now known would eliminate the slight, but not negligible, radiation which every atomic plant throws off, nor the remote but still omnipresent chance of a nuclear accident which could take thousands of lives. The building of an additional twenty plants along the banks of the Connecticut—which some estimates call for, in order to meet future demand for electricity—would be a clear invitation to an ecological disaster.

In the end I began to susject that there is no harmless way to meet the demands for power of a rising population, with rising living standards—much less for a new herd of millions of electric cars. Every additional kilowatt levies some tax upon the environment, in one form or another. The Fourth Law of Thermodynamics seems to be: "There is no free lunch."

Every time you look at one of the marvels of modern technology, you find a by-product—unintended, unpredictable, and often lethal. Since World War II American agriculture has performed miracles in increasing production. One result was that we were able for years to send a shipload of free wheat every day to India, saving millions from starvation. The by-products were: (1) a steady rise in India's population; (2) the poisoning of our streams and lakes with insecticides and chemical fertilizers; (3) the forced migration of some ten million people from the countryside to city slums, as agriculture became so efficient it no longer needed their labor.

Again, the jet plane is an unquestionable convenience, capable of whisking a New Yorker, say, to either the French Riviera or Southern California in a tenth of the time he could travel by ship or car, and at lower cost. But when he reaches his destination, the passenger finds the beaches coated with oil (intended to fuel planes, if it hadn't spilled) and the air thick with smog (thanks in good part to the jets, each of which spews out as much hydrocarbon as ten thousand automobiles).

Moreover, technology works best on things nobody really needs, such as collecting moon rocks or building supersonic transport planes. Whenever we try to apply it to something serious, it usually falls on its face.

An obvious case in point is the railroads. We already have the technology to build fast, comfortable passenger trains. Such trains are, in fact, already in operation in Japan, Italy, and a few other countries. Experimental samples—the Metroliners and Turbotrains—also are running with spectacular success between Washington and Boston. If we had enough of them to handle commuter and middle-distance traffic throughout the country, we could stop building the highways and airports which disfigure our countryside, reduce the number of automobiles contaminating the air, and solve many problems of urban congestion. But so far we have not been able to apply the relatively simple technology needed to accomplish these aims, because some tough political decisions have to be made before we can unleash the scientists and engineers. We would have to divert to the railroads many of the billions in subsidy which we now lavish on highways and air routes. We would have to get rid of our present railway management—in general, the most incompetent in American industry—and retire the doddering old codgers of the Railway Brotherhoods who make such a mess out of running our trains. This might mean public ownership of a good many rail lines. It certainly would mean all-out war with the unions, the auto and aviation industries, and the highway lobby. It would mean ruthless application of the No Growth principle to roads, cars, and planes, while we make sensible use instead of something we already have: some 20,000 miles of railways.

All this requires political action, of the most radical kind. Until our Great Slob Society is willing to take it, technology is helpless.

My final apostasy from the American Creed was loss of faith in private property. I am now persuaded that there no longer is such a thing as truly private property, at least in land. That was a luxury we could afford only when the continent was sparsely settled. Today the use a man makes of his land cannot be left to his private decision alone, since eventually it is bound to affect everybody else. This conclusion I reached in anguish, since I own a tiny patch of land and value its privacy above anything money can buy.

What radicalized me on this score was the Department of Agriculture and Dr. Ian McHarg. From those dull volumes of statistics which the Department publishes from time to time, I discovered that usable land is fast becoming a scarce resource—and that we are wasting it with an almost criminal lack of foresight. Every year, more than a million acres of farm and forest land is being eaten up by highways, airports, reservoirs, and real-estate developments. The best, too, in most cases, since the rich, flat bottom lands are the most tempting to developers.

Since America is, for the moment, producing a surplus of many crops, this destruction of farmland has not yet caused much public alarm. But some day, not too far off, the rising curve of population and the falling curve of food-growing land inevitably are going to intersect. That is the day when we may begin to understand what hunger means.

Long before that, however, we may be gasping for breath. For green plants are our only source of oxygen. They also are the great purifiers of the atmosphere, since in the process of photosynthesis they absorb carbon dioxide—an assignment which gets harder every day, as our chimneys and exhaust pipes spew out ever-bigger tonnage of carbon gases. This is a function not only of trees and grass, but also of the tiny microorganisms in the sea. Indeed, its phytoplankton produces some 70 per cent of all the oxygen on which life depends. These are delicate little creatures, easily killed by the sewage, chemicals, and oil wastes which already are contaminating every ocean in the world. Nobody knows when the scale will tip: when there are no longer enough green growing things to preserve the finely balanced mixture of gases in the atmosphere, by absorbing carbon dioxide and generating oxygen. All we know is that man is pressing down hard on the lethal end of the scale.

The Survivable Society, if we are able to construct it, will no longer permit a farmer to convert his meadow into a parking lot any time he likes. He will have to understand that his quick profit may, quite literally, take the bread out of his grandchildren's mouths, and the oxygen from their lungs. For the same reasons, housing developments will not be located where they suit the whim of a real-estate speculator or even the convenience of the residents. They will have to go on those few carefully chosen sites where they will do the least damage to the landscape, and to the life-giving greenery which it supports.

This is one of the lessons taught by Ian McHarg in his extraordinary book, *Design With Nature,* recently published by Natural History Press. Alas, its price, $19.95, will keep it from reaching the people who need it most. It ought to be excerpted into a pocket-size volume—entitled, perhaps, "The Thoughts of McHarg"—and distributed free in every school and supermarket.

The current excitement about the environment will not come to much, I am afraid, unless it radicalizes millions of Americans. The conservative ideas put forth by President Nixon—spending a few billion for sewage-treatment plants and abatement of air pollution—will not even begin to create the Survivable Society. That can be brought about only by radical political action—radical enough to change the whole structure of government, the economy, and our national goals.

How the Survivable State will work is something I cannot guess; its design is a job for the coming generation of political scientists. The radical vision can, however, give us a glimpse of what it might look like. It will measure every new law, every dollar of investment by a cardinal yardstick: Will this help us accomplish a zero rate of growth and a stabilized environment? It will be skeptical of technology, including those inventions which purport to help clean up our earthly mess. Accordingly it will have an Anti-Patent Office, which will forbid the use of any technological discovery until the Office figures out fairly precisely what its side effects might be. (If they can't be foreseen, then the invention goes into deep freeze.) The use of land, water, and air will not be left to private decision, since their preservation will be recognized as a public trust. The landlord whose incinerator smokes will be pilloried; the tanker skipper who flushes his oil tanks at sea will be hanged at the nearest yardarm for the capital crime of oxygen destruction. On the other hand, the gardener will stand at the top of the social hierarchy, and the citizen who razes a supermarket and plants its acreage in trees will be proclaimed a Hero of the Republic. I won't live to see the day, of course; but I hope somebody will.

This Hurts Me More Than It Hurts
Mr. Harrington

April, 1957

DEAR MR. HARRINGTON:[1]

Enclosed please find Form 1040 and two quarts of my life blood—or, as your boys would say, the equivalent thereof.

The operation hurt plenty, and has left me weakened, dazed, and peevish. It is my duty, I guess, to give you a report on my enfeebled condition, since you will be expecting to tap my veins again next year—and right now even a vampire bat would not regard me as a hopeful prospect.

What hurt most was the three weeks of torture—most of it unnecessary—which you forced me to go through while I was trying to figure out how much blood money I had to send you. It's only fair to admit that your Tax Forms and Instructions are less appalling than some of those concocted by your predecessors. But they still add up to a cruel and unusual punishment of the kind forbidden by the Constitution. (See Amendment VIII, Line 2, and enter balance here and on Line 1, Schedule D Summary on Page 3.)

They were designed, apparently, by a bureaucratic sadist with a permanent grudge against the English language. The result is a thicket of Spanish-bayonet prose impenetrable to anybody except a Philadelphia lawyer, accompanied by a CPA and two sherpas with machetes. Look, if you can bear it, at those last five paragraphs on the back of Schedule D. I have pored over them, in my braver moments, for the best part of a month—and I still don't know whether I am a fiduciary, a decedent, a carryover, a surviving husband, or a collapsible corporation. My pulse and blood-count point to the latter.

Couldn't you hold out a few dollars, Mr. Harrington, from the $73 billion you expect to collect this year, and hire a writer to translate

1. At the time this was written Russell C. Harrington was head of the Internal Revenue Service.—J.F., 1973

your horrendous documents from fiscalese into English? Nobody fancy. You wouldn't need a Hemingway or a John Ciardi for a job like this—just an honest hack, with calloused finger-pads and a working knowledge of the language. I could name you a dozen—all sound Republicans—who would leap at the chance. You could get them cheap, too, especially during the first two weeks in April, when they need every penny they can scrape up.

Such a translation not only would ease the aches and bafflements of millions of your serfs. It also would eliminate what now amounts to an additional, unfair tax, never authorized by Congress. You wouldn't mind; this extra tax never reaches your vaults anyhow, because it is a levy on time, not income. If I could have worked at my own trade during the hours I wasted trying to decipher your marrow-chilling demands, I could have earned almost enough to pay the quarterly install-ment on my Declaration of Estimated Tax. (See Line 17-b, Page 1, and Instructions, Page 8.)

Don't think I fail to appreciate *your* problems, Mr. H. I do, indeed, and my heart would bleed for you if it had a drop left. I realize that you didn't stud your instructions with all those verbal fishhooks just to lacerate us ordinary, or dopey, taxpayers. What you had in mind, I am sure, were two of your other duties—duties which are both diffi-cult and contradictory:

(1) You have to catch The Sharpies—those specialists in the barely-legal buck, who can afford to retain lawyers by the platoon to figure out new ways to evade your net. This presumably accounts for that poetic passage, full of Empsonian ambiguities, about "Wash Sales" Losses. (Refer Section 1091, Internal Revenue Code of 1954.) And I can see what you were hinting at when you whipped up your General Rule for Annuities (Schedule E and Page 13) with all its clotted syntax and bristling formulas. The warning is clear enough: Better a man should cut his throat than start messing around with those annuities.

(2) At the same time you have to leave a few loopholes, no bigger than an oil pipeline, for the benefit of The Blessed Few. This isn't your fault, of course. Congress ordered you to poke those holes in your net, as a kind of legalized political pay-off. But it must be hard

for you to devise language which will permit a farmer or an oil man to squirm out of paying taxes on a good share of his income, and yet clamp tight on every grocery clerk and filling-station operator.

Embarrassing, too, if the common taxpayers—who don't vote in blocs like the farmer, or chip into campaign funds so generously as the oillionaires—should happen to read it. They might not understand. That, I suppose, is why you offer farmers a special Schedule F and Additional Instructions, which are not distributed to the common herd; and why oil men can send in for Form O, on which they may claim their special 27½ per cent depletion allowance in privacy.

I didn't understand myself until my Congressman explained it to me. He pointed out that when God put oil in the ground He intended it for people of saintly character, like Clint Murchison and H. L. Hunt and Sid Richardson and Glenn McCarthy. It would be un-Christian to expect them to pay taxes on their whole take, as the worldly do. Moreover, their oil wells will run dry some day, and we have to give them an incentive to go out and hunt some more.

A little bitty incentive won't do. Some of The Blessed already are taking in a million dollars a day, and you can't ask a man with that kind of money to get outdoors and hump himself for peanuts. Besides, they have a lot of extra expenses—financing the campaigns of Congressmen who understand about the oil and gas business, for example. Sometimes even their generosity is misinterpreted; look at all the trouble that oil company had with Senator Francis Case.

So anybody who really tries can see why a 27½ per cent rebate for oil people is none too much. Just the same, I think you are prudent not to call their special blessings to the attention of the rabble.

Actually, the only thing wrong with this depletion business is that you don't carry it far enough. Take the case of old Joe Louis. He left a little of his youth on the canvas, along with the blood and sweat, every time he crawled out of the ring. Even Joe, the best of our time, had only so many fights in his system, just as an oil well has only so many gallons of crude.

Yet nobody gave him a depletion allowance—and today I understand that he owes you more than a million dollars which he has no chance of paying off, no matter how hard he works for the rest of his life.

Not even another Emancipation Proclamation could get Joe out of bondage to the Internal Revenue Service. This bothers me sometimes, because I can't help feeling that maybe we owe Joe Louis more than he owes us, on account of that evening when he took Max Schmeling apart. When Schmeling went down, screaming, the Nazi myth of racial superiority collapsed with him. What was that worth to us in the war years that followed?

Or look at the way we treat artists. Until you see a novelist who has just finished a book, Mr. Harrington, you don't know what a depleted man looks like. He is a natural resource too; maybe the most important one we've got. A civilization can get along without oil—Plato's Greece managed fine without a drop of it—but unless it produces poets and sculptors and story-tellers and philosophers, it isn't a civilization at all. So you might think it sound public policy to encourage such people with the same tax incentives you give to the other flowers of our culture, like Messrs. McCarthy and Hunt.

What you do give them, of course, is a fiscal kick in the belly. Many a writer spends most of his life in poverty, while he is working up to one first-rate book. Then, if it sells well, he may earn a fair amount of money in a single year—and you promptly grab the bulk of it. This is a dandy way to drive the temperamental ones to drink, and the practical ones into the dry-goods business; but maybe it isn't the best way to foster The Good Society. Couldn't your Treasury experts find some way to grant artists the same kind of depreciation write-off that you allow for drill presses or vending machines? They depreciate just as fast, and are harder to replace.

Please don't think I am complaining about my own taxes. I'm depleted, all right, but I'm neither a Joe Louis nor an artist, so that last suggestion wouldn't apply to me. It is true that I moaned like a banshee when I finally worked my way to that last dread figure (Line 12, Page 1) but after I had stared at it for a couple of hours I quieted down to a mere whimper.

Because—I keep telling myself—the things I need most can't be bought except with tax money.

This household needs a lot of things. The car is four years old and wheezing a little. That roof gutter on the north side will have to be replaced one of these days, the stairway carpet (I am told) is a sheer disgrace, the upstairs plumbing isn't too sound, and all the women who live here say they are practically in rags. The car probably will hold out for another year, though, and the rags that fill every drawer and closet in the house still look fetching enough to me.

The thing that won't hold out much longer—and isn't a bit fetching, either—is our school. It should have been torn down twenty years ago. Instead it is bulging with kids—35 in some classrooms—and the kind of education they get shouldn't happen to a dog. The teachers get paid less than truck drivers, and one of the best of them has to wait tables at a country club on weekends in order to feed his family. (Our community pays its teachers better than the average, too.) If we don't do something drastic, and fast, the youngsters are going to come out of that school knowing even less arithmetic than I do—and, as you can see from the attached, that would be catastrophic.

Something else I'd like to buy is nicer Sunday afternoons. It would be worth a good deal not to have to spend them in a two-hundred-mile traffic jam, inhaling carbon monoxide, hanging onto my temper with gritted teeth, and listening to my blood pressure climb notch by relentless notch. And before the weekend is over, I would like to get a few hours of serenity in a quiet stretch of woods, uncluttered with billboards and beer cans, or on a clean, uncrowded beach. These are getting to be about the scarcest commodities in America and—like the schools—the only way I can pay for them is with taxes. So maybe the money you take for national parks and highways and pollution control and regional planning are the best dollars I spend. That is why I wrote the enclosed check cheerf—well, not quite cheerfully, but at least with resignation.

The reason I can't be entirely cheerful is that I'm uneasy about what you people are doing with the rest of the money. You all seem happy because Modern Republicanism has at last accepted the basic ideas of the New Deal. But don't you think that sort of thing can be carried a mite too far?

The basic economic idea of the New Deal (so far as there was one) came straight from John Maynard Keynes. He argued that the government ought to spend a lot of money in hard times, to boost the country out of the slump, and that in good times it ought to save money and pay its debts, in order to level off the boom before it reaches a dangerous peak. Whether the whole theory is sound or not, it seems pretty clear that you can't run a sound economy on just half of it—the easy half.

Yet here we are, high on the upper reaches of the biggest, longest boom in history—and Washington still seems to be operating on the depression half of the Keynesian gospel. According to the new budget, the government will fork out sheaves of green money next year at a rate which will make Franklin D. Roosevelt look like a Vermont miser. Even the non-military parts of it are more lavish than anything That Man ever dared suggest.

At the bottom of the depression, for example, FDR was considered a reckless fellow because he spent a billion dollars a year to rescue our bankrupt farmers. Now twenty-five years later, they still seem to need rescuing—but this time it will cost five billion. Harry Truman during his last free-handed year in office didn't come close to that.

Isn't it time, Mr. Harrington, for somebody to ask whether our everhungry farmers are worth all this rescuing? If they can't stand on their own feet, after all these years and billions, when will they? Wouldn't it be better for the country—and for their characters—to let a few million of them learn to be self-supporting in some less chronically busted business?

Another puzzling item is that $210 million you people have budgeted for reclamation projects. Building dams may be a good way to make jobs in a depression—but why build them now, when everbody is worrying about inflation, not unemployment? The Interior Department wants to build these projects, as I get it, to bring more land into cultivation, to raise more crops which we don't need. At the same time the Department of Agriculture—about ten blocks away—wants to spend $984 million for its Soil Bank to take 40 million acres *out* of cultivation.

You can see how this sort of thing unsettles a taxpayer who is a little confused already by all that fine type of Form 1040. He gets to wondering whether somebody couldn't introduce Mr. Seaton to Mr. Benson—perhaps at the golf course—and let them chat about whether they want more crop land or less. Maybe their little talk would save only a few hundred millions—but to a citizen in my wan and shaken state even that looks like something.

Naturally I realize that nobody in Washington can waste much time on such chicken feed when the really big money—$45 billions of it—is being spent on defense. This is a sacred subject, of course, and I hesitate to bring it up. But there are a few points I wish somebody would straighten out for me.

Everybody wants all the defense we need, regardless of cost. No argument about that. But does anybody really know what an adequate defense program *ought* to cost?

Certainly I don't; there is no conceivable way for me—or any other private citizen—to find out. Nor do the newspapers, our traditional watchdogs over public expenditures. In this field, they are barred from looking at the facts, because of the necessity of secrecy. (Although most newspapermen believe that a great many more facts are classified "Secret" than actually need to be; every bureaucrat is under an almost irresistible temptation to use that label to cover up his mistakes and extravagances.)

Congress doesn't know either. No Congressional committee has anything like the time, or the staff, for anything more than a once-over-lightly survey of the military estimates. And I doubt whether the Secretary of Defense and his staff are much better off. They have to spend the bulk of their time on the overwhelming job of day-to-day administration, and coping with Congressional committees. I belong to that small minority which suspects that Charles E. Wilson, for all his indiscretions, may be a pretty good man for the job—but I know that there are corridors in his own Pentagon which he has never penetrated, and dozens of multimillion-dollar installations when he can never visit. His days, too, have only 24 hours.

One thing we do know is that an enormous apparatus has been developed to pressure the Administration and the Congress for ever-growing military appropriations. It includes the highly efficient propaganda machines of each of the armed services. It also includes the industries—a large fraction of the nation's total—which have a stake in defense contracts. It includes every town with an Army post, or air field, or defense plant which it would like to have expanded. (No Chamber of Commerce ever asked to have such an installation closed down; that is why we are still operating some forts originally built as outposts in the Indian wars.)

Pressure for more spending also comes from the powerful veterans' lobby, and from every foreign nation which would like to get a few hundred tanks or planes for free, and from an army of scientists who have discovered that they can finance almost any sort of research—with a lavishness beyond their most grandiose dreams—if only they can find some way to label it "Defense."

(For instance, Werner von Braun, the rocket genius we imported from Germany, undoubtedly has contributed a lot to the development of guided missiles. He is quite frank, however, in admitting that his real interest is in developing a space ship which will someday travel to the moon. This is a harmless ambition, shared by nearly every boy under twelve—but I can't think of any reason why the taxpayers should pay for his toys. Does anybody really know how much of the millions we have handed over to the von Braun team is being spent on practical weapons, and how much on space cadetery?)

Such futuristic boondoggles are probably small change, however, in comparison with the money we are wasting on obsolete weapons. As everybody knows, once the government starts spending money for something it is incredibly hard to turn off the tap. We kept building battleships, for example, a full generation after they were out of date, and the last remnants of the horse cavalry still survive. So it is hard not to wonder whether we are now building tanks which would have been very useful in World War II, or planes which already have been made obsolescent by the new missiles.

This all adds up to one question, which must be bothering a lot of taxpayers just as much as it bothers me: Has the budget got out of control?

We can see the pressures—almost irresistible pressures—which have built up for more spending. Nowhere can we see any organized pressure for economy. Moreover, the governmental machinery for controlling the purse strings was designed for an earlier and simpler era. Each of its parts—the Congressional committees, the Budget Bureau, and the rest—are pitifully vulnerable to the spending pressures. They have neither the independence nor the manpower to look at each demand with a searching, icy eye.

Is there anybody in Washington, then, besides George Humphrey, who really cares? His piercing screams of frustration are the most frightening thing of all. For if George Humphrey can't get the budget under control, who can?

Maybe you know the answers, Mr. Harrington, and if you do I sure wish you would enclose them on a little slip of paper when you send me your sheaf of Forms and Instructions next spring. It would be a lot easier to cope with this annual ordeal if I didn't get that sinking, no-bottom feeling when I write out the check. (Line 18, Page 1.)

Why Nobody Can't Write Good

January, 1964

SHE had just been graduated from one of the more expensive women's colleges and now she was looking for a job in publishing. Her grades were good. She had majored in English, with special attention to eighteenth-century poetry; and she confessed, flapping her eyelashes modestly, that she had written a little verse of her own. Her speech was civilized, her clothes were in unobtrusive good taste, her nails were clean and her appearance was presentable—indeed, quite fetching.

But when she took the routine employment test it was at once apparent that she couldn't spell, construct a grammatical sentence, or write a paragraph of coherent prose. Moreover, she was astonished that anybody expected her to do these things. She assumed that we had some drudges in a back room who took care of such grubby details. What she wanted, she explained, was "to do something creative."

The suggestion I offered was meant to be helpful, and I'm pretty sure that I put it in a fatherly—well, anyhow an avuncular—tone without the faintest hint of a leer; but she didn't take it well. In fact, she seemed to regard me as both flippant and impertinent.

Her case is by no means unusual. On the contrary, every businessman knows that it is a rare day when he can hire either a woman or a man who is capable of writing reasonably competent English. It is easier, one executive recently told me, to find people trained to write the mathematical binary language of computers.

Such complaints are becoming frequent enough to suggest that the almost-vanished art of writing has become an expensive problem for American business. The dean of the Harvard Business School, for example, reports that "an incredible number of college graduates who apply for admission can't write a passable sentence"—and he is supposed to get the cream of the crop. Langley Carleton Keyes, the head of a Boston advertising agency, has deplored the "enormous wasteful-

231

ness" which results from "the great amount of dull, difficult, obscure, hackneyed, wordy writing in business." Several of the better law schools have started intensive programs in writing because—as Thomas M. Cooley, dean of the University of Pittsburgh law school, put it—"the graduates of our colleges, including the best ones, cannot write the English language," much less draft a cogent brief. The State Department has just launched a course in elementary composition for its officers, who frequently cannot comprehend one another's memoranda. And Washington University in St. Louis is starting a special project, at the cost of $135,000 a year, to translate the incomprehensible jargon of social scientists into English.

Most alarming of all is the discovery that a lot of teachers can't write either. Dr. Harold Martin, of the College Entrance Examination Board's Commission on English, found that a third of the English teachers in secondary schools were unfit to teach their subject.

Which should surprise nobody. For we have people who make it their business to teach binary computer language, or French or Russian or Swahili. But today nobody—with a few honorable exceptions, to be noted in a moment—seems to feel that it is really his job to teach the writing of English.

Listen to Professor Paul Roberts, the author of several well-known English texts:

"Everybody who is not an English teacher," he says, "seems to think that English teachers have had special training in English composition and in how to teach it. We have not had. We have been trained in English and American literature, in Old English philology and structural linguistics. Nobody has been trained in composition. . . ."

If you spend a little time around the English department of any big university, you will discover that this is an understatement. The satraps in charge of graduate work there have no interest in training people to teach children to write. What they are interested in is producing Ph.D.s—and producing them according to a formula handed down almost unchanged from the medieval universities of the Old World. They are, moreover, afflicted by feelings of inferiority, because they see most of the big money and prestige flowing to their colleagues in the science departments. Hence they try their best to imitate the scientists, in an effort to prove that their scholars are just as scholarly—indeed, just as scientific—as anybody across the road in the physics lab. Above all, they insist that every Ph.D. candidate must make some "original contribution to knowledge."

As an academic outsider you may think this an unreasonable demand. For the English scholar is not free to explore the limitless reaches of the physical universe in search of his "original contribution." He is limited to the finite body of English and American literature. This means he must write yet another dissertation on James or Melville or some other famous chestnut; or he must dig up some obscure eighteenth-century poet who hasn't already been explored to tatters. Such poets are getting mighty scarce—and when found, it is obvious that they are obscure for the best of reasons. So by the time the poor candidate has spent three years poring over his subject's hamstrung syntax and beclouded rhetoric, any natural feeling he may have had for the English language probably has been smothered for good.

If not, in most universities his preceptors will soon take care of that. They will see to it that his dissertation is not written in plain, straightforward English—that would be distressingly unscholarly—but in the peculiar argot known as Pedagese or Academic Mandarin. (For representative samples, see the bound doctoral typescripts moldering in the stacks of any university library, or any issue of *Publications of the Modern Language Association.*) In due course, then, the fledgling scholar is awarded a velvet hood to wear in academic processions and a parchment license to teach English.

His first job almost certainly will be the teaching of Freshman Composition in some college: a task for which, as Professor Roberts pointed out, he is totally unequipped. He will loathe it, for this reason and because the pay is poor and the prestige worse; he is, in fact, considered the low man on the academic totem pole. Moreover, he probably will conclude that his labors are hopeless, because his classes are far too large to teach writing in the only way it can be taught: that is, by painstakingly analyzing every sentence of an assigned paper with each student individually, pointing out his mistakes and making him do it over—and over and over—until he gets it right. Even if he had the time and stamina, his pupils would rebel against such methods; for the one thing they learned about English in high school is that it is unimportant.

Oh, maybe an occasional fussy English teacher had carried on about it—but the high-school math and history and social-studies teachers couldn't have cared less. They seldom assigned written papers or essay-type examinations, since their classes (the old problem) were too big, and it is easier to grade true-and-false "objective" tests. In any case, they didn't bother about errors in spelling and grammar; their attitude, implicit if not openly expressed, was: "Just get down the facts and don't worry about the language." Most of them, indeed, were so insecure about their own English that they would have flinched from correcting a mistake in rhetoric, even if they had considered that part of their duties.

This was not always true. To quote Professor Roberts again: "In the last hundred years there has been a steady decline in the use of writing in the general educational process. It used to be that no one had to teach composition because everybody taught it. The student was writing all the time, not only in his literature course but also in history, in economics, even in science and mathematics. It was every teacher's responsibility, and not just the English teacher's, to keep the student up to a respectable standard and to show him how to improve his prose."

And he concludes gloomily that "very likely we can never go back to such a system, but this is no argument for having special courses in writing taught by departments of English"—because that wouldn't help either. "Students write badly. They take courses in English composition and they still write badly. And nothing has been achieved except the ruin of departments of English."

With his elders in such despair, who can blame the young instructor with his shiny new Ph.D. if he scuttles away from Freshman Composition as fast as he can manage it, and begins to teach courses in Chaucer or Milton's Use of Imagery—which is, after all, what he has been trained for?

Meanwhile, the university turns out another generation of illiterates, some of them with Ph.D.s. And the graduate schools of law and business, in desperation, launch programs in elementary composition, to give their students what they failed to acquire during the previous sixteen years—because it was nobody's business to teach them.

At this point the taxpayer may begin to wonder whether we really need all those English Ph.D.s., educated at such vast expenditure of money and talent. Wouldn't it be more sensible to train a few hundred thousand people specifically for the teaching of English composition? Maybe—O heretical thought—it isn't really necessary to make a man get a Ph.D. before permitting him to teach a writing class? Maybe a different kind of union card would be more practical?

If the taxpayer is also a businessman, plagued by illiterate employees (and his own inability to write a lucid memorandum) he may begin to suspect that our whole school system isn't worth the billions we pour into it, so long as it turns out such defective products. He is not likely, however, to devote much energy to seeing whether the school system might be improved. Usually he will just grumble in private, curse the eggheads who run the schools, and vote against the next school bond issue—as the citizens of my own community did just a few weeks ago.

Fortunately not everyone has abandoned hope. In both high schools and colleges a small band of stubborn teachers still believes that it is not only possible but essential to teach kids to write. They are convinced that American society will not permit itself to drown in the rising tide of incoherence . . . that sooner or later it will realize that no nation can survive a breakdown in communications (remember the Tower of Babel?) . . . and that it will then insist on the changes, however painful and expensive, necessary to rebuild a common skill in the use of language. After all, language is the most valuable tool *Homo sapiens* ever invented, and he is not likely to abandon it for good.[1]

When that day comes, they hope to be ready with a whole kit of new ideas for the teaching of English. The intellectual ferment now going on among them may well be the liveliest anywhere in the field of education. (Or so at least it seems to me, after spending a good

---

1. Its value, in the crudest dollars-and-cents terms, is nicely illustrated by Frederic G. Donner, chairman of the board of General Motors, the world's biggest manufacturing firm. He is of course one of the world's best-paid executives. While at the University of Michigan he got straight A's (except for one B in history) and graduated with a Phi Beta Kappa key. One of his old professors remembers that Donner "had a great skill in writing and an excellent vocabulary. From that I assumed he could think clearly."

deal of time recently with English teachers in classrooms and at their professional meetings.) The result may be an upheaval in the teaching of English comparable to the recent revolution in the teaching of mathematics and science.

The structural linguists, for example, are developing new kinds of grammar which ought to be more logical, and therefore easier to teach, than the traditional variety. (So far, at least three different approaches have emerged, and it is not yet clear which may eventually prove the most useful.) The College Entrance Examination Board already has embarked on an ambitious program for retraining teachers, working out new curricula, and making TV films to show how outstanding teachers go about their jobs. The teachers' professional associations—there is a surprising number of them—are getting together in conferences all over the place to define what they call "the basic issues" in the teaching of English, and to figure out new ways to rejuvenate their trade.

What is likely to come of all this? Here are a few guesses, based on scores of reports, speeches, and bull sessions from which I've tried to sieve some of the ideas now boiling up among the professionals:

1. We are going to have to attract a lot more—and a lot better—people into the business of teaching English. Trained English teachers are already in short supply, and because of low pay and discouraging working conditions they are getting scarcer.

2. A cataclysmic shake-up is coming both in university English departments and in teachers' colleges. It will be resisted fiercely, because professors with a vested interest in their ancient academic habits are about the world's most deeply entrenched conservatives. But it will come. One result may be a new degree—perhaps labeled Ph.M., for Master of Philosophy—which will be awarded to people specifically trained for teaching language skills and who are not forced to waste years in the brain-numbing irrelevancies of the present English Ph.D. programs.

3. The taxpayer will have to shell out a lot more money for the teaching of English. For, done right, it is a hideously expensive undertaking. It requires higher salaries to attract enough good people. It demands smaller classes. It calls for a big investment in the colleges, in order to train the regiments of additional teachers needed in our

grade and high schools. (This may, of course, mean that the taxpayer will decide to spend less money on scholastic frills, such as driver education, home economics, vocational agriculture, and football.)

4. Teachers in other subjects—from social studies to chemistry—will have to assume once more some responsibility for making their students toe the mark in their use of language. The creeping slobbism which is endemic in many schools cannot be checked so long as a youngster is permitted to get by with sloppy writing in every classroom except one.

This too will be bitterly resisted. When Dr. Albert R. Kitzhaber of the University of Oregon recently suggested it in an influential book, *Themes, Theories, and Therapy: the Teaching of Writing in College* (McGraw-Hill), he stirred up an astonishing uproar among the pedagogues in other fields. The tone of their comments is indicated by a burlesque review of his book which appeared in the *Newsletter* of the Institute of Early American Culture and History of Williamsburg, under the title "Why Nobody Can't Write Good." Supposedly written by a history teacher, it read in part:

"It is unbelievably incredible for someone to write that other professors than in English courses should teach students, which is not their job to do. In American History, to show a specific example, the professors in actuality should stick to the subject and the facts about it, and they should not meddle in someone else's course. In fact, English hasn't got anything to do with History, which proves that his whole book is irrelevant."[2]

But Kitzhaber will find some allies, too, in the other departments. Already many teachers are coming to realize that sense and style can't really be separated—that a student who can't write clearly can't think clearly. For the physical act of putting words on paper is an essential part of the thought process. Until you put a thought in words—sharply and precisely—it isn't a thought at all; it is just a kind of fog rolling around inside the skull.

Consequently, I think it likely that more and more schools will reduce their dependence on true-and-false tests, and will require an

---

2. I *think* the *Newsletter* was kidding, but quite possibly the review is genuine. I know a number of academic historians who write just like that.

increasing amount of written work in all classes, as the better prep and high schools have been doing all along. It is conceivable that the different departments may someday get together in the planning of assignments. Then, instead of having to write both an English theme and a history paper over the weekend, Johnny will have only one task: a paper on, say, The Causes of the American Revolution—for which he will be responsible to his teachers both in history and in English. Instead of racing to slap something down any old how, he will be expected to spend twice as much time in organizing his facts, thoughts, and language. And if either teacher is dissatisfied, he can insist that Johnny do the job over again. Thus Johnny will get the idea, eventually, that anything worth putting on paper is worth the very best writing he can possibly achieve.

5. This may sound utopian, but I have hopes that the colleges will someday refuse to admit any student who cannot read and write. This would be a truly revolutionary step. For most colleges, it would immediately cut enrollments by at least half (thus solving the overcrowding problem). It would force the high schools to teach English properly—and the taxpayers to put up the money for it, if they want their little darlings to get into college. It would eliminate all those dreary courses in remedial English for undergraduates—and for students in law, business, and other postgraduate schools. It would help a lot to reduce delinquency, since an inadequate grasp of reading and writing is one of the commonest causes for school dropouts. It would cut unemployment and relief costs, since until a man has acquired the basic skill in using his native tongue he has little chance to learn the other skills necessary to earn a living.

And it would give some assurance that when a college graduate walks into an office in search of a job, he probably has at least the minimum qualifications necessary to perform it.

I should live so long.

How to Rescue America from Plumbers, Carpenters, and People Like That

A somewhat Irish proposal for wiping out slums,
emptying the prisons, opening up new jobs for Negroes,
saving the taxpayers' money, decreasing crime, and
fixing the building-trades unions, all at one magnificent stroke.

January, 1967

JOSEPH F. X. Muldoon is a retired plumbing contractor, an unforgiving man, a connoisseur of Irish whiskey, and (he says) a freethinker. When he called me a few nights ago to help him appraise a new bottle, just imported from some unheard-of distillery in Limerick, I suspected that he was having another Free Thought. Old Joe's notions flow best in the presence of both a shot glass and an audience; and when he can't find a more sympathetic listener, he sometimes drafts me.

Before the bottle was a third empty, I had to tell Joe, with the candor of an old friend, that this time his ideas were not only ridiculous but dangerous. Did he want to get his teeth kicked in?

"They are false teeth anyway," he said, "and at my age I am willing to risk martyrdom for the good of mankind, and to get even with my old enemies in the plumbers' union. If somebody doesn't stop those pirates—and their brother buccaneers in the carpenters', painters', bricklayers', and electrical workers' trades—I'm telling you that New York is doomed.

"Why are the slums spreading like mildew in a damp basement? Because nobody, not even City Hall, can afford to fix up the old tenements, much less build the fifty thousand new houses we need every year.

"Why are building costs so outrageous? Because the construction trades are holding a cutlass at the public's throat, that's why. Not that I'm against honest unions—I used to be a union man myself—but these crafts, in this city, have turned their unions into something very like a conspiracy against society.

"For example, as of this night all of the plumbers in Manhattan have been on strike for nearly four months. Not over any real grievance, mind you, but because a power struggle is going on inside Local No. 2 between a couple of union bosses, Jack Cohen and Mike Pappalardo. I'll bet you a Stillson wrench to a lead pipe that they will stay out until after the next union election.

"And why shouldn't they? The union members aren't suffering. They are all working, every man jack of them, in New Jersey and Westchester and Long Island. Plumbers are so scarce, you see, that they can take their pick of jobs outside of New York, even while they are keeping the city's construction industry closed down tighter than a soldered joint.

"Who does suffer? Thousands of sick people, because the city can't open up five new hospitals which are practically finished except for the plumbing. Kids in four school districts where new buildings couldn't be completed in time for the September term. All those families who couldn't get into their new apartments last October first—New York's traditional moving day—on account of no running water.. A lot of them already had given up their old leases, and where are they now? Going bankrupt in some hotel, or doubled up with begrudging relatives, that's where. Ah, there will be many a broken home before this strike is over."

While Joe was refilling his glass, I hinted delicately that maybe he could be a little biased, as a hangover from his old wars with the plumbers' union. After all, didn't a poor pipe bender have a right to try for more money and better working conditions, just like anybody else?

For an elderly gentleman with high blood pressure and a short-fused temper, that kind of question was definitely unhealthy. He choked and shook his wattles for a good three minutes before he got his voice back.

"What do you mean, more money! They already get an arm and a leg every time they fit a faucet. For a six-hour day their pay comes to $7.29 an hour, including fringe benefits, *plus* double for overtime.

It's a rare plumber who doesn't make at least $300 a week. And his working conditions, if you can call it work, would make a nurse or schoolteacher shriek with envy. There he sits, with a helper to wipe his brow and light his pipe and pick up his tools, while he moves like the tide in Bantry Bay, barely fast enough to be discerned by the human eye."[1]

If the construction industry offers so good a deal, I asked, how come it is so short of labor? Why don't a couple of million unemployed people swarm into those sweet $300-a-week jobs?

"Because the unions won't let them, you idiot," Joe said. "If you aren't a union member you can't work—and most locals accept only a few new apprentices each year. And those few, as it happens, are nearly always the sons or nephews of old members. An unemployed Negro has as much chance of joining one of their locals as the New York Yacht Club. Didn't you know that the building-trades unions are about the most exclusive and segregated institutions you can find, short of the Ku Klux Klan and the John Birch Society?

"They don't see it that way, of course. They feel they have a God-given right to monopolize these particular jobs, and to pass them along in their families." Joe reached over to his desk and began to fumble through a drawer full of old letters, family photographs, and newspaper clippings. Finally he found the clipping he wanted.

"Here," he said, "is a letter printed in the *New York Times* of August 3, 1963. I regard it as a very fair statement of the building mechanic's creed."

It read:

Some men leave their sons money, some large investments, some business connections, and some a profession. I have none of these to bequeath to my

---

1. Other building tradesmen in the New York area, I found out later, get roughly comparable pay. Carpenters, for instance, have a contract calling for $6.93 per hour, including fringe benefits. Electrical workers get $7.70 per hour—and in their case the fringes include a provision that the employer pays the employee's share of social-security taxes, to boot. For bricklayers, the base wage plus fringe benefits comes to $7.74 an hour—about three times the general industrial wage. As the *New York Times* has pointed out, the building-trades unions never "pay any attention to the guidelines or to any other anti-inflation program. Their motto always has been to grab everything they could get. . . ."

sons. I have only one worthwhile thing to give: my trade. I hope to follow a centuries-old tradition and sponsor my sons for an apprenticeship.

For this simple father's wish it is said that I discriminate against Negroes. Don't all of us discriminate? Which of us when it comes to a choice will not choose a son over all others?

I believe that an apprenticeship in my union is no more a public trust, to be shared by all, than a millionaire's money is a public trust. Why should the government, be it local, state, or federal, have any more right to decide how I dispose of my heritage than it does how the corner grocer disposes of his?

(Signed) Charles Kelly
Wantagh, Long Island

"It is true," Joe said, "that in the last few years the old monopoly has loosened up a little. In the old days, if a contractor tried to hire a Negro or Puerto Rican, his whole crew would walk off the job in a flash. Now a few of the locals—under pressure from the government and the National Association for the Advancement of Colored People—are grudgingly accepting an occasional Negro apprentice. But there is still no sign that they will ever be willing to throw the job market wide open.

"My plan would do exactly that.

"We'll start with the prisons," he said. "Probably a majority of the poor devils inside them are there simply because they couldn't earn an honest living outside. Especially the Negroes. They make up a disproportionate share of the prison population, and no wonder. When a youngster grows up in a slum, with a third-rate education, a broken home, or maybe a father out of work, and with no chance to get an apprentice's training, how can he learn to hold down a skilled job? I don't blame him—much—if he takes to mugging or dope peddling, out of desperation or sheer boredom.

"In theory, at least, most penitentiaries try to teach their inmates some useful skills. Traditionally, convicts have been put to work making something that the state needs—license plates, for example, or prison uniforms. But since these crafts aren't much use to a man once he has been turned loose, naturally he is likely to drift back into crime.

"Recently, however, some prison industries have begun to branch out into more practical lines of training. In Texas, convicts can learn to be dental technicians by making false teeth for state-hospital patients. Or they can retread tires for the state's automobiles, roast and blend coffee, and make soap for the state institutions. As a result, Texas is saving about $2 million a year, and at the same time giving at least some of its criminals a chance to earn an honest living in the future. California goes even further. Its convicts make furniture and stationery for state offices, and toys for children in orphanages. Iowa gets most of its official typewriters repaired by prison labor. And a couple of federal penitentiaries are training their inmates to become computer key-punch operators. All of which is a good thing—but it doesn't go far enough.

"What I propose is that we teach convicts all the construction trades, and put them to work on public building projects. The plan might work something like this:

"As soon as a prisoner arrives at, say, Sing Sing, he would get a thorough screening by the resident psychiatrists. If he seems to be a really hard case—an irredeemable criminal type—he would be locked up in the old-fashioned way. But if he looks like a reasonably hopeful candidate for rehabilitation, he would be offered basic training in the building trade of his choice. The course would last just as long as he needs to acquire the fundamental skills. A fast learner might pick up the essentials of carpentry in four months. A slower man who enrolls in an electrical-installation course might need a couple of years.

"His training would be quite different from that which an apprentice ordinarily gets on the outside. As part of their featherbedding policy, the unions have of course stubbornly opposed the introduction of modern methods—whether paint-spray guns, power saws, or prefabricated components. The resulting inefficiency has forced up construction costs even more than the outrageous wage scales. In contrast, our Prisoners' Rehabilitation Program would use only the latest tools, the most efficient methods. Consequently, our graduates would have a considerable advantage when they start looking for a job on the outside—enough, maybe, to offset the prejudice of some employers against hiring convicts.

"As soon as our convict is able to pass a qualifying test, he could become a special kind of trusty. He would be assigned to a team of construction workers which would leave Sing Sing, under minimal guard, to work an eight-hour shift on a slum-clearance or urban-renewal project. If he behaves himself, working conscientiously and not trying to escape, he can look forward to an early parole. Otherwise, back he goes to the lockup. Moreover, while working he would get the statutory minimum wage of $1.50 an hour, to be paid into a savings account so that he would have a modest nest egg when he is finally released. Under those terms, I don't think many would try to run away."

"Your scheme will never work," I said. "For one thing, the Teamsters Union would refuse to deliver building materials to any project employing prison labor . . ."

"In that case," he interrupted, "we would deliver it by state truck, protected by an armed guard. Besides, if the government ever succeeds in putting Jimmy Hoffa behind bars, as it may any day now, he might take a more kindly attitude toward his fellow inmates."[2]

"Even so," I said, "the notion is politically impossible. Because no governor or state legislator is going to risk a fight with the building-trades unions."

"Are you sure?" Joe said. "Take a careful look at all the good things the Muldoon Plan would accomplish—every one of them packed with political vitamins. First of all, we could build a lot of public housing at a fraction of the present cost. The slum dwellers and the taxpayers won't forget that at election time. Then we would be training tens of thousands of Negroes to fill decent and much-needed jobs. That ought to fetch the support of the civil-rights organizations.

"Best of all, the Plan would break the monopoly of the building-trades unions, and most of their political power along with it. As soon as a few thousand skilled, but nonunion, building mechanics are available, the contractors—and the city government—will no longer have to knuckle under to every piratical demand the unions make. What if the unions do so strike? The contractor can go right ahead with the job, using our Sing Sing graduates—and he can get rid of all those ridiculous featherbedding work rules at the same time.

"But if the unions are half-smart, outright strikebreaking will seldom

---

2. Hoffa did go to prison not many months after these lines were written; and he did emerge, in due course, as a vocal advocate of penal reform—though not, alas, of the Muldoon Plan.—J.F., 1973

be necessary. They wouldn't want to see the labor market flooded with a lot of qualified but nonunion workers. Therefore the Muldoon Plan will, I hope, force them to abandon their closed-shop policy, and replace it with the union shop, already common in a good many other industries. That is, an employer could hire anybody he likes—with the understanding that the new man will join the union as soon as he goes on the payroll. That would put a stop to the unions' segregationist and monopolistic practices, and end the artificial shortage of labor in the building trades. But it would still preserve all the legitimate functions of a labor organization.

"In any case," Joe went on, "the old political maxim that it is suicide to tangle with a union simply doesn't hold true any longer. Not when the union is unpopular with the public. Remember that Bobby Kennedy first became a national political figure because of his investigation of the Teamsters Union and his crusade to put Hoffa in jail.

"Now the building-trades unions are about as unpopular as a drunk at a wedding. Did you ever know a householder who hasn't been gypped, at one time or another, by some plumber or painter or electrical-repair man? They are disliked even within the labor movement because they have been feuding with the industrial unions ever since the AFL-CIO was founded. And, as with the Teamsters' Union, many of their locals are notoriously corrupt.

"I could cite you dozens of cases. At least one local on Long Island is controlled by the Mafia. Another has had three of its officers indicted for conspiring with plumbing contractors to cheat the city out of $778,000 on twenty-three school-construction jobs. Just this fall an official of the Brotherhood of Painters, Decorators, and Paperhangers was indicted for taking $840,000 in bribes over an eight-year period. That is downright greedy, even in an industry where it is commonplace for union bosses to shake down the employers, under threat of strikes. And out in San Francisco a couple of honest officials of a painters' local were murdered, when they began to ask embarrassing questions about the way its welfare funds were handled.

"This sort of thing has become so commonplace that a politician could become a hero, I tell you, if he started a real campaign to clean up the building-trades unions. And the only way that can be done is by breaking their monopoly control of the job market. Why it might turn out to be the grandest political opportunity since Tom Dewey took on Murder, Inc."

At this point I informed Joe that I had absorbed all the oratory and whiskey that I could manage for one night. He has the Irish gift for eloquence and for magnificent dreams, and in another half-hour I might have begun to take him seriously.

As a matter of fact, when I think back to that conversation I sometimes wonder whether the Muldoon Plan is really as impractical as it sounded. After all, De Valera looked pretty visionary, too, on that spring morning in 1916 when he marched off to the Irish rebellion. . . .

Women's Lib and the Caperton Girls

February, 1972

U N T I L she died a few months ago at the age of eighty-seven, my mother held strong opinions on every conceivable subject except one. Women's Lib baffled her. She never could figure out what the movement was all about, and my efforts to explain it seemed merely to increase her exasperation.

"Liberation from what?" she would ask.

"Well, men, I guess."

"Fiddlesticks!"

She had never felt oppressed for a moment in her life, and the idea that other women might rear and whinney against male domination was simply beyond her grasp. Her attitude toward men was one of wary affection, like that of a lion tamer toward her performing cats. If she didn't watch them carefully they might try to get out of hand, but it was then her duty to put them, firmly and kindly, back into their places; and she never had the faintest doubt that she could do it. If she got clawed now and then, well, that was just the nature of the beasts, and she didn't resent them for it.

All the current talk about careers for women puzzled her too, because she had no trouble starting her own career at the age of seventeen. It was then about the best job available in the Texas Panhandle, for men or women—easier and less dangerous than punching cattle, which is what all her brothers and boyfriends did, and better paid to boot. A good cowhand at that time got $30 a month and found. As teacher of a one-room school, she got $35. The work also carried more prestige than anything except landowning; and she set out at the same time to become a landowner.

She had a dozen pupils of both sexes, ranging from six years old to seventeen. The biggest was a boy her own age and nearly twice as heavy, who let it be known at 8:05 A.M. on the first morning of school that he had no mind to take orders from any girl, much less

247

little Georgie Caperton whom he had known practically all his life. She picked up a chunk of firewood from the box beside the Franklin stove and knocked him down. When he got up spluttering she knocked him down again. By 8:10 A.M. there was no doubt about who was foreman in that classroom, and she told me that she never again had any serious disciplinary problems—nothing that she couldn't handle with a cottonwood switch.

Didn't the children ever complain to their parents about such peda-gogical methods?

"Of course not," she said. "They knew that if they did they would get another switching at home."

The Wheeler County school board offered her the job because she was better educated than most people thereabouts. For two years she had attended Goodnight College—more of a high school, really, than a college, but at that time the only place in north Texas offering any learning above grade school. It was a private undertaking, started in 1898 by Colonel Charles Goodnight, Indian fighter and pioneer cattle-man, near his ranch at the little settlement of Clarendon. He had never had any formal education after he was nine years old, but he felt that the North Plains needed some culture and that it was his clear responsibility to provide it. After all, he had settled the country, building the first house in the Panhandle—a one-room sod hut, rem-nants of which are still standing in Palo Duro canyon—and for decades had led the community in everything from suppressing rustlers to im-proving the breed of livestock. So when he decided that the next neces-sary step toward a civilization was a college, he took $30,000 out of his own bank account to put up a building and import a faculty, including one Ph.D. from Heidelberg.

The college survived for only a decade or so, because there wasn't enough money in the community to support it. The students paid what tuition they could, often in beef and hides, and the boys—who usually commuted on horseback—tended a small garden and dairy herd on the back lot. The girls lived in and helped pay their way by doing the housekeeping. On at least one occasion the whole student body, together with the faculty and the Goodnight ranch hands, had to turn out with wet brooms and gunnysacks to fight a prairie fire that threatened to wipe the place out. To hear my mother tell it, the college operated much like a modern commune. Complete equality of the sexes, in both rights and responsibilities, was taken for granted—although sexual permissiveness was of course unheard of, like drugs and liquor on campus. (Colonel Goodnight would never tolerate whiskey even in his bunkhouses and line camps, on the theory that any man who drank was liable to mistreat his horses.) Undergraduates never dreamed of rebelling against the Establishment, because there wasn't any establishment as far as the eye could reach, barring a windmill and a barbed-wire fence. Their role was to learn to found some kind of establishment in an all-but-empty country.

About her studies my mother was never very specific, although to the end of her life she remembered a little Spanish, Shakespeare, and music. She also persuaded the school board that she was qualified to teach the only subjects required: reading, writing, arithmetic, and history. Politics also may have had something to do with her appointment. Her father had served as a Confederate cavalryman under General Joe Wheeler, as had a good number of other post–Civil War migrants to the Panhandle: hence the christening of Wheeler County. Fellow veterans weren't about to let the Caperton family starve, if a teaching job for one of its girls would help—and hunger, though not actual starvation, was no stranger in those parts. The staple diet for most families was beef, beans, and cornbread, with maybe an orange for each of the kids at Christmas. And for the first few years after moving west from Alabama, the whole Caperton family—a big one—lived in a two-room soddie. To build it, they simply dug a rectangular hole in the ground about three feet deep and maybe twenty-by-twelve feet in area; above the ground they built up sod walls for another four feet and roofed it over with cedar posts, brush, and a layer of sod. In a country without timber, aside from a little cedar and cottonwood in the canyons, such architecture was the only choice. It served well enough: warm in winter, cool in summer, and since the door—the only opening—faced east, it kept out the ceaseless wind. Eventually, when the family got established in the cattle business in a small way, they managed to haul in enough lumber from the nearest railroad depot to build a proper house. Today it would be considered substandard, but my mother remembered it as luxurious; for one thing, it had a wooden floor.

So did her own house, or hut, when she embarked on her career as a landowner, soon after she started teaching school. Under the Homestead Law anybody could file a claim on 160 acres of unoccupied government land. To "prove up the claim," you had to live there for at least a year, build a house, and produce some kind of crop. The law was originally designed for the Middle West, where a farm family could make a reasonable living off 160 acres. In north Texas, however, it made little sense, because only about twenty inches of rain fell a year. The only feasible crop, therefore, was the native grama and bunch grasses—and a mere 160 acres of such pasture didn't begin to make a ranch big enough to support a family.

So it was customary for every child in a family to file a claim as soon as he or she was old enough, with the idea of adding the new acreage to the original family homestead. Additional land could usually be purchased for about twenty cents an acre from bachelor cowboys or railroad grants, until enough was accumulated for a decent-sized ranch—normally a minimum of two or three sections, each measuring a square mile, or 640 acres. A big ranch, such as Colonel Goodnight's or the XIT, might run well over a million acres.

My mother filed her claim on a piece of land nearly half a day's ride from the home place, and her father and brothers put up the one-room shack where she was to live out the required year. Her school was only a couple of miles away, and a few other homesteaders' shanties were within equally easy range, so she never felt too lonesome. Besides, any cowboy whose work brought him somewhere near was sure to drop by for a chat and a cup of coffee; pretty girls were scarce, and none of the five Caperton sisters ever lacked company for long. She also had the companionship, such as it was, of Little Blue, an elderly retired cow pony on whom she depended for transport.

Didn't a teenaged girl ever get scared under such circumstances?

"Yes," she said. "I got real scared once. I was about halfway to school one morning when a hailstorm broke. Some of the hailstones were nearly as big as baseballs, and if one of them hit me, I was pretty sure it would crack my skull. So I took the saddle off Little Blue, held it over my head, and ran the rest of the way to the schoolhouse."

What happened to the horse, I asked.

"Oh, he got a few lumps, but the hailstones didn't really hurt him. His old head was too thick."

She was never sentimental about horses, and to my knowledge she never got aboard one except when necessary. Riding as a sport never occurred to her, for the same reason that truck drivers don't go plea-sure-driving on Sunday mornings.

Incidentally, I suspect that her memory exaggerated the size of those hailstones. In that same country, however, I have seen them as big as golf balls, pelting down with enough force to dent car tops and knock the shingles off houses, so her fright wasn't just a case of girlish hysteria.

The U.S. Land Commission Office in Texhoma, where she had to file her homestead claim, was then being run on a part-time basis by a young man who also dabbled in politics and put out the weekly newspaper. Like other land commissioners throughout the West, he realized that the Homestead Law couldn't be applied too literally in the semi-desert climate of the Great Plains. Consequently he wasn't bigoted in his inquiries into how much farming a homesteader actually did, or even whether an applicant was of legal age. His duties did require him, however, to check on every claim from time to time to see whether the claimant was in fact living there. Perhaps he inspected Miss Georgie Caperton's homestead more often than was strictly necessary.

She didn't mind. As she remembered it a quarter of a century later, he was about the first man she had ever met who didn't have to make his living on horseback, or keeping store—certainly the first who owned a derby hat. He was better educated, too, than most eligible young men thereabouts, having finished the best part of high school in the effete East: i.e., Marietta, Ohio. Already, moreover, he had had the gumption to homestead a place of his own—not on the dry and windy plains, but in southeastern Oklahoma where there was enough rainfall most years to raise a crop of corn, cotton, or broomstraw. Before her homesteader's year was out, she had made up her mind to marry him. I don't think either of them ever regretted it.

Their mother raised all the Caperton girls to be experienced managers of men. Because she was too busy running the household to pay much attention to the younger children, she handed that responsibility over to her daughters as soon as they were old enough to change a diaper; they became, in effect, a built-in nursery and day-care center. Their home on Sand Mountain in Alabama, where most of the brood was born before the family moved west, was a log cabin, surrounded by woods and a few thin acres of crop land. Their life was not much different from that of Appalachian country people today, as described by Robert Coles in the November issue of *Harper's:* a hard scrabble all the way. Sometime in the misty past, before the first Capertons had migrated from Scotland, they had acquired a coat of arms of doubtful authenticity, bearing three boars' heads and a Celtic motto. Nobody of her generation could read the motto, but my mother would always claim that it meant "Root, hog, or die."

At least that would have been appropriate, since all the children beyond the toddling stage were expected to carry their full share of work. For the girls, the upbringing of their younger brothers was just a starter. They also shucked corn, picked wild berries, made soap out of bacon grease and leached wood ashes, and did the laundry over an outdoor fire in the same big kettle used for boiling soap and scalding pigs. They knew that these chores, plus any number of others, were just as essential to the family's survival as the work done by the boys. They never had any feeling of subordination to males.

On the contrary, they grew up knowing that one of their prime duties in life was to keep menfolks from doing something foolish. For all of the Caperton men were, as my mother put it, "a little wild." George, her father, evidently fitted the traditional pattern of Confederate cavalrymen: debonair, charming, reckless, and hot-tempered. (The only scar he got from the war was from a knife wound inflicted in a campfire brawl with some of his fellow troopers.) He also was given to sudden extravagances, such as buying a piano that the family could ill afford, or a fast colt instead of the mule he really needed. From time to time, moreover, he drank too much.

Several of his sons inherited some of these traits: one died an alcoholic, another was killed in an accident while racing a quarter horse. It was hardly surprising, then, that the Caperton women regarded liquor as the devil's favorite weapon. Before her marriage, my mother asked her fiancé to promise that he would never take another drink—a pledge he kept with no strain, since he too had been raised in a strict Methodist family. Even in his relatively carefree bachelor days he had never drunk anything more than an occasional glass of beer at a political rally. His reputation for sobriety helped reconcile her family to the marriage—although George Caperton never could quite forgive his daughter for marrying a Yankee.

In addition to protecting the men under their jurisdiction from the evils of drink, the Caperton women considered themselves guardians against sin in all its other guises, notably gambling and wastrel habits. Consequently my father never touched a card or bet on a horse; but his wife couldn't quite manage to suppress his inclination to speculate in land and livestock, which he insisted was investment, not gambling. As a result, on two occasions—the depressions of 1920 and 1932—he lost everything and found himself deeply in debt. These disasters reinforced my mother's conviction that frugality was a cardinal virtue. She cut down my father's old suits to make clothes for me and my brother, saved his worn ties to make piece quilts, and cooked on a wood range long after most of our neighbors had shifted to gas or electric stoves. Even in her old age, when she didn't really need to be so thrifty, she insisted on saving scraps of leftover food that any ordinary housewife would have tossed in the garbage pail; and I don't think she ever took a taxi without feeling a twinge of guilt.

Regular churchgoing was of course regarded as a prophylaxis against sin. My mother saw to it, therefore, that the whole family went to Sunday school and two services on Sunday, and usually to a prayer meeting or church supper in midweek. She also took us to hear every traveling revivalist who came to town and enrolled me early in the Epworth League, the Methodist equivalent of Hitler's *Jugend*. The upshot of this enforced piety was that I felt, when I was old enough to leave home, that I had heard enough sermons for one lifetime; I have avoided churches with marked success ever since.

By no means, however, was my mother the most churchly of the Capertons. One of her sisters joined an obscure Baptist sect notable for its austerity; it held that everything pleasant, including music in church, was sinful. Her husband, a robust, lusty cattleman—known as Whispering Till, because he could seldom get his voice down below a bellow—put up with this for a good many years. Then he ran off with a show girl from a traveling carnival.

Among her maxims for the governance of males, one of my mother's favorites was: "The devil finds mischief for idle hands to do." My brother and I were saved from idleness, so far as she could help it, from the time we were big enough to make ourselves useful. At the age of six, for example, my list of chores included taking care of a pen of chickens, smelly, addlebrained creatures that I loathed. Most Sundays, moreover, I had to catch a rooster, chop off his head, and clean and pluck him for dinner—an assignment I loathed even more, since a determined rooster is a fairly even match for a small boy. To this day I have no appetite for chicken in any form.

The anti-idleness program also included such jobs as chopping firewood, stoking and cleaning the furnace, mowing lawns, peddling comb honey from door to door, delivering papers, and selling the *Saturday Evening Post*. For the household chores I got no allowance—Mother didn't hold with such foolishness—but I did keep anything I earned from outside enterprises. I was encouraged, however, to set aside a tenth of these earnings for Sunday school collection, and to salt away at least half of what was left in a savings account, against the day I might go to college.

All this, I am afraid, sounds a little grim; which would be misleading. Like all small boys, I developed a considerable talent for passive resistance, thus defeating many of my mother's schemes to lead me into the paths of industry and righteousness. She gave up on piano lessons, for instance, before I was ten, and at all times I contrived to spend more hours at play than at work. Besides, for all her determination, she didn't have a grim bone in her body. She loved gaiety of all kinds—at least those that didn't cost much money—and was forever organizing picnics, fishing trips, taffy pulls, and hayrides. She also loved to dance (as my father, alas, did not), and one of her abiding sorrows was that neither she nor anybody else could teach me how to waltz. A boy who couldn't waltz, she felt, was as ill-educated as one who couldn't ride, shoot, fish, swim, or handle an ax.

She disapproved of fighting, but she disapproved even more of my getting licked. When I came home from school one day, bloody and blubbering, at about the age of seven, she insisted that my father give me boxing lessons. Though she didn't know it, he was nearly as un-skilled in that art as I was; but he dutifully brought boxing gloves for both of us, and sparred with me in the backyard until he thought I was passably nimble, or he got bored. I must have learned something, because I seemed to hold my own at recess from then on; and when I finally did get to college I was able to earn part of my expenses by boxing occasionally in welterweight matches at American Legion and Elks Club smokers.

In public life, as in the home, she believed that women were divinely appointed to serve as custodians of morals. She worked hard for the Women's Christian Temperance Union and for its main cause, Prohibition; and she was an early, enthusiastic advocate of women's suffrage. She also held strong, if sometimes eccentric, political opinions, which occasionally led to a certain amount of domestic strife. The earliest arguments I can remember between her and my father were about politics—for she was a hereditary Democrat and he was a hereditary Republican, and neither ever succeeded in changing the other's mind. At an age when I could barely count pennies, much less understand the Gold Question, she took me to a Chautauqua lecture by William Jennings Bryan, who was as interminable as he was illustrious. When I began, after the first hour or two, to squirm and whine, she told me to hush up.

"Never mind if you can't understand the words," she said. "He is a great Democrat, and you should be edified to be here."

I wasn't. But again I learned something; when I was asked, many years later, to help write speeches for Democratic Presidential candidates, I made them short and I avoided the Gold Question.

One of her more original political notions was that all bachelors should be heavily taxed. The Christian duty of every man, she believed, was to get married early, raise a family, and support it as best he could. Any shirker manifestly should be made to feel the teeth of the public fisc. Sometimes, usually after she had been condoling with an old maid, she went further.

"An old bachelor," she would proclaim, "is the meanest thing in the world. If I had my way, I would shoot them all."

I wish she had lived to discuss that proposition some day with Betty Friedan or Gloria Steinem. She would, I am sure—well, fairly sure—have tried her best to be gentle and understanding. She realized that she had grown up. with advantages no longer available to them, and perhaps never again to any but a negligible number of American women—notably an early chance to sprout confidence and self-reliance under the best of growing conditions. She would have sympathized, too, with Women's Lib in its complaints about the current crop of young men, whom she mostly considered a sorry lot—lazy, uncurried, rarely harness-broken, and unschooled in the deference they owe to the more responsible sex. But she also believed that those failing were largely the fault of today's women, who had failed to enforce Decent Standards; and for the whining self-pity that seems to afflict so many Lib types she would have had no patience whatever. If she had ever heard one of those lectures in which Miss Steinem tells women "how to seize control of your own lives," I suspect my mother would have exploded. Seize indeed!

Any woman who ever lacked control of her own life after the age of ten had, by the Caperton lights, only herself to blame.

Letter from Leete's Island:

Field Notes on the Manners, Morals, and Customs of the Connecticut Yankee

January, 1969

WHEN I was growing up in Texas, I learned that New Englanders are a mean-spirited race, stingy, Puritanical, taciturn, and shrewd. This was received doctrine in a family which consisted on one side of unrepentant Confederates and on the other of poor farmers who had for generations believed that they were harshly used by Yankee mortgage-holders in Boston and Hartford.

Now that I have been living among Yankees for nearly a year, I am beginning to suspect that such a view—still common throughout much of the South and West—might be a little myopic. They are indeed peculiar people, different in many ways from the Americans I have known elsewhere; but the differences are not what I had expected. Hence these notes on what I have discovered so far about the real character of New Englanders, or at least their Coastal Connecticut subculture.

The observation post, or blind, for these sightings is an old yellow farm house perched on a bluff above the shore of Leete's Island. It is a good spot for surveillance: to the south, of the gulls and sail boats on Long Island Sound, to the north, of Yankee behavior. To the east and west lie woods, alarmingly overpopulated with woodchucks who also need some surveillance if I can ever get around to it.

Four hundred years ago the Island actually was one, a member in good standing of an archipelago now known as The Thimbles. The shallows between it and the Connecticut mainland gradually silted up, however, and turned into salt marshes. When causeways were thrown across these marshes to carry a road and the New Haven railway, Leete's Island became, to all intents, a peninsula; but during big hurricanes it turns back into an island again for two or three days at a stretch.

Few New Yorkers have ever heard of it (as I had not until a

couple of years ago) but, unknowingly, most of them see a bit of it every day. For much of New York City is built of Leete's Island granite, a distinctive pinkish-gray stone which forms the spine of the peninsula. Because glaciers had scoured away much of the top soil, the granite was easy to quarry and it could be loaded directly onto barges for cheap shipment to the city, a hundred miles to the southwest. It was used, therefore, to build such monuments as the Brooklyn Bridge and the base of the Statue of Liberty, and also for street curbings and the stonework in many an office building—including Two Park Avenue, where this magazine is published. The quarry—the only industry the Island ever had—is closed now; it couldn't compete with reinforced concrete. But the families of a few of its Italian and Croatian stonecutters still live in the neighborhood.

Although some of them have been around for generations, they are still regarded as newcomers—as my wife and I will be, for as long as we live. Fair enough, too. A really settled resident in these parts is someone like my neighbors, William and Lawrence Leete. They raise dairy cattle and cut cord wood on land which came down to them from an earlier William Leete, a governor of colonial Connecticut. He landed in 1639 with the shipload of English emigrants who founded the village of Guilford four miles east of here. Their names are all listed in the local records, although the name of the ship—a 350-tonner—somehow has been mislaid. Of the twenty-five names on that list, fifteen are still common in the township. So much for the myth of American hyper-mobility.[1]

For my purposes, the Leete's Island business district is just the right size. It provides the necessities for bodily and spiritual comfort, but no more.

It consists of three wooden buildings, all painted the same dull shade of red. The largest is Bill Robinson's store, not much bigger

---

1. The Quinnipiac Indians gladly sold Guilford Township to the colonists, because for generations they had been fighting a losing war with the Mohawks and Pequots. At the time of the deal, the Quinnipiac tribe was down to forty-seven men and in danger of being wiped out by the next Mohawk raid. So much for the myth of the noble savage, supposedly happy and tranquil until the coming of the whites.

than a freight car but roomy enough to stock the essentials, from bread and tobacco to the *New York Times*. On the other side of the parking lot is the liquor shop, run by Noreen Contois and her Great Dane, who may well be the most popular resident of the Island. He suffers, alas, from cysts in his feet which make it necessary for him to wear stockings. All the men hereabouts whose feet are big enough save up their worn socks for him.

The third building is the railway station, about the size of a box stall, with a dirt floor and a plank bench along the back wall. Since the New Haven line has long been in bankruptcy, the station hasn't been painted in living memory and its scabrous appearance is an embarrassment to the community. A few years back Bert Stickney wrote the manager of the road, offering to paint the station at his own expense. He got back a nice letter saying thank you, no; if nonunion labor so much as laid a brush on any New Haven structure, the company would have a strike on its hands.

Anyhow the station does provide shelter from the rain and a frayed tie with the outside world. A one-car local stops there twice a day—at 7:15 A.M., heading for Stony Creek, Pine Orchard, and eventually New York, and again at 6:00 in the evening, on its way back toward Guilford and New London. Usually it carries at least one Leete's Island passenger each way, and on summer weekends it may have five or six. Some days, of course, it doesn't show up. The New Haven's venerable rolling stock tends to get discouraged and quit under adversity such as a snowstorm, or a heavy dew.

As you can see, there is nothing superfluous about either the train service or the community it serves. After putting up for twenty-five years with the superfluities of New York—including noise, dirt, people, chaos, and a cornucopia of goodies that I don't want—I find the spareness of Leete's Island especially satisfying.

The business district is a strategic place for watching Islanders. For example, Dorothy Emery, a widow who lives just up the road in what used to be a quarryman's house; she and Jake, her late husband, turned its eleven acres, including an abandoned quarry pond, into the best example of landscaping on the Island. Or her next-door neighbor, Doc Holley, a retired Negro pharmacist and highly regarded elder of the community; he sent his son through Yale medical school, and his views are often sought on subjects ranging from local herbs to real-estate values.

A broader spectrum of Yankee character is on view just beyond the woods in Guilford, where chores or business take me a couple of times a week. After nearly four hundred years it is still a minute village, which looks as if it might have been designed by Grandma Moses as The Classic New England Country Town—complete with elm-shaded green, monument to the Union dead, white church spires, tinker's shop, Odd Fellows Hall, and lots of eighteenth-century saltbox homes. This appearance is entirely deceptive, for reasons to be noted in a moment.

Guilford is, however, full of prime specimen Yankees. One of my favorites is Doris Montgomery, who runs our bank: once the Guilford Trust Company, now a branch of the Second National of New Haven—the only *Second* National bank I ever heard of. I'm told that she is a sound banker with a firm grasp of computer bookkeeping and price-earnings ratios; that I'm not competent to judge, but I do know that she is a warm-natured woman who somehow makes her bank feel as comfortable as a farm kitchen. It is, apparently, a matriarchy. Occasionally I've glimpsed a man behind one of the back desks, but the important jobs—from the safe-deposit vault to the teller's windows—are all handled by women. There is a playpen, with assorted toys, in the lobby, and one of the girls is always glad to take domestic messages or mind a bag of groceries while a customer tends to other errands around town. For twenty-five years I had an account in a New York City bank just across the street from my office. In all that time none of the bank's employees ever learned to recognize me; every time I cashed a check I had to identify myself, and the teller invariably looked up my account to see if the balance would cover it. At Doris's bank all of the ladies knew me by the time of my second visit, and they apparently carry my balance in their pretty heads.

The boys in Page's hardware store, next door to the bank, have this same knack. They now know as much about my house maintenance problems as I do, and often tell me a better (or cheaper) way to mend a chest of drawers or fence rabbits out of the garden patch.

From such people, and a few dozen others whom I've come to know pretty well, I am working out a tentative revision of my inherited concept of New Englanders.

Taciturn they are not. At the drop of a subject, they are willing to discuss anything, in a detail which even a New York taxi driver would consider garrulous. They don't seem to be notably Puritanical either nowadays, although they do take their pleasures more quietly and discreetly than most of my Texas friends. It is true that they generally are careful about money—one of my neighbors cuts his own hair—but since I'm a close man with a nickel myself, that doesn't bother me.

What did puzzle me for quite a while was their feelings about money. Stingy doesn't define it at all, and I don't know any other word that is quite right either.

Take the case of one of my neighbors. He owns several hundred acres of woodland and pasture, near the shore and therefore worth at least $5,000 an acre. Any morning he could sell it to a subdivision developer for enough to keep him in comfort for the rest of his life, in a beach chair on Biscayne Bay or the Riviera. Yet he keeps on, at well past middle age, living the hard frugal life of a New England farmer—getting up at 5:00 A.M. to milk the cows, split cord wood, mow salt hay, and plow the bottom-land with his team of big red Belgium draft horses. Clearly he likes this style of life better than any other he can imagine. And his wife once explained, a little haltingly, that nothing could ever persuade them to sell an acre . . . it had been in the family a long time . . . they don't want Guilford to turn into another suburbia . . . they love the woods, and think of them as a kind of private trust, to be kept the way God made them, for at least their lifetimes and maybe longer.

To paraphrase Ada Louise Huxtable, these are people who do not think that the most beautiful thing in the world is a buck.

This attitude is by no means universal, of course. We have plenty of fast-buck operators around here; they have, for instance, despoiled several miles of shoreline with a clutter of vacation cabins. (If you scratch the heart of almost any American you will find, I suspect, a trace of the land speculator.) But these public enemies are largely neutralized by other people who have a genuine concern for the environment. A surprising number of them seem intent on making a decent life, not just for their own families but for the whole community; and not only for today, but for the long future.

One such is Helene Piggott, the only real-estate agent I ever met who is not hell-bent on converting every possible square foot of ground into ready cash. She, instead, devotes a good part of her time to the Guilford Land Conservation Trust, which is acquiring, by gift or purchase, all the open land it can lay its hands on. Together with the local Audubon Society it has rescued, in the nick of time, hundreds of acres of woods and estuary marshes.

So "mean-spirited" is another term I've had to discard in thinking about New Englanders. "Shrewd," however, is a word I can stand by. I am coming to believe that in certain respects they are smarter than most Americans I have known. At times they even rise to a rare kind of wisdom in the management of their common affairs. The rest of us could, I think, learn a lot from them about the difficult art of city living.

City living? Yes, that is exactly what I mean. For all of their bucolic look, Guilford and its Leete's Island suburb are part of a great city: the Super-Metropolis which blankets the Atlantic coast from Bangor, Maine, to Norfolk, Virginia. In an article which he wrote for *Harper's* ten years ago, Christopher Tunnard called it the Atlantic Urban Region. Washington planners often describe it as The Northeast Corridor. Whatever you call it, it is a single blob of people—forty million of them—concentrated in a six-hundred-mile strip with an average density of about a hundred per square mile. Each of its segments—Leete's Island as well as Harlem, Boston, and Baltimore—is tied to all the others with a thousand cords, mostly invisible. They are all interdependent, for their livelihood and their culture. Their big problems are common ones, which none of the component communities can solve alone. But the Connecticut Yankees are tackling these problems, it seems to me, with better sense than most of the other people who inhabit the Super-City.

For one thing, they don't huddle so close together. When you drive through Connecticut, much of it looks like farming country or even wilderness. But this is a happy illusion. The whole state is essentially industrial; only 3 per cent of its people make their living from farming.

All the rest work in factories, or in the service trades—from filling stations to universities—which are industry's handmaidens. Yet most of Connecticut's manufacturing is not jammed together in huge, grimy, slum-raddled concentrations, such as New York's garment district or the steel centers of Gary and Pittsburgh. (There are a few exceptions, such as Bridgeport and New Haven; but even they are comparatively small cities, and they are coping rather hopefully with their typical urban woes.) The distinctive characteristic of the state's industry is its scatteration through hundreds of little towns and open countryside. Modern technology makes this kind of site planning feasible for a wide range of industry.

Guilford, for example—in spite of its Grandma Moses guise—is really a manufacturing town. It has more than thirty factories, making a broad variety of products: pharmaceuticals, magnetic wire, conveyor belts, precision tools, flexible tubing, electrical fittings, and photocopiers, to mention only a few. Yet it has no "factory district." The plants are dotted at wide intervals all over the 46 square miles of the township. One occupies a converted trolley barn; others are tucked away in the forest or screened by landscaping so that a casual visitor is unlikely to notice them.

All of them are fairly small, with work forces ranging from three or four men up to a couple of hundred. Most are in fields requiring modern technology, or at least considerable skill; wages, as a result, are relatively high. A case in point is the Guilford Brass Foundry, a mile down the road from our home. It is a modest shop, no bigger than a good-sized barn, surrounded on three sides by woods. To my wife it looked like just the place to take a prized old brass kettle which needed mending. The manager looked at it with interest, but shook his head.

"Twenty years ago we would have been glad to take on this kind of job," he said, "but we can't do it now. We're too busy trying to catch up on our orders for radar components."

He sent her instead to Tinker Hubbard, an elderly gentleman who can fix anything from a lawn mower to a turret lathe. Such work is as much hobby as profession, since he comes from an Old Family and owns a lot of land hereabout.

A Guilford factory hand can go home for lunch, if he is of a mind to, often on foot. He is more than likely to own a skiff with an outboard motor, which he uses for fishing on evenings and weekends, and a shotgun for hunting ducks in the marshes. Oysters, clams, and mussels are a familiar part of his diet, since they can be had for the taking, in season, in a dozen bays and estuaries. (I have collected the makings of an unsurpassable *moules marinières* in ten minutes from the tidal ledge at the edge of our yard; in a New York restaurant it would cost at least five dollars.) Anyone who can't be bothered to catch his own fish can pick them up at the town harbor, which accommodates a small commercial fishing fleet. And the three markets offer excellent locally grown meats and vegetables at prices a Manhattan housewife wouldn't believe.

All this may have something to do with the fact that none of my informants could remember when Guilford last had a strike—although several factories are organized and labor is anything but "docile." (Docility is not a Yankee characteristic.) The men aren't afraid for their jobs, either, because unemployment is negligible; jobs are going a-begging, in fact, in a number of trades.

That is one reason why the town's welfare budget is only $16,675 for the current year. The other is that hardly anybody is willing to go on the poor rolls so long as he (or she) can lift a hand. I know several grandmothers who are ironing shirts and cleaning other people's homes when they ought to be in bed nursing their arthritis. Such work is not, however, regarded as unrespectable. Nor is any kind of work, so far as I can tell, considered menial or dead-end. On the contrary, a man is not fully respected unless he can turn his hand to most anything, from rough carpentry to electrical repairs. Most people actually *like* manual labor, apparently. Scott Gordon, a highschool boy who sometimes helps around my yard, wears his hair fashionably long, but he also holds down eight part-time jobs—not from hunger but because he is saving money to pay for his car and motorboat and college fees. As I said, a peculiar people.

Hardly anybody around here is either very rich or very poor. Only one home, built to house the art collection of the retired director of research for Olin Mathieson, is really elaborate, although a good number of homes on Sachem's Head and Clapboard Hill Road suggest that their owners are, in the local phrase, "comfortably well-off." On the other hand, there are no slums. The typical dwelling is a modest frame house, often (like my own) more than a century old. A few look cramped or shabby; but nearly all of them, except those in the center of the village have a little land, often several acres, fringed with sumac and juniper and lilac. Both woods and water are within easy walking distance for any active youngster, since two rivers wind through the township and much of its land is in publicly owned forest.

There is no ghetto either. Negroes have lived in Guilford ever since it was an underground railway station before the Civil War, and increasing numbers of Puerto Ricans have been moving in recently to work in the factories. They live all over the place, wherever they can find a house. That isn't easy, because building land seldom comes on the market and mortgage interest rates are high. The resulting housing shortage forces some workers to commute to Guilford from as far as New Haven, sixteen miles to the west.

Nevertheless the town is growing—cautiously and reluctantly. The towns I knew out West all wanted to grow as fast as possible, and welcomed any new business firm, from a slaughterhouse to a strip-tease joint. Not Guilford. By common consent, it encourages only those businesses which are "consistent with . . . the community character," and then only when "subject to strict controls on nuisances and pollution." These controls are set forth in a tight zoning code and in the "Comprehensive Plan of Development"—a document adopted four years ago after many months of study and debate in town meetings. It anticipates a doubling of the township's population, to about 20,000, by 1985. Most people aren't happy about that, but they realize that no community within the Atlantic Urban Region can escape the population explosion. Hence the plan, which is intended to channel the coming growth in an orderly and rational fashion, and to provide in advance for the necessary schools, sewerage lines, roads, parklands, beaches, and public buildings.

To my amateur eye, it is a thoughtful piece of work—an ingenious accommodation of tradition to change. It was drafted by the town's professional planning staff, with the help of an outside consulting firm, but it reflects pretty accurately (I think) the feelings of the whole community. It turned out that way for two reasons.

First of all, Guilford is small enough and stable enough to be a true community. Everybody knows everybody else, or feels he does. Personal, responsive government is still possible. One day soon after we moved here a rainstorm clogged up a culvert under our road and sent a small flood streaming into the garden. When I asked Douglas MacLise next door what I ought to do about it, he said: "Why, call Milton Bullard, of course." Mr. Bullard is our First Selectman—in effect, the Mayor. He answered his phone at once, and said he would see what could be done. No promises; but before midafternoon the town engineer had unplugged the culvert. Only someone accustomed to the sluggish labyrinths of New York bureaucracy can understand how miraculous that seemed.

Mr. Bullard, and the other two selectmen, and the planning and zoning commissioners, and everybody else at Town Hall can't help knowing how their bosses feel about any given subject, even before it comes up in town meeting. They talk to a good share of us every day.

The other reason is an aspect of the Yankee character. It seems to be contagious, spreading from the oldtimers to the Italian, Croat, Puerto Rican, and Texan newcomers who are trying, like myself, to become New Englanders by adoption. Nearly everybody is infected with a lively concern for the present state of the community, and its future.

This does not make for a placid and harmonious atmosphere. I have seen old friendships broken up by such explosive questions as the design of the new police station. (Should its architecture be modern or phony-colonial? The phony-colonialists won, and their opponents, including most of the resident architects, are still fuming.)

But it does mean that every issue gets discussed until it is frayed at the edges, in our weekly paper, and the bank lobby, and Bill Robinson's store. It means that busy men—company presidents, Yale professors, and Al DeBay (who, being a carpenter, is probably the busiest of all)—devote their considerable talents to community affairs. When a conclusion does emerge—right or wrong—it is likely to represent fairly well the sense of the meeting. This, I guess, is what is meant by "participatory democracy." An exhausting exercise, but bracing.

When I was in high school I learned from Don Marquis, one of my literary heroes, about The Almost Perfect State. I have been looking for it—and writing about it, in one way or another—ever since; though I am no longer so hopeful as I once was of finding it in one lifetime. Now, as time gets short, I would be willing to settle for The Reasonably Decent Society. And, with a nervous glance at my Confederate ancestors, I am about ready to admit that these New Englanders may know something about it that the rest of us don't. At least they are trying hard to create a little part of the Super-City which will combine modern industry with a humane way of life, and a respect for the land, the water, and the past. How they come out might well be a matter of some interest to the rest of America.

A Case of Termination

February, 1973

T O understand her letter you ought to know something about Dorothy.

She was a strong-minded woman. Some called her eccentric, but since eccentrics are about as common as blue jays in our town, that was no reason for special remark. Until you got to know her ways, though, she could be a little disconcerting. If she thought you were talking nonsense, for example, she would say so, loudly, and command you to shut up. When she decided she didn't like a book she was reading, she was likely to throw it into a far corner of the room. "Scoundrel" was her softest term for people she disapproved of—the real estate man who cut a road through her favorite woods, or the banker who had once refused her husband a loan, to mention only a couple on her long hate list. She never forgave her enemies, because she considered forgiveness "part of that damn fool Christianity non-sense." But to her friends, who were far more numerous, she was so fiercely devoted that she would not abide a critical word about any of them.

A few days after my wife and I moved to Leete's Island, a small community in eastern Connecticut, she stomped into our kitchen, uninvited, emitting a rapid commentary on something—I couldn't quite make out what—in the voice of an enraged sergeant major. When she paused for breath, my bewildered wife said, "I don't believe I caught your name."

"Of course you didn't," Dorothy said. "I haven't told you yet."

She then simmered down to a mild uproar and explained that she wanted to welcome us to the neighborhood, having heard about our arrival from a mutual friend. From then until her death we saw her at least once a week and never knew a dull moment in her company.

At that time she was in her late seventies and had been widowed for about six months. In her younger days she had been an editorial assistant at the *Ladies' Home Journal* and had written short stories and articles for *The New Yorker, The Saturday Evening Post,* and other magazines. Her themes usually had been passionately feminist—Women's Lib a generation ahead of time. So it did not surprise me to hear (from others, never from her) that her marriage had been a trying one. For by all accounts (except Dorothy's) her husband Jake had been a difficult fellow—moody, demanding, and quick-tempered. She never spoke of him with anything but affection, and her most cherished memories were of the long hiking trips they had made, decades earlier, through the Quebec woods, each carrying a forty-pound pack. Yet at one time, according to the oral history of the town, she and Jake had decided on divorce. To announce it, they invited all their friends to the biggest party they had ever attempted. It turned out to be such a success that they called off the divorce and lived happily ever after—or at least in a reasonably amiable state of truce.

After her eightieth birthday, the rheumatoid arthritis that had plagued Dorothy for years took a turn for the worse. She was in severe and increasing pain; neither medication nor physical therapy was much help; and eventually she could get about only with the help of a walker, a few agonizing steps at a time. She never uttered a word of self-pity, but she did resent her growing dependence on friends and on the town's visiting homemakers' service. Most of all she dreaded the day when she would become completely bed-bound; and though her wits (and tongue) remained as sharp as ever, she feared that her wits might begin to falter without her realizing it, as so often happens with elderly people.

When the visiting homemaker came one morning last spring, she found Dorothy in a coma. The town ambulance got her to a New Haven hospital within half an hour, but she died several days later without gaining consciousness.

Her affairs turned out to be in meticulous order, down to the payment of the last bill and balancing of her final bank statement. Arrangements had been made for her modest house, with its stream, pond, and eleven acres of woods and gardens, to go to a biological research station for use as a nature area—thus saving the land she had tended with such loving care from the real estate developers she loathed. She left instructions for cremation, and no funeral service. Her elderly car and most of her small savings went to her close friend and helper, Viola, a Negro woman who had stayed for dinner with her every Wednesday night. In Viola's care she left carefully considered bequests for each of her other friends—books, a vase, a picture, and the like.

To Viola she also had entrusted a handwritten letter, with the request that a copy should be sent to each of her "dear friends" shortly after her death. It reads, in part, as follows:

This message was started in November 1971. I have reread it and added to it from time to time but made no basic changes.

To those whom I dearly value, this is an explanation, and a confession, and a plea. For if this ignorantly managed attempt is successful, I ask you to be happy for me—and ultimately for yourselves too.

Long ago I accumulated the means for this act; with no morbid intentions; with no sense of guilt; merely cherishing the feeling that if the time ever came when I thought it far better to fall asleep and never wake, I had the very great good fortune to have it in my power to do so. I seem always to have felt that one could—and even under given circumstances should—be the rightful judge of that moment. (It always seemed so distant and unlikely!)

I began really to feel it only after Jake's death when I began to feel truly alone—in the very critical sense of loss of mutual dependence. I felt too old and dilapidated to undertake new obligations of any validity.

The time may be long or short, I do not know, because I want no despondency involved when the precise moment comes. I'm sure it'll take a bit of doing, but it is not quite exactly a matter of courage or cowardice, except as it is the courage *of* cowardice and fear (and common sense?). I want to go while I can still enjoy my friends who are so good to me and who I know can still enjoy me; while I can still feel a not too unfavorable balance between the happiness and competence and interest and even limited usefulness of my days—and the difficulties and discomforts and pain and expense involved in trying first to maintain that balance and then later merely to prolong life.

At that point I waited (it is now early April) and the effort is steadily increasing.

I think it will not be long now, for once clearly decided, I can feel the decision setting its own time-quickening schedule . . . I've just had a splendid hour of sunshine and comradeship in this my best loved room, and it is *that* which seems real and everlasting—with the other just a grim and foolish nightmare that I'll awaken from. But the inexorable stark truth lies the other way around, and that cherished splendid hour will last only as long as memory lasts. . . . The reasons for the *when* as well as the reasons for the *why,* make it a tightly woven complex of tough small fibers that result in a determined act when determined on.

Two things bother me about that letter. The first is that Dorothy felt it necessary to write it—she who never in the years I knew her had felt any need to explain or apologize for whatever she did. The second is that her last act had to be "ignorantly managed" and the "means" had to be accumulated surreptitiously and "long ago." Presumably, whatever drug she used had lost some of its potency; hence the prolonged coma at the end.

Yet I am glad she wrote it; for it has led me, over the months I have been thinking about it, to reverse a lifelong conviction. I have quoted from the letter at some length in the hope that it may persuade at least a few others to a similar change in belief—to the conviction that our society's whole attitude toward suicide is profoundly wrong.

I was raised like most Americans in the belief that suicide is an immoral act. Under some circumstances, I still believe that to be true. But in Dorothy's circumstances, what she did now seems to me not only sensible but morally praiseworthy. Even the word "suicide" seems wrong to me in such a case, because it is so heavily encrusted with connotations of disapproval. I would rather call it a case of termination.

Dorothy had no children, no dependents, no close relatives. Her wasting body would soon become a grief and burden to her friends, as it was to her. Recovery was out of the question. Her decision then seems a natural one, like that of the old Eskimos who know when the time has come for them to drift off on an ice floe into the final cold.

Yet she—who had no patience whatever with foolish social conventions—felt some social compulsion to explain and justify her decision. In a more rational society she would have felt no such need, taking it for granted that her friends would understand and approve. And in such a society she—who hated anything surreptitious—would have been able to carry it out more openly and more surely.

Aside from the clergy, the main obstacle in the way of a more rational attitude is the medical profession. Paradoxically, too, it is the medical profession that has made a change in public values long over-due. For, thanks to modern medicine, the average life expectancy no longer is thirty-five years, as it was in my grandfather's time. Nowadays (when overpopulation has become a worldwide problem) any number of people can expect to drag on into their reluctant eighties. The nursing homes are full of them, in misery, pain, and longing for the end.

Out of a fairly wide acquaintanceship among medical men, I have known only two doctors who agreed with Dorothy's view that a person has a right to die at the time of his choosing. One of them told me that he normally let a patient slip away without "heroic measures" whenever both of them knew the case was hopeless. The other goes further. When a patient asks to be helped along, as he puts it, he takes the necessary action.

Perhaps a good many other doctors secretly behave the same way. But most of those with whom I've discussed the matter still believe that it is their duty to keep a patient alive to the last possible moment, by whatever means. That is an imperative imposed upon them by their training, by the tradition of their profession since Hippocrates, and by the Judeo-Christian moral code. I respect their conviction, but I believe the time has come to reexamine it, as has been done to so many other items in the traditional moral code in recent years.

This is not a matter for legislation. That may be needed eventually, in those states where attempted suicide, or the abetting of it, is listed as a crime. Indeed, a "Death with Dignity" bill recently has been introduced in the Florida legislature—so far as I know the first of its kind anywhere. But the first necessary step is a change in the public consensus. That will happen only as the end product of long discussion—in print, in conversations among friends, and most importantly in consultations between laymen and physicians. Once doctors come to realize that many of their patients feel as Dorothy did, it will be easier for them to rethink their own positions. Then there may be fewer cases, so familiar to all of us, where a life is prolonged for weeks or months at the cost of great suffering to the patient and financial and emotional bankruptcy for his family.

So far as I know, the only organized effort in this direction is being made by the Euthanasia Educational Council, 250 West 57th Street,

New York 10019. (Euthanasia is derived from the Greek term for "good death"; in this, as in so many other aspects of philosophy, the ancient Greeks were way ahead of us.)

To anyone who wants it, the Council will send a copy of a document it calls a Living Will. It reads:

> To my family, my physician, my clergyman, my lawyer:
>
> If the time comes when I can no longer take part in decisions for my own future, let this statement stand as the testament of my wishes:
>
> If there is no reasonable expectation of my recovery from physical or mental disability, I request that I be allowed to die and not be kept alive by artificial means or heroic measures. Death is as much a reality as birth, growth, maturity and old age—it is the one certainty. I do not fear death as much as I fear the indignity of deterioration, dependence and hopeless pain. I ask that drugs be mercifully administered to me for terminal suffering even if they hasten the moment of death.
>
> This request is made after careful consideration. Although this document is not legally binding, you who care for me will, I hope, feel morally bound to follow its mandate. I recognize that it places a heavy burden of responsibility upon you, and it is with the intention of sharing that responsibility and of mitigating any feelings of guilt that this statement is made.
>
> Signed————